SAVED BY HOPE

Dr. Richard C. Oudersluys

SAVED BY HOPE

Essays in Honor of
Richard C. Oudersluys

Edited by
James I. Cook

William B. Eerdmans Publishing Company
Grand Rapids, Michigan

Library of Congress Cataloging in Publication Data

Main entry under title:

Saved by hope.

    "A bibliography of the writings of Richard C. Oudersluys": p. 185.
    CONTENTS: Hesselink, I. J. Richard C. Oudersluys: Biblical scholar for a
new age.—Ridderbos, H. The Christology of the fourth Gospel.—Morris, L.
Love in the fourth Gospel. [etc.]
    1. Bible—Criticism, interpretation, etc.—Addresses, essays, lectures. 2.
Oudersluys, Richard Cornelius, 1906- Addresses, essays, lectures. 3. Oudersluys,
Richard Cornelius, 1906- Bibliography. I. Oudersluys, Richard Cornelius, 1906-
II. Cook, James I., 1925-
BS540.S24   225.6   78-5416
ISBN 0-8028-1736-X

Contents

Preface

No word is more beautifully descriptive of the gospel of Jesus Christ than hope, with its concomitants, trust and expectation. And there is no more appropriate word to set to a volume whose particular intent is to honor Richard C. Oudersluys upon the occasion of his seventieth birthday and the completion of a distinguished teaching career of thirty-five years at Western Theological Seminary. Christian hope is never merely wishful thinking, a consoling dream of the pious imagination; it is ever grounded on the divine act of salvation accomplished in Jesus Christ. As Anton Biemolt Professor of New Testament, our colleague articulated this gospel and its glad hope in lectures, sermons, and prayers with a spirit and eloquence whose echoes continue to sound in the ministries of his many students. "Saved by hope," as Paul phrased it, confesses that the work of salvation has been completed by Jesus Christ, but in such manner as always to be accompanied by the hope that what is now experienced genuinely but partially will one day be known in its fullness.

When one man bears responsibility for teaching the entire range of New Testament studies, there is small space for narrow specialization. Even the development of special interests will be balanced by work on the numerous and varied materials that must be taught. It is fitting, therefore, that the contents of this *Festschrift* maintain that balance. One third of the essays recognize Professor Oudersluys' special interest in the Gospel according to John; the others reflect his interest and work in the synoptic Gospels, the parables, the theology of Paul, the canon, and the covenant.

The fact that this volume represents the affection and effort of many people lays upon me the pleasant duty of expressing sincere thanks to those who have contributed the essays; to the Göttingen publishing house of Vandenhoeck & Ruprecht for permission to translate and publish the essay of Professor Eduard Schweizer and to Professor Gerhard F. Megow of Hope College for making the initial translation; to Mildred Schuppert for the bibliography of Professor Oudersluys' writings; to

William B. Eerdmans, Jr., for his cooperation and encouragement; to colleagues I. John Hesselink, Lester J. Kuyper, Donald J. Bruggink, and Norman J. Kansfield for their counsel and help; and to Hilary Coppen (Durham, England), Eleanor Hoffman, and Estella Karsten for their expert assistance in the preparation of the manuscript.

JAMES I. COOK
Editor

Abbreviations

NovT	*Novum Testamentum*
NovTSup	*Novum Testamentum Supplement*
NTA	*Neutestamentliche Abhandlungen*
NTD	*Das Neue Testament Deutsch*
NTS	*New Testament Studies*
PGC	*Pelican Gospel Commentaries*
RB	*Revue Biblique*
SJTh	*Scottish Journal of Theology*
SJThOP	*Scottish Journal of Theology Occasional Papers*
SNTSMS	*Society for New Testament Studies Monograph Series*
StBTh	*Studies in Biblical Theology*
StNT	*Studien zum Neuen Testament*
StUNT	*Studien zur Umwelt des Neuen Testaments*
TDNT	*Theological Dictionary of the New Testament,* ed. by G. Kittel and G. Friedrich
ThBl	*Theologische Blätter*
ThW	*Theologische Wissenschaft*
WMANT	*Wissenschaftliche Monographien zum Alten und Neuen Testament*
ZThK	*Zeitschrift für Theologie und Kirche*

Richard C. Oudersluys: Biblical Scholar for a New Age

I. JOHN HESSELINK

Any teacher who has taught for thirty-five years in the same institution is bound to have made a major impact. This is certainly the case with Professor Richard Oudersluys, who taught at Western Seminary without interruption from 1942 until 1977. The one whom we honor in this *Festschrift*, however, did more than teach faithfully and effectively during that long period. He conducted the school through the transition from an uncritical, popular approach to the text of the New Testament to responsible, historical, critical exegesis.

He was not the first instructor at Western Seminary to come to the Scriptures without the traditional dogmatic presuppositions. The missionary-theologian Albertus Pieters had broken the ground a generation earlier by challenging accepted dogmas with fresh insights from Scripture. Lester Kuyper, Professor Oudersluys' close friend and a colleague for more than thirty years, had also begun to initiate midwestern Reformed Church ministerial candidates into new insights into the Old Testament. (Much earlier, from 1913 to 1917, Dr. John W. Beardslee, Jr., had taught in a similar manner, but his stay was too short to make much of an impact.) Even so, it was left to Richard Oudersluys to pioneer in New Testament studies and in the nuances and riches of the Greek Testament. The fact that Western Seminary attracted and challenged so many able young persons to the life of dedicated biblical scholarship and church leadership during the post-war era was due in large measure to his influence. That era brought to the campus a generation of students which would not settle for unexamined traditions and a superficial understanding of the New Testament. Many of them wanted to know what was happening in contemporary New Testament scholarship, what the issues were, and how they should be met. In Professor Oudersluys they found the answers they sought. It was he who ushered Western Seminary into the new age of New Testament studies. He kept abreast of the best in current scholarship without succumbing to faddism. In him a deep faith commitment was joined to an open and honest approach to the Scriptures.

In the course of Professor Oudersluys' teaching ministry accents and concerns have changed from decade to decade, but one thing has remained the same: a serious and profound wrestling with the message of the Scriptures and a concern to share it with others. Modesty and integrity have so graced his long career that they have often prevented him from enjoying the recognition that his ability and achievement deserve. With this *Festschrift* we hope to rectify that imbalance and to honor one who richly deserves some lasting plaudits.

I. Preacher

When Richard Oudersluys became a professor of New Testament, the church lost a preacher. Not that he ceased preaching when he came to the Seminary; but the exercise of his preaching gifts was held in abeyance for a time because of other demands. It is difficult to be both a good teacher and a good preacher, but in our friend's case former skills took on new luster with the passing years. The skills were always there, but age and experience added to his preaching both passion and a common touch.

There was little in Richard Oudersluys' background to encourage him to become a minister. Born in Grand Rapids, Michigan, in 1906, the eldest child and only son (four sisters were to follow) of a cabinetmaker, he did not grow up in an ordinary Reformed Church home. His parents came from a very strict, ultra-Calvinistic offshoot of the Dutch Reformed Church known as the Nederduitse Gereformeerde Kerke (Netherlands Reformed Congregations). Their membership was in a congregation on Turner Street that was served regularly by ministers brought from the Netherlands. The use of an organ for congregational singing was forbidden, the worship services generally continued for two hours, and all sermons were delivered in the Dutch language. Although Richard's grandfather had been an elder in this congregation, his parents were never more than baptized members, for they were taught that only those of very advanced years and of nearly impeccable Christian character should make confession of faith and come to the Lord's Table.

Such circumstances were hardly conducive to inspire a lad to consider the ministry as his vocation. Thanks to the leadership of their mother, however, the Oudersluys children eventually attended English services and Sunday School at the Bethel Reformed Church in Grand Rapids. There Richard's faith was nourished and his leadership qualities were given opportunity to develop. He was active in the Christian Endeavor Society, sang in the church choir, and, while still in his teens, taught a Sunday School class.

Two ministers were particularly influential in his spiritual development. The one, the Reverend John C. Van Wyk, was very evangelistic. After a series of revivalistic meetings led by a guest speaker, Pastor Van Wyk concluded the week with a sermon on a text from Revelation 3: "Behold, I stand at the door and knock . . ." This dramatic appeal was instrumental in moving Richard to make a decision for Christ and make public confession of his faith at the age of fifteen—in those days considered to be rather early for such a decision! The other minister who made an enduring impact on this young Christian in his later high school and early college years was Dr. Bernard J. Mulder, later to become influential throughout the denomination as editor of the *Church Herald* and Secretary of the Board of Education. Rather different in temperament and style from his predecessor, Pastor Van Wyk, Dr. Mulder also was an able student and powerful proclaimer of the Word. These two men in particular were vehicles of inspiration and models of ministry for the young Oudersluys, encouraging him to respond to God's call to be a minister of the Word.

This response, however, was not to come until several years later. Acting upon his father's advice, Richard majored in commercial subjects in high school and then specialized in business administration at Grand Rapids Junior College. But in an experience reminiscent of John Calvin, he eventually realized that it was necessary to forsake his father's direction in order to realize a higher calling. Determined to enter the ministry, he enrolled in Calvin College. Once again, two men were to be especially formative in the development of the young scholar: Dr. William Jellema, professor of philosophy, and Dr. Ralph Stob, professor of Greek. Both men were outstanding teachers, capable of bringing out the best in their students and inspiring them to lofty goals. Fired by their vision, Richard read Plato in the original Greek with special joy. With a major in classical languages, he graduated in 1929 and proceeded to enroll in Western Seminary in Holland.

At Western he benefited from the skilled teaching of Professors Albertus Pieters and Siebe Nettinga, but once more there were two men who played key roles in his development. Dr. John Kuizenga was of special help in theological maturation and Dr. John R. Mulder was instrumental in renewing his vision of the lofty place of preaching within the life of the church. He had already demonstrated special gifts in this regard when as a college student he was frequently called upon to speak at various church gatherings. His sensitivity to the nuances of language served to enhance his oratorical talent. Not surprisingly he was chosen class speaker when he graduated from the Seminary in 1932. Moreover, his reputation as a preacher was such that he was called immediately to be the minister of the First Reformed Church in Milwaukee.

Soon after his ordination he married Marian De Young, also from Grand Rapids. In the following years they were blessed with a daughter, Judith, and two sons, Richard, Jr., and Mark. This very close-knit family played an important part in the development of the young pastor.

In the early 1930's Richard Oudersluys continued to make his mark as a preacher. He found preaching—especially in the context of a sophisticated congregation like First, Milwaukee—to be both a challenge and a delight. His reputation as a pulpiteer was such that within a few years of entering the pastorate he received, in rapid succession, calls from three major congregations in Michigan: the First Reformed Church in Grand Haven, the Central Reformed Church in Muskegon, and the Third Reformed Church in Holland. The last of these calls was especially attractive to Richard, but he did not feel he was ready to undertake so heavy a responsibility.

Shortly thereafter he received one of the most flattering inquiries of his career—a letter from the Eastern Clergy Bureau of the Presbyterian Church which informed him that the National Presbyterian Church in Washington, D.C., was interested in him. Their invitation to submit a resumé in order to initiate further discussions was declined in the conviction that God had called him to a ministry in Milwaukee. In these decisions, as in most subsequent ones, the influence of his wife Marian was a significant factor.

Although he was soon to be led in another direction, Richard Oudersluys continued to be an effective preacher throughout his career. His love for preaching never diminished, even in the midst of his later arduous academic involvement. From his first days in the ministry until his retirement from Western Seminary forty-five years later in 1977, he has always cherished the privilege of being a minister of the Word of God. He has proclaimed the Word as he taught it, honestly, seriously, and faithfully.

II. Teacher

Although experiencing genuine satisfaction in the pastorate, Richard Oudersluys' keen mind sought additional challenges in the area of biblical studies. The New Testament in particular fascinated him, and his strong background in classics at Calvin College had provided him with the necessary equipment to pursue graduate studies in New Testament. Again his wife was influential in the decision to investigate possibilities for advanced work. Because of its proximity the Divinity School of the University of Chicago was a natural choice, although its theological tradition was not the most congenial for a conservative young pastor.

His graduate program at the University of Chicago was at first limited to summer sessions. The consistory of the Milwaukee church approved of this arrangement for their pastor as long as he returned to conduct worship on Sundays. During his last two years in the pastorate, Richard took an additional term each school year. This involved rising at five o'clock on Monday mornings in order to board a commuter train which would enable him to attend classes at Swift Hall by 8:30 a.m. He would remain in Chicago until Wednesday noon and then return to Milwaukee to make pastoral calls and conduct the midweek service. Thursday morning he would go back to the University, and return home on Friday afternoon.

This regimen proved too strenuous, however, even for a disciplined, gifted, and now somewhat experienced young pastor. It was also taking its toll on his family life. So after nine and a half years in Milwaukee, in the summer of 1941 he resigned his pastorate in order to devote full time to his New Testament studies at the Divinity School of the University of Chicago.

The financial burden which this move imposed on the family of four was mitigated when Richard became a student assistant for Professor W. R. Willoughby. The stipend thus received freed him to work closely with his major professor, Ernest Cadman Colwell, one of the leading American New Testament scholars of the twentieth century. Colwell had been reared in a conservative Methodist background and thus was both supportive and critical of Richard's conservative stance. Colwell's meticulous scholarship and strong personal interest in the young Reformed scholar proved to be another major influence in the shaping of the latter's development as a New Testament theologian.

Two events, almost simultaneous, conspired to prevent Richard Oudersluys from completing his doctoral dissertation. When Robert Hutchins became President of the University of Chicago, he selected Ernest Colwell to be his vice-president. This meant that Colwell had to resign his position at the Divinity School. In the meantime Jacob Vander Meulen, professor of the New Testament at Western Seminary, retired. Acting swiftly, the Seminary's Board of Trustees invited Richard Oudersluys to succeed Vander Meulen on the Western faculty. And so in the summer of 1942, after only one full year of residence study at the University of Chicago, the Oudersluys family moved to Holland.

The first years were difficult, not only because of the suddenness of the move and the challenge of orienting to a new career, but also because of World War II. Students were few and demands in the church were many—especially for preaching. Moreover, his classical studies and his later work at the University of Chicago had done little to provide Professor Oudersluys with a comprehensive theological framework for his teaching. Accordingly, during his first ten years at Western Seminary he was continually developing his own theological position. He was not content to be a mere technician, a Greek scholar and exegete who did not see the larger biblical-theological consequences of his work. In those critical years assistance in his theological quest came through a work by an older Reformed biblical scholar: Geerhardus Vos's *Biblical Theology*, which first appeared in 1948 but had been given in lecture form for many years at Princeton Seminary. In some ways it was a seminal work—at least from a conservative Reformed standpoint—although it was dated by the time of its publication because of its failure to interact with contemporary theological developments. Professor Oudersluys found this shortcoming corrected by works of two other influential biblical theologians who were quite different in their approach but who basically shared Vos's understanding of an eschatologically oriented progressive revelation. Oscar Cullmann's *Christ and Time* (E.T. 1951) and Otto Piper's *God in History* (1939), together with Vos's *Biblical Theology*, gave the maturing young professor all the clues he needed to work out his own biblical theology. This theological approach moved increasingly to eschatology and the kingdom of God as the organizing center of biblical revelation.[1] Although in many ways it was akin to the *Heilsgeschichte* (salvation-history) approach particularly associated with the name of Oscar Cullmann, Richard Oudersluys was always his own man. In his later years he was also very appreciative of the works of the Kampen biblical theologian, Herman Ridderbos, whose conclusions served to confirm his own convictions.

These convictions have been expressed lucidly and eloquently in his own "Theology of the New Testament," a book-length syllabus of 139 single-spaced pages. This scholarly study was given to students in mimeographed form in 1962 and was intended for publication. Unfortunately, the press of duties and an undue modesty have prevented this valuable work from being submitted to a publisher. Friends of our honoree will want to encourage him to prepare this syllabus for publication so that it can be appreciated by a larger readership.

The lineaments of Professor Oudersluys' theological perspective are evident even in a casual perusal of this *magnum opus*. After a brief preface, in which are traced the fortunes of biblical theology, he discusses the nature of New Testament theology. Beginning with the redemptive-historical event of Jesus Christ, he proceeds to its rootage in the Old Testament, and then takes up the history of salvation in the Old Testament. In Part III, the major portion of the work (pp. 24-127), the theology of the New Testament, as such, is developed. The key category is the *kerygma*, discussed first in the synoptic Gospels, then in John, Paul, and the Epistle to the Hebrews.

A brief discussion of the theology of the consummation follows this analysis of the *kerygma* in the New Testament. The concluding two sections of Part III are about the final events and the triumph of the kingdom. Here the underlying motif of his contribution comes to the fore. The entire New Testament "must be studied in the light of a central eschatological event, Jesus Christ revealed as God's Messiah and his inauguration of the Kingdom of God."[2] Rejecting the extremes of either a one-sided realized eschatology or a futuristic apocalyptic, Professor Oudersluys seeks to hold in biblical balance an inaugurated eschatology which does not eliminate the temporal aspects of God's consummation of history.[3]

It is interesting—and probably theologically significant—to note that his "Theology of the New Testament" concludes with a brief treatment of the final glory of God and a lengthy quotation from the venerable Princeton Calvinist, B. B. Warfield.[4] What is significant about this is that although no one has been more aware of and sensitive to the latest developments in biblical theology than Richard Oudersluys, in the last analysis he never moved very far from his early moorings. His mature theological position was much broader and deeper than that of his early days, but all of his sophisticated scholarship and understanding never led him to forsake the faith of his fathers. Occasionally students have raised questions about their professor's orthodoxy, but most if not all of them, in looking back, recognize that it was their immaturity, not Professor Oudersluys' orthodoxy, that was the problem.

Several other aspects of our honoree's teaching career should be noted. In the earlier years of his service at the Seminary he also assisted the Bible and Religion Department at Hope College. Particularly during the early post-war years when the student enrollment increased so suddenly he was often in demand to teach courses both in Greek and in biblical studies. Hope College, recognizing his scholarship and special gifts in teaching and preaching, awarded him the Doctor of Divinity degree in 1945.

Another aspect of Professor Oudersluys' career at Western is the diversity of his offerings and his willingness to share or surrender certain courses as more specialized scholars were added to the faculty. During his years at the Seminary he has taught courses on subjects as diverse as church administration and the Constitution of the Reformed Church in America, on the one hand, and archaeology, worship, and homiletics, on the other.

He has also made major contributions in two non-curricular phases of seminary life. As chairman of the library committee for many years, he played a key role in the construction of the present library (a structure which was not in the original plans for the Seminary). Equally important has been the advice and counsel he gave to the Seminary librarians through the years. His knowledge of current biblical and theological literature was invaluable in making crucial decisions for acquisitions at a time when budgets were very low and general faculty input was minimal.

Professor Oudersluys' other major extracurricular contribution was his involvement with the *Western Seminary Bulletin* (1947-1955), the first official scholarly publication of the Seminary, and its successor, the *Reformed Review*. Together with his close friend and colleague, Lester Kuyper, he was instrumental in founding the *Bulletin*, and an examination of "The Writings of Richard C. Oudersluys" listed at the end of this volume reveals that he published twenty major essays in the *Bulletin* and the *Review*. Because the list of book reviews in his bibliography is selective, it may be noted here that, in all, he wrote seventy-seven reviews for these two journals alone through the Fall, 1976, issue of the *Reformed Review*. During his last year of full service at the Seminary he also acted as editor of the *Reformed Review*, a fitting way to close a long career devoted to solid scholarship for the benefit of the Seminary, the church, and the academic world.

It is appropriate to conclude this sketch of our friend's career as a professor at Western Seminary by recognizing his outstanding effectiveness as a teacher. From the outset he was a very popular instructor, even though he made heavy demands on his students. There were periods—especially the activist '60s—when certain types of students were impatient with his quiet insistence on laying the careful exegetical foundations they judged to be no longer relevant. But he was always highly respected by all students. Moreover, there is general agreement among those privileged to study under him that he has been one of the finest classroom lecturers in the history of Western Seminary.

To impress students when one is young and fresh, or when one is in his academic prime, is one thing. To continue to challenge and stimulate students to the very end of one's career is quite another matter. What has been most impressive and heartwarming is to see how Richard Oudersluys' last years have been among his best. This is the judgment of many recent students. One illustration will suffice. One of his most popular courses for many years has been an elective on the parables and miracles, one of his specialties.[5] When this course was offered the fall term of his final year, only middler and senior students were eligible. Because of the large enrollment the academic dean asked the members of the middler class if they would postpone this experience with the understanding that the course would be offered again during the spring term. This was the first time in the history of the Seminary that an elective course was offered twice in one academic year.

III. Churchman

Seminary professors are often criticized for being out of touch with the realities of parish life. Pastors sometimes complain that professors do not really understand their problems, and lay people frequently feel that seminary faculty members do not speak their language. There is some basis for these misgivings, but Western Seminary professors have always been exceptionally active, concerned churchmen. This has been so much the fact that at times the above criticism could even be turned around to say that some Western professors have given so much time to the local church and the denomination that their academic output has suffered. In the case of Richard Oudersluys there has been an ideal blending of solid scholarship, superior classroom performance, and a steady, significant contribution to the life and work of the church.

Mention has already been made of his preaching, a gift he has continued to exercise throughout his long academic career. But preaching is only one aspect of his great concern for parish and church. Few professors—outside the specialists in the area—have invested so much time and energy in the production of instructional material for catechism and Sunday School. While a pastor in Milwaukee, he published in rapid succession his four catechetical books for children. One incentive was to provide suitable materials for his own offspring! The durability of this contribution is seen in the fact that some of these volumes are still in print.

In the long run, however, much more time was spent writing a weekly lesson exposition based on the International Sunday School Lessons for the *Boys' Guide* and the *Girls' Guide*. This task was begun in the pastorate (1935) and continued well into his seminary career (1961). During this same twenty-six-year period (1935-1961) Professor Oudersluys contributed a weekly column on the Christian Endeavor topic for the *Sunday School Guide*. It is noteworthy that one of the major contributions of one of the most erudite professors in the history of

Western Seminary was to the children and youth of his denomination.

Nor were his contributions confined to the Reformed Church in America. In 1940 he wrote a series of six articles about Jesus for *Forward*, a magazine produced by the Board of Publications of the Presbyterian Church in the U.S.A. In addition, from 1948 until 1962 he wrote a weekly column, "Insight Into Difficult Passages," for the *Adult Uniform Lessons*, a quarterly published jointly by the Presbyterian Church, U.S., the United Presbyterian Church, and the Reformed Church in America.

Other contributions appeared in the official denominational weekly the *Church Herald*, and its predecessors, the *Leader* and the *Intelligencer-Leader*, including a series of short expositions on familiar texts frequently misunderstood. Without being exhaustive, this review of his publications provides ample evidence that Richard Oudersluys was willing and able to share generously of his life and learning with the children, youth, and adults of the church.

It could be argued that, for all of that, a theological professor remains isolated from the issues of daily life as long as he restricts his contributions to the pen and the pulpit. But that has not been the way of our colleague. In the midst of his teaching, preaching, and writing he somehow found time to teach lay-leadership training classes in New Testament studies in Holland, Muskegon, and Grand Rapids; to teach Sunday School classes at his own church, the Third Reformed Church in Holland; and to teach courses at midweek services in churches throughout western Michigan. In earlier years, again often with Lester Kuyper, he frequently represented the Seminary on mission-fest tours in various parts of the Midwest. He also made major contributions during the 1960s to the Reformed Church's Commission on Liturgy,[6] and during the 1970s to its Theological Commission. Another area of extended concern and involvement was the former Board of Domestic Missions. In particular he was interested in the work of the new immigrant churches in Canada and for several years was chairman of the Committee for Canadian Work. Thus there has never been a period when he was not actively involved in some phase of congregational as well as denominational church life.

What is especially impressive is the way Richard Oudersluys has continued to give unstintingly of himself as retirement approached. In his late sixties, an age when most men are enjoying retirement, he has maintained a pace rarely achieved by many younger men. He has continued to carry a full teaching assignment, has lectured frequently at various conferences and consistory retreats, and has occasionally taught simultaneously on Wednesday evenings and Sunday mornings. In 1974-75, at the age of sixty-eight, he joined a local pastor and two seminarians to form a ministry team that spent several hours each Wednesday evening in a Grand Rapids congregation. He was not the team leader, but simply one among equals. Those fortunate students and the minister and members of that congregation will long remember his participation as a singular act of unselfish devotion to Christ.

In these many ways the man known primarily as a teacher and scholar has been an active churchman, willing to contribute to the life and work of the whole church whenever and wherever possible.

IV. Friend

Richard Oudersluys is a quiet, reserved, and unassuming man. He can slip in and out of a crowd—as he often does in his home church on Sunday mornings—without being noticed except by the people who happen to be at his side. His many achievements accordingly often go unnoticed. Like any man he appreciates recognition, but unlike most he does not advertise his accomplishments. This is not to suggest that he is either unknown or unappreciated. In his own quiet, modest way he makes his mark. In a remarkable way he is the embodiment of the gentleman and the scholar. As far back as this writer can remember, Richard Oudersluys has possessed certain qualities that set him apart. To those who did not know him well he sometimes appeared rather detached. He was always cordial and gracious and did not lack a sense of humor, but there was a reserve bordering on aloofness at times which prevented many people from drawing close to him.

To his colleagues, however, he was always loyal, considerate, and cooperative. Two relationships in particular should be singled out. His arrival as a professor at Western Seminary had been preceded by that of Lester Kuyper,[7] an Old Testament scholar, who had begun to teach at his alma mater two years earlier. They had been friends since their days at Western, although their personalities and temperaments were quite different. They had gone in opposite directions since their graduation, but as colleagues they shared the same concern: to approach the Scriptures reverently as the very Word of God but at the same time to use the historical-critical method as honestly and diligently as possible in order to understand the true meaning of the text. Although both of them were firmly rooted in the Reformed tradition and were always loyal to it, their probing, questioning ways inevitably evoked occasional misunderstanding and suspicion. They were not always in agreement, but through the calm and storm of three decades they supported each other. Moreover, as has already been noted, they collaborated in various ventures and were largely responsible for the academic upgrading and updating of the Seminary in the post-war period.

When James Cook joined the faculty in 1963 in order to assist Professors Oudersluys and Kuyper in the biblical languages, another beautiful relationship developed. Although a junior professor and former student of both of his senior colleagues, James was treated as an equal from the outset. In addition, he came to enjoy an unusual affection and esteem on the part of his colleagues in the biblical department (including that of the fourth member, Professor John Piet). The deep and tender friendship that evolved between James Cook and Richard Oudersluys has been a model of Christian love.

In less intimate settings the same dimensions of friendship could not be expected, but many people from quite different backgrounds would claim Richard Oudersluys as a good friend, one who is kind, gentle, and generous rather than withdrawn or aloof. These friends range from long-standing acquaintances at the Third Reformed Church in Holland to the members of the Social Progress Club with whom he has met monthly for almost twenty-five years. In the latter group, consisting largely of professional men, he was challenged to present papers on social, economic, and political themes. These friends hold Richard Oudersluys in high esteem not only for his insights and incisive presentations, but also for his fairness and openness to new and differing ideas.

Friendships of a different sort were made during sabbaticals at the University of Basel in Switzerland and the University of Cambridge in England. Scholars from other parts of the world came to know and appreciate Professor Oudersluys when they visited the Western campus. Many of these friends are represented in this *Festschrift*.

These friendships notwithstanding, it must be conceded that for most of his academic career Richard Oudersluys was content with the rather formal relationship between professor and student. He was always courteous, helpful, and respectful, even with indifferent and recalcitrant students, but very few of them came to know him as a friend—at least during their student days. One reason was his innate personal reserve; another was the closeness of the Oudersluys family. The family circle, especially the relationship between husband and wife, was so close-knit that there was apparently little need or desire to go beyond it for intimate social relationships.

All of this changed suddenly on April 3, 1973, when Richard and Marian were returning from West Virginia after a visit with their son Richard, Jr., and his family. A tragic automobile accident resulted in the immediate death of Marian, and left Richard with serious injuries. For several days his condition remained critical and many of his friends and colleagues feared that even if he did recover his health, his teaching career was probably at an end. It was not simply his age and the physical effects of the accident; it was also a question as to whether he could recover emotionally from so great a personal loss.

But a veritable miracle occurred. Not only was there an amazing recovery from the effects of the accident, but there was also a powerful determination to carry on as before. A replacement had been acquired to teach his courses for the remainder of the last term, but within a few weeks he was back in the classroom, teaching all his courses. It was not an easy task, but he did not solicit sympathy or special treatment. At the same time, he did not pretend that the grief was not deep and the loneliness painful—even after the months stretched into years.

Nevertheless, this tragedy has been slowly and gently edged with touches of light. In the mysterious providence of God, what might have destroyed a man and an illustrious career became the means to an altered life and a revitalized career. This was more than the mellowing that comes with age; more even than the deepening of a sensitive Christian life, tempered by tragedy. In Richard Oudersluys there was also a deep and wondrous stirring with the result that qualities and virtues which before had been veritably hidden now burst forth in a fresh springtime of service.

One remembers with gratitude that the Seminary community was a wonderful instrument in this recovery and renewal. A host of friends rallied around Richard in his hour of need, but over the years it was especially his colleagues who helped him during the day-to-day struggle. As loving hearts reached out and touched him, he opened up and responded in ways not known before. The students soon sensed a change. Here was a Richard Oudersluys who now shared with them the fullness of his heart and mind. The emotions, the affection, and the love had always been there, but only those within a small circle were privileged to glimpse this side of the gentleman and the scholar. Now the circle was suddenly enlarged and countless people—students above all—came to recognize and be blessed by a warm faith and deep piety which before had been almost hidden. The preacher, teacher, and churchman wielded new influence as a compassionate counselor, confidant, and spiritual guide. In ways new and wonderful he had become a friend.

Those of us who have contributed to this volume are representatives of countless others who pay tribute to this friend who has enriched our lives and who has served the church of Jesus Christ so faithfully as a servant of the Word. Our prayer is that, in the future as in the past, Richard Oudersluys may know the blessing of a continuing ministry to the glory of God.

NOTES

1. Among his publications see especially:
"The Resurrection and the Christian Life," *Western Seminary Bulletin*, 2, no. 4 (March, 1949), 3-5.
"Biblical History and Faith," *Western Seminary Bulletin*, 7, no. 2 (September, 1953), 1-4.
"Eschatology and the Church," *Reformed Review*, 16, no. 4 (May, 1963), 8-18.
"Eschatology and the Holy Spirit," *Reformed Review*, 19, no. 2 (December, 1965), 3-12.

2. "The Theology of the New Testament: A Syllabus" (mimeographed, Holland, Mich., 1962), p. 118.

3. *Ibid.*, pp. 119ff.

4. *Ibid.*, p. 127.

5. See:
"Preaching the Parables and Miracles of Jesus," *Western Seminary Bulletin*, 5, no. 2 (September, 1951), 5-8.
"The Parable of the Sheep and Goats (Matthew 25:31-46): Eschatology and Mission, Then and Now," *Reformed Review*, 26, no. 3 (Spring, 1973), 151-161.

6. His long-time interest in this subject is evident in the following articles and essays:
"The Place and Need of a Formulated Liturgy in the Reformed Church," *Church Herald*, May 18, 1951, p. 24.
"The Revision of Our Liturgy," *Western Seminary Bulletin*, 8, no. 4 (March, 1955), 1-4.
"Liturgy in the New Testament," *Reformed Review*, 9, no. 4 (June, 1956), 45-55.
"The New Liturgy: The People's Book," *Church Herald*, June 14, 1968, p. 14.

7. Lester Kuyper retired in May, 1974, but continues to teach at the Seminary on a part-time basis. Cf. the *Festschrift* in his honor, *Grace Upon Grace: Essays in Honor of Lester J. Kuyper*, ed. by James I. Cook (Grand Rapids: Wm. B. Eerdmans, 1975).

1: *The Christology of the Fourth Gospel: History and Interpretation**

HERMAN RIDDERBOS

I

The way the image of Jesus is depicted in the Fourth Gospel continues to arouse discussion. There is often talk of the "riddle" of the Fourth Gospel—the totally unique witness of this book to the person and work of Jesus Christ in his life on earth, a witness that seems quite removed from the historical Jesus-image of the synoptics. In other words, it is the relation between the historical reality of Jesus' life and John's interpretation of this reality—which can be called (for better or worse) his "Christology"—which is continually under consideration in biblical and dogmatic theology. Some recent developments in this discussion bring to the fore what in my opinion is essential for understanding the Fourth Gospel and solving its so-called riddle.

Some scholars feel the Fourth Gospel bears the character of a theological interpretation to such an extent that they deny the author any historical intention at all. This does not mean that he was such a poor historian, but rather that he has consciously and purposely portrayed the image of Jesus in a mystical or symbolic way. His purpose was not to recount history, but to express his ideas about the divine person and message of Jesus in historical images. Although these idealistic and mystical interpretations of the Gospel (for instance, that of F. C. Baur, father of the Tübingen school, and that of A. Loisy, the French priest noted for his part in the so-called "modernist controversy") do not receive much support nowadays, radical historical criticism of the Fourth Gospel is still alive. For Bultmann, in his well-known commentary, the Gospel has hardly any historical value. What counts for him is

*This article was first published in Professor Ridderbos' recent book *Studies in Scripture and Its Authority*, Copyright © 1978 by Wm. B. Eerdmans Publishing Co.

John's *interpretation*. The characteristic of this book, according to Bultmann, is that the works of Jesus as the Revelator are described in the language of mythology, specifically in what he calls the gnostic myth of the Redeemer, a supernatural being who descends from heaven, brings people real knowledge, and then returns to God. In the gnostic conception of reality, however, the glory (*doxa*) of the Redeemer is a hidden glory, visible only to those who are able to discern this glory with the eyes of faith, to people who are spiritually sighted, not blind. According to this underlying gnostic conception the keyword in the Gospel, "the Word became flesh" (John 1:14), is to be understood in terms of the complete hiddenness of the revelation, which is designated by the word "flesh." This saying means: the Word became man and nothing else but a man. This is the great paradox, the *skandalon* in the revelation of Jesus Christ. He came to reveal the glory of God, but there was in him nothing glorious or divine that could be seen and recognized other than by faith. The Christology of the Fourth Gospel as Bultmann explains it therefore appears to be of a *kenotic* nature.

To be sure, Bultmann is aware that the Fourth Gospel also contains a number of tremendous miracles, in which the glory of the Redeemer seems to reveal itself in all clarity for the eyes of all people. But Bultmann does not consider that the miracles in the Fourth Gospel had this significance for the author. In relating the miracles in their spectacular form, he was merely joining the tradition. For him miracles had only symbolic significance; they meant nothing in themselves. They are just another sort of *kerygma* and can mean something only for those who understand their deeper, symbolic reality. The whole Gospel is therefore nothing but a mythological expression of the *kerygma* that in the encounter with Jesus Christ one is confronted with the Word of God. Not the knowledge of the "historical Jesus," but the existentialistic decision (*Entscheidung*) with which he confronts us, is important.

Remarkable is the criticism of Bultmann by the well-known scholar Ernst Käsemann. On the one hand, as a pupil of Bultmann, coming out of the same radical tradition, he approaches the historical reliability of the Gospel no less critically than does Bultmann. According to Käsemann, the Fourth Gospel, measured by our concept of reality, is more fantastic than any other book of the New Testament. He, too, believes that the book originated in heretical circles of a gnostic character and that the evangelist has described the historical Jesus on the basis of a gnostic concept of reality. That is why he could work with the historical tradition so freely and imaginatively, because historicity in itself does not have much value for the gnostic. On the other hand, Käsemann's conception of the Christology of the Fourth Gospel is precisely the opposite of

Bultmann's interpretation. While Bultmann argues that the glory of Jesus in the Fourth Gospel is a totally hidden one and the Redeemer became man and no more than man, Käsemann says that the Fourth Gospel is surely meant to give a description of the abundant glory of Jesus in the flesh. His is a completely different—and, in my opinion, much better—explanation of John 1:14. Of course it reads "the Word became *flesh*," but then follows "and dwelt among us . . . and we have beheld his glory." The incarnation was not a means of *concealing* the glory, but in fact of *revealing* it. It is the glory of the divine Logos of God, which has revealed itself in overwhelming majesty in the flesh, which has empowered him to perform the greatest miracles, which enabled him to dispute with his opponents with unlimited superiority, which resulted in his going into death as the triumphant one. That is why one cannot by means of demythologizing the Gospel remove the divinity of Jesus without destroying the core of the Gospel. The image of Christ in John is not that of a man and nothing but a man, but rather of God walking on the earth. And according to Käsemann, this is how it is intended. The Gospel is not simply concerned with the *kerygma*, in the existentialistic sense of that word, but especially with the *person* of Jesus. The witness of the divinity of Jesus is really the content of the message of John—in sharp antithesis to what Bultmann says.

Käsemann's explanation of the intention of the Fourth Gospel strikes me as far nearer the truth than Bultmann's. With Bultmann all things center on the existentialistic message of the decision the individual has to take *against* the visible world, *against* what is available for us and what we can dominate ourselves, and *in favor of* the invisible world, which is not within our reach. This is the only way a person can really become human. And it is, in Bultmann's view, the "christological" message of the Fourth Gospel that brings us to this confrontation, to this paradoxical decision, as the only way of freedom and salvation. The big issue in the Fourth Gospel is therefore not Christology as such but anthropology; not the nature of Christ but the nature of salvation.

It is exactly in this respect that Käsemann differs from Bultmann. The dogma of the Fourth Gospel is not that of Bultmann's demythologizing and existentialistic interpretation, but is the dogma of the revelation of Jesus Christ in his divine glory as the Son of God. This christological dogma in the real sense of the word is the very core and heart of the message that confronts us in the Fourth Gospel. That is why, Käsemann says, the church has accepted this Gospel in spite of its possibly heretical origins and that is why the church even today cannot evade a confrontation with this message without thereby setting aside the real meaning and purpose of the Gospel of John.

In this respect Käsemann's criticism is on target. Soteriology depends on Christology, and you cannot change this order. But the consequence of this position, it seems to me, is that the question of historicity comes back with its full force. According to Käsemann the Christology of the Fourth Gospel has a naive, docetic character, originating in its gnostic background, revealing itself in its free and sometimes fantastic treatment of the historical tradition. But how then can we possibly accept the real message of this Gospel, as Käsemann has pointed it out so consistently, without falling back into a new (or old!) idealistic Christology, in which at decisive moments a spiritualistic ideology has to replace the failing historical revelation? This is the Achilles' heel of Käsemann's attempt to combine an unbiased interpretation of John's message with radical historical criticism.

More and more students of the Fourth Gospel are becoming convinced that an ahistorical approach to it is untenable, whether in the idealistic manner of F. C. Baur or the existentialistic manner of Rudolf Bultmann. It cannot be denied that John wanted to write history. The Gospel as a whole, with all its historical, chronological, and topographical details, is proof of this. Therefore one can observe a turn in the tide of opinion, in the judgment also of many whom one cannot reproach with undue conservatism or fundamentalism. C. H. Dodd, for instance, argues that the Gospel of John undoubtedly is more a theological than a historical work, but he strongly maintains its historical basis and value.

There are recent indications which point emphatically to Palestine for the historical background of the Gospel and, indeed, to a time before the fall of Jerusalem. The accuracy of various topographical references in the Gospel has been established by such experts in Palestinian archaeology as W. F. Albright and Joachim Jeremias. Since the excavation of Bethesda and its colonnades it can no longer be maintained that the five arcades mentioned in John 5 were only symbols of the five books of Moses, as some people used to do. It is no less important that the Qumran writings have opened up a rich source of comparable material proving at least that for the explanation of various Johannine ideas and motives it is not necessary to look so far afield as has often been supposed.

One cannot maintain that to the evangelist of the Fourth Gospel only the *kerygma* and not history is important. What he—like the other Gospel writers but in his own way—tried to make clear was that Jesus' life was filled with the glory of God. He recorded everything so that his readers would believe that *this* Jesus of history, who dwelt among us, is the Christ, the Son of God (20:31). The story of this Jesus must bring forth faith; faith has not brought forth the story, much less the history. This is no less fundamental for understanding the Fourth Gospel than for the other three.

Nevertheless, there is interpretation of history, too, in all four Gospels. But in the Gospel of John the element of interpretation is extremely important and, I think, manifest. This is perhaps why the historical meaning and character of the Gospel has been doubted, misunderstood, and rejected again and again.

II

This element of the interpretation of history is dominant in the Gospel from its very beginning. Everything told about Jesus stands in the supra-earthly glory of the prologue, the glory of the Logos who was with God, in whom was God. This is the glory (*doxa*) which dominates the whole Gospel. In John this glory is not only the projection of the later glory of the resurrection of Christ, but is the glory of the pre-existent Son of God, the glory from the beginning. It is perfectly clear that the evangelist, by placing the whole story of Jesus in the light of this prologue, intends to give a very special interpretation of the story of Jesus of Nazareth.

Other evangelists give their interpretations of this history, too. But there are real differences between John and the synoptics. The Gospel of Matthew, for instance, also has an all-dominating prologue—the genealogy of Jesus of Nazareth, which is traced back to Abraham. But it makes a difference whether the interpretation of the history of Jesus has its starting point in Abraham or in the eternal Logos who was in the beginning. The question may arise whether the glory is not overexposed in John. Can the abundant glory in which John places the history of Jesus be harmonized with the humanity of Jesus and not conflict with the reservation which was typical in Jesus' self-revelation—not only in the synoptics, but also in John's Gospel itself? In his farewell discourse (recorded in John 14-17), Jesus himself says: "I have yet many things to say to you, but you cannot bear them now. When the Spirit of truth comes, he will guide you into all truth. . . . He will glorify me, for he will take what is mine and declare it to you" (John 16:12ff.). And yet, time and again in the Gospel it is as if the veil has been removed already and Jesus speaks without this reservation, for example, when he says of himself "before Abraham was, I am" (8:58), or when he speaks of the glory he had with the Father before the world was (17:5, 24), or when he says that the disciples will see the Son of man ascend to "where he was before" (6:62).

There are indications that in his description John is already removing the veil lying over the revelation of the earthly Jesus. Indeed, we sometimes do not know for sure who has the word in this Gospel, the earthly Jesus or the Gospel writer who witnesses about him. This is especially true of those curious parts in John 3—vv. 12-21 and 31-46—where, as in the prologue, Jesus is spoken of in the third person: not "whoever believes in *me*," but "whoever believes in *him*." But also in passages where Jesus is introduced in the first person, he sometimes speaks in an undisguised fashion about his pre-existent glory, and then it seems as if all boundaries between his eternal and earthly existence disappear.

At this point we have to take into consideration again what Jesus said to his disciples in the last discourses about their future witness to him. Among other things, he said that when he himself was no longer with them, the Holy Spirit would teach them everything and remind them of all he had said to them (14:26). Exactly the same thing is said in 15:26: "*he* will be a witness to me; and *you* also are witnesses, because *you* have been with me from the beginning." There is thus a close connection between those who were with Jesus from the beginning as ear- and eye-witnesses and the witness of the Spirit. The operation of the Spirit will be more than merely sharpening the memory of the apostles concerning the exact words of Jesus; it will also be teaching them, expounding all that Jesus had taught.

It may rightly be asked whether we are here given an indication, a clear hint, that the evangelist is himself aware that he is giving the words of Jesus in a new interpretative and creative form. This might explain the words of 16:25 that Jesus has up to now spoken in figures (*paroimiais*), but that the hour is coming when he will speak plainly of the Father. May we assume that that hour comes in the Gospel itself when (in our judgment) the veil is already removed and Jesus seems to speak freely of his Father? In other words, here in the testimony of the evangelist to the readers of the Gospel, the Spirit, who explicates everything, is already jointly declaring the word. Through the Spirit as his witness Jesus is speaking plainly of the Father, also in the words of the Gospel. That is why there is this sort of duality: on the one hand the tradition and the memory of John as eyewitness, on the other the teaching by the Spirit, as a result of which there comes about the removal of the veil which had been laid over the self-revelation of the glory of Jesus.

Perhaps we can say that the historical image gets, as a result, a surplus value, because it is seen now in the light not only of the later exaltation of Jesus, but before all things in the light of the Logos, who was from the beginning. This image of the historical Jesus is not only drawn with the help of memory and tradition, but also with the aid of the Spirit. The Spirit taught them who Jesus really was and what was the secret of his glory. And John himself refers for this image to what Jesus had promised him and the other apostles in his last discourses with them.

III

As a result of this does the image of Jesus given by John become less historical, even docetic? Is the Fourth Gospel (as some have said) the Gospel of a God wandering over the earth, no longer the Gospel of the man Jesus of Nazareth? I think it can scarcely be questioned that John himself regards Jesus as a real man. You can even cite the Fourth Gospel especially to prove that Jesus was a man of flesh and blood. It is the Gospel of John which lays stress on the fact that water and blood came out of the side of the dead Jesus; that, in his life, he showed human needs, became tired and thirsty, wept at the grave of his friend, was deeply moved by the prospect of his own impending death (19:34; 6:7; 11:35; 12:27). In addition the Gospel constantly mentions Jesus' *obedience* to the will of his Father, to which he had to *submit* himself, even when this would lead him into deep *humiliation*. All this can scarcely be contested.

But the question remains whether it is not true that all these human traits and features are deeply overshadowed by Jesus' divine glory and his unity with his Father, so that his humanity is totally absorbed by his deity and his incarnation (1:14) is nothing but a temporary medium through which God's glory in him was revealed to the people. According to Käsemann, who styles the Christology of the Fourth Gospel as naive and docetic, this docetism is especially evident in the way John speaks about the death of Jesus. In the Fourth Gospel, according to Käsemann, the glory of Jesus so controls the total development that fitting in the passion becomes a problem. It comes into the picture only at the end, as a sort of appendix. Naturally the Gospel writer could not bypass Jesus' death. He finally solves the problem by describing the passion as a sort of glorification. The cross is no longer the accursed tree but the proof of his divine love and his glorified return out of the exile to the Father. That is why, with a peculiar wordplay, the Fourth Gospel sometimes speaks about the cross as the exaltation of Jesus (3:14; 8:28; 12:32, 34) and other times as his glorification (7:39; 12:16, 23; 13:31; 17:1, 5).

Still, with this not everything has been said about John's interpretation of Jesus' death. Even though on his way to the cross Jesus showed himself to be the mightiest (the officers and soldiers arresting him in

Gethsemane fall down; 18:6), John describes his suffering from other viewpoints as well—for instance, from the viewpoint of humiliation and self-surrender as the bitter cup his Father gives him to drink (18:11); and as "hating of his life" (12:25). Also it becomes abundantly clear that John sees the death and self-humiliation of Jesus as necessary for those who belong to him. Only when the grain of wheat falls into the earth and dies does it bear fruit (12:24). Jesus is, according to the word of the high priest, the one who dies *for* the people (11:50, 51). For their sake he sanctifies himself; that means he consecrates himself to death (17:19), and only if he washes their feet in humiliation do they have a part with him. Thus John the Baptist, at the very beginning of this Gospel, can call Jesus the Lamb of God who took away the sin of the world. In all this we have not even spoken of the so-called sacramental discourses (John 6), in which Jesus speaks of the eating of his flesh and the drinking of his blood as the meat and drink for eternal life. No matter how much in the Fourth Gospel's description of the death of Jesus his glorification receives strong emphasis, it is not yet the case that his death is nothing but a return, a passage, an exaltation. The writer of the Fourth Gospel not only presupposes the Christian tradition with regard to the meaning of Jesus' death (cf. also 1 John 2:2), but he also brings it to expression, though partially and incidentally. This also means that the flesh was not only the medium of the revelation of his glory, but also the way he had to sacrifice himself for his people (10:11), bearing their sins.

All these features can hardly be reconciled with a docetic Christology. Quite properly others have pointed out that it would be more correct—on their grounds—to call the Christology of the Fourth Gospel anti-docetic. They also appeal for this opinion to the First Letter of John, which clearly and purposely rejects docetism: "Every spirit which confesses that Jesus Christ has come in the flesh is of God, and every spirit which does not confess Jesus is not of God. This is the spirit of antichrist" (1 John 4:2, 3).

Still, the more firmly this is maintained, the more the question comes to the fore of how it all can be harmonized with the mighty, actually blinding light that floods through the whole of the Fourth Gospel from the prologue in chapter 1. Can one really speak of incarnation and of being man when the subject of the incarnation is the Logos, who has been with God and has been God before the world was? The question comes up anew when Jesus testifies of himself "before Abraham was, I am" and when he prays in chapter 17 that God will glorify him with the glory he had with God before the world was. Is the humanity not inevitably absorbed in the divinity, the *vere homo* sacrificed to the *vere deus*? Is such a Christology "from above" not automatically docetic, and can there be a starting point for a genuinely non-docetic Christology other than the revelation of the historical Jesus—which means a Christology "from below"?

I am not here asking how we can fathom the mystery of the incarnation of the Son of God. Nor is it my intention to go into the dogmatic formulations the church has used in its efforts to bring to expression the mystery in human words (pre-eminently at Chalcedon, but also afterwards). All those questions and definitions are coming up again in the present theological discussion, especially the formula of the non-personal human nature of Christ. I am not suggesting that I can answer all these questions. All I mean to discuss here is the question of exegesis and biblical theology: How could the author of the Fourth Gospel, who spoke (as we have seen) so massively about the humanity of Christ (even after his resurrection; cf. 20:20, 27; 21:13) and did not shrink from the tremendous harshness of the expression that the Logos "became flesh," at the same time make in his prologue the divine Logos the subject of his whole Gospel? This question is related to another old problem: How did our author come to know and understand the Logos itself?

IV

To start with the last question, there is a tendency to think that the Gospel writer had previously had a certain dogmatic or philosophical knowledge of the figure of the Logos and that in the light of that knowledge he wanted to acquaint his readers with the person of Jesus. This is the presupposition of all interpretations which say that John derived the figure of the Logos from the religious philosophy of that time—from Philo or the Hermetic writings (as C. H. Dodd suggests) or from the gnostics (Bultmann's view)—to introduce Jesus in this way to his Hellenistic contemporaries. This is indeed a Christology "from above," from a transcendent a priori—in this case the philosophical abstraction of a Logos, no matter from whatever syncretistic origin it comes.

It seems to me that there are insurmountable objections to this interpretation. First of all, the idea of such an abstract, philosophical, more or less personified Logos, who would have stood as a kind of intermediate principle or being between God and man is apparently not the motive for the author of the Fourth Gospel to start his prologue with the opening words of the Torah. Furthermore, in the following chapters of the Gospel any hint that the name Logos would point to such a philosophical background is lacking. There is in other words nothing in the Fourth Gospel even to favor such an interpretation of the name

Logos, much less to warrant speaking in terms of proof for it.

The question is thus justified the more: How can anyone imagine that the evangelist would have taken as the all-dominating starting point of his message such a philosophical abstraction? His whole Gospel, as a matter of fact, consists of a witness to the total uniqueness of Christ. How could he then have reduced this witness to the lowest common denominator and made it dependent on a figure out of the syncretistic religiosity or philosophy of his time?

The real key to understanding John's speaking of the Logos must be sought in the identity of the opening of the prologue and that of Gen. 1:1—"in the beginning." This is confirmed by the opening of the First Epistle of John: the Logos of which the evangelist is speaking is the dynamic, creating Word of God which called the world into being. To be sure, Genesis 1 does not speak of the Logos in the personal sense of John 1. Some have explained this "personalization" with reference to parallels in the Wisdom literature, where Wisdom is also introduced as speaking from the beginning. Likewise the Torah is sometimes described as being from the beginning with God. By analogy, John is said to have spoken of the Logos as the personified Word of God. But still the difference is essential. The Logos in the prologue of John is not just a personification but a Person, and, at the same time, a person of whom it is said that he was with God and that he was God—an idea that has no analogy whatever within the framework of traditional Jewish thinking but would have been judged there as totally unacceptable if not blasphemous.

Therefore, John's concept of the Logos cannot be classified with contemporary pagan and Jewish speculations or personifications, without thereby infringing on its unique character. What must come to the fore here is not John's indebtedness to contemporary religious or philosophical ideas about creation, but the overwhelming revelation of the historical Jesus himself. When the evangelist wants to express the glory of him whose witness he is, he cannot speak of this glory in any other way but in divine categories, because this glory exceeds everything that preceded him in history, even the glory of Moses. That is why the evangelist falls back on the dynamic, creating Word at the beginning of all God's ways, the Word that called forth light out of darkness and created life: the Logos of life that was from the beginning. "The life was made manifest and we saw it, and testify to it, and proclaim to you the eternal life which was with the Father and was made manifest to us" (1 John 1:2).

What is new is that in the prologue to the Gospel and in the opening of John's First Letter this Word and light and life are introduced as a person, albeit that the person and his salvatory significance are spoken of alternately. We might better say that Logos has not yet become the standard title of the pre-existent Son of God. What is said of the Logos can be said of the light, too: that it has been with the Father from the beginning. It is not just the name of the Logos that counts, it is he himself, who was in the beginning, who also can be named life and light, who has been revealed now. For what is said is that God's creative speaking from the beginning, his light- and life-bringing word, has become flesh and blood in Jesus Christ and has dwelt among us. And so from now on this Word, this life, this light can be spoken of in the personal categories of "*he was*" and "*I am.*" What brought the evangelist from the divine deeds to the person is not the philosophical material from another religious world, but the beholding of God's glory in Christ about which he speaks in John 1:14.

The reflection on this and the giving of the name in the concrete sense of John 1:1 were certainly matters of time, or better, matters of the witness of those who had been with Jesus from the beginning. We may point out here that in the Old Testament and later Judaism when expression had to be given to the divine character, whether of the Messiah or the Law or Wisdom, it was often referred back to the glory of God in the beginning. One could say that lines had been drawn into which reflection could move itself. But what a prophet or a pious Jew was never able to say John said, because the proper explanation of this speaking about Christ as the Logos lies in the way the glory of God revealed itself in the person of Jesus. "He who was from the beginning" is not just a personification or idealization of how the divine glory *functioned* in the life of Jesus of Nazareth, as the Wisdom and the Law can be glorified in pre-existent personifications. It was the oneness of his person and his work, of what he did and who he was, it was the revealing of his unity with the Father, not only in love and obedience but also in will and authority, which empowered the evangelist to speak about Jesus Christ as he did in the prologue.

Therefore, the point of departure of the prologue does not lie genetically in the eternal Logos but in the historical Jesus. John does not speak about Jesus on the basis of a certain pre-knowledge of the Logos; he can speak as he does about the Logos only because he had come to know Jesus. That is why it is not strange that the name Logos is not mentioned any further in the Gospel. Jesus Christ is the great subject of the Gospel, and on the basis of his revelation it is possible to speak of the Logos as is done in 1:1-4. This does not mean that the Logos had become an attribute of or a fancy name for the earthly Jesus. No, in order to know who Jesus is one has to go back to the beginning. Without knowing how wide and high and deep the work of God has been at the beginning, one cannot understand the dimensions of the glory, of the grace, and of the truth of Jesus Christ. But the converse is also true: to be able to speak in this way, one must have seen the glory of Jesus Christ. Nobody has ever seen God, and nobody will ever know him as he is, unless that person has seen the glory of him who dwelt among us. And that is the story of Jesus of Nazareth. John is a Gospel writer, not "after all" but from the very beginning of his book. Like his predecessors, he testifies and witnesses about Jesus as he *was* when he walked and dwelt among us.

If we may understand the "Christology" of the Fourth Gospel in this way (and that is, even in its most profound and divine pronouncements, an approach "from below"), then the humanity of Jesus cannot be regarded as docetic. Without the revelation in the flesh—that is, without his entry into history and into the depth of human existence—the glory of the Son of God would not have been revealed. Without this humanity there could not possibly have been talk of the divine person in this distinctiveness. This does not solve all the problems concerning the person of Jesus Christ. In the Gospel of John the human character of his feelings, his deliberations, his decisions cannot be doubted for a moment (cf., for example, 12:27ff.; 19:26). At the same time there is, especially in the "I am" sayings, a consciousness of power, authority, and oneness with God which appears to transcend the human ego. Thus we should avoid on the one hand a onesidedness which, fully recognizing the divine image of Jesus in the Fourth Gospel, does not find sufficient place for its humanness and ends up in a docetic Christology; and on the other hand the conception that the true human nature and ego of Jesus Christ can only be maintained if the pre-existence of Christ as the Son of God, the Logos who was with God and who was God, is understood as a theological postulate, an ideal glorification of God's revelation in the man of Nazareth. For the way the glory of God in the Fourth Gospel reveals itself personally in the flesh and blood of Jesus Christ supposes a pre-existence by nature, not just in idea alone.

It is another question whether we can do more than avoid onesidedness in either direction, whether we can subsume under one formula what the author of the Fourth Gospel testified about the glory of God in the flesh of Jesus. My aim in this essay has been no more than to understand this Christology, not on the basis of an abstract conception of the Logos nor a theological presupposition about the nature of the Son of God, but on the basis of the historical revelation of God in Christ.

2: *Love in the Fourth Gospel*

LEON MORRIS

Love is one of the great themes of the Fourth Gospel. The noun agapē
occurs seven times in that writing (as against once each in Matthew and
Mark and not at all in Luke), the verb *agapaō* thirty-six times (apart from
1 John, which has thirty-one occurrences, the highest number elsewhere
in the New Testament is thirteen in Luke; Matthew has it eight times and
Mark five), and the verb *phileō* thirteen times (Matthew five, Mark one,
Luke two). These statistics are impressive but they do not tell the whole
story, for the idea of love is often present when the actual word is not
used. The traditional description of the author of this Gospel as "The
apostle of love" testifies to the centrality of love in what he wrote. It is
plain in this writing that the Father loves the Son and that he loves people
too, that the Son loves the Father and that he loves his own, and that
people are called upon to live in love.

There is a problem with the command to love "one another." Does
this mean that believers are simply to love other believers and confine
their love to the redeemed community?[1] If so, what should be their
attitude to the world outside the brotherhood? If not, why does not John
say so plainly? There is a real problem here, and we must bear it in mind
throughout our study. But we begin with the love of God.

The Love of the Father

In his great high-priestly prayer on the night before the crucifixion Jesus
spoke of love a number of times and at one point he said, "You loved me
before the foundation of the world" (17:24). The love of the Father for
the Son is not a love originating in time nor one brought about by
anything that the Son did. It is part of the eternal nature of things. The
Father loves the Son always. That must be taken as basic.

God's eternal love for his Son has its manifestation in the incarnate life of the Son. "The Father loves the Son, and shows him all things that he himself does" (5:20), which has implications for the way the Son lives. "The Father loves the Son, and he has given all things into his hand" (3:35), which is a way of saying that in his earthly mission the Son was not separated from the Father's love and, further, that that love provided him with all things necessary for the fulfillment of that mission. Once John says that the Father loves the Son because he lays down his life (10:17). This does not, of course, mean that the death of the Son is the meritorious cause of the Father's love. We have already noticed that the eternal love of the Father for the Son is plainly recognized in this Gospel and that it must be taken as basic. Here the point is that the Son is doing the will of the Father in dying for the world. The love of the Father is such that he wills the salvation of mankind even at such cost, and when the Son lays down his life the love of the Father for him is the seal that this death is that which the Father wills.[2] The cross quite obviously shows us the love of the Father for the world and the love of the Son for the world. John is saying that, rightly understood, it also shows us the love of the Father for the Son. In line with this the Son prays that the love with which the Father loved him "might be in them" (i.e., the disciples; 17:26). We never find the thought that the love of the Father stops at the Son. It is extended ceaselessly to those for whom the Son died, so that the Father may be said to love the redeemed with the love with which he loves the Redeemer.

Accordingly, Jesus speaks of the Father as loving the disciples as he has loved the Son (17:23). Or again Jesus may speak of loving them as the Father has loved him (15:9). In both ways of putting it, it is the love of the Father that is the standard. That is real love, and all other loves may be known as love only as they stand up to the test of comparison with that great love.

As might be expected, there are occasions when the love of the Father is specifically said to extend to those who have cast in their lot with his beloved Son. "The Father himself loves you," Jesus said, "because you have loved me and have believed that I came out from God" (16:27). The word "himself" is emphatic. The Father is not unwilling to receive men: he does not need to be persuaded before he will love them. Nor do the words mean that it is only because the disciples love Christ that the Father comes to love them, as though they had somehow earned the Father's love. Rather, as Augustine long ago remarked, "He would not have wrought in us something He could love, were it not that He loved ourselves before He wrought it."[3] Our love is at best an answering love. John is telling us that the Father is pleased when men and women respond to what he has done in them with love to the Son. As they love the Son and put their trust in him, they find that they are the objects of the love not only of the Son but of the Father as well. Notice that faith is linked with love. The two go together in the thinking of the fourth evangelist. We must bear in mind further that in passages like these it is not the origin of God's love that is in mind, but its continuance.[4]

The thought that to be loved by Christ is to be loved by the Father comes out elsewhere as when Jesus says, "He that loves me will be loved by my Father, and I will love him and will manifest myself to him" (14:21). This follows a reference to the importance of keeping Christ's commands as an evidence of love to him, and the sequence is repeated a verse or two later when Jesus says, "If anyone loves me, he will keep my word, and my Father will love him, and we will come to him and make our abode with him" (14:23). Love is not some airy-fairy "spiritual" thing that exists in the realm of pure thought. Love must be demonstrated in the real world where people, often unpleasant people, live. To obey Christ's commandments, to keep his word, in that kind of world is to show a real, not a theoretical, love. And that love does not go unrecognized by the Father. The Father loves the person who loves like that, and so does the Son. The result is that he who really loves enters into fellowship with his Maker, that fellowship in which he knows what it is to have God live in him while he lives in God.

The love and the unity of believers have evidential value. In his prayer Jesus said, "I in them and you in me, that they may be perfected into one, so that the world may know that you have sent me and have loved them just as you loved me" (17:23). The implication appears to be that the community is not to be an inward-looking one. Its members are to have a due regard for the way they are seen by the world outside. And it is important that they be so unified that people outside will recognize them for the recipients of the Father's love. Jesus is not saying that they should so live as to convince people of how loving they are. They are sinners, not great and outstanding and loving people. But they are loved by God and that makes all the difference. God's love is to be seen in the fact that it brings about a unity that transcends any merely earthly unity. The love that does this is the love with which the Father loves the Son (v. 26), so it is a great and abounding love. That love is to be "in them," which means that it "is to become the determining power of their life."[5]

Does God then love only those who are in the community of believers? Not at all. In one of John's most memorable sayings we read, "God so loved the world that he gave his only Son, so that everyone who believes in him might not perish but have life eternal" (3:16). This is an express declaration that the love of God is wide enough to cover all mankind.[6] No one is beyond the scope of God's love. The love with which he loves us is a love that depends on what he is rather than on what we are. It is not a love drawn out from an unwilling or neutral deity by the attractiveness of men. It is a love for all people, not just the attractive ones. And it is a love that is concerned to give the greatest of all sacrifices in order that they might be saved. This means that those whom God loves were perishing apart from that love. They were sinners. But because he is a God who loves, their sin could not be the last word. God's love found a way to save them from perishing and to open up the way of salvation.

This is the great thought of the Fourth Gospel. "God did not send his Son into the world to condemn the world, but so that the world might be saved through him" (3:17). Salvation from sin, not judgment for sin is the Father's purpose in sending his Son. And John tells us in set terms that he wrote his Gospel so that his readers might come to believe in Jesus as Christ and divine Son and in this faith might have life eternal (20:31). His whole Gospel is full of the thought. One of the expressions that recurs is "the Father who sent me," and the question that arises is "Why did the Father send the Son?" We have just seen the answer in terms of love and the cross, and this answer is implied everywhere. God sent his Son to bring mankind back to him. His love was as great as that.

This comes out in other ways. In the Prologue we read, "There was a man sent from God whose name was John" (1:6), and the writer goes on to detail how the preaching of this man formed a strong testimony to Jesus (cf. 5:33, 35). Indeed, in this Gospel the one thing John the Baptist does is to bear witness to Jesus. He is constantly pointing people to him. The entire mission and message of John the Baptist is an indication of God's care for sinners, for God "sent" him. The mission shows us God's concern, and the recording of it shows us John's.

The Prologue has other evidences of the love of God. It tells us that the Word became flesh and dwelt among us (1:14). It speaks of him as "full of grace and truth" (*ibid.*).[7] It says that it is "of his fullness" that all have received (1:16). It speaks of "grace upon grace" (*ibid.*). It informs us that, while nobody has ever seen God, the only begotten has set him forth (1:18). In none of these verses is the love of God expressly mentioned, but how can we understand any of them apart from that love? The evangelist is telling a story of love, of that great divine love which sent the Word to dwell among us (though that meant all the condescension involved in becoming flesh) so that we might receive God's good gift. "Grace" is one of the great Christian words, and it is eloquent of God's concern for unworthy sinners. And why should the Son set the Father forth unless it were to bring men and women out of their bondage to sin and lead them into the place of blessing and of love?

As we move from the Prologue to the body of the Gospel the same concern is constantly manifested. The love of God is everywhere. But it will be more convenient to consider the remaining sections under the heading "The Love of the Son," for the Father has chosen to do his work through that Son. It is not that the love of the Son is more real than that of the Father. That is nonsense. It is rather that the way we see the love of the Father is in what he has done for us in the person of his Son Jesus Christ.

The Love of the Son

During the discourse in the upper room Jesus spoke of doing what the Father commanded "in order that the world may know that I love the Father" (14:31). Curiously this is the one place in John, and for that matter the one place in the whole New Testament, where Jesus is explicitly said to love the Father. That love is implied everywhere, but this is the one place where any of the New Testament writers gives it expression. It is fundamental to Jesus' life, and the whole of that life was lived in trust in the Father and obedience to his will. Jesus comes back to the thought of his concern to keep the Father's commandments a little later (15:10), adding that he abides in the Father's love. Love and doing the will go together.

This is seen also in the love Jesus has for his followers, for he said, "He who has my commandments and keeps them, he it is who loves me; and he who loves me will be loved by my Father, and I will love him and manifest myself to him" (14:21). We have already noticed that this kind of saying does not mean that the divine love is earned by what men do. God's love comes first. But Jesus is saying that there is a close tie between the love of the Father and that of the Son for us, on the one hand, and the love and obedience that is the response to that divine love on the other. Christ is not indifferent to the way we respond, and he considers the keeping of his commands important. That is the way we enter into the fullness of the blessing and receive the manifestation of Christ. Probably much the same is in mind in the command, "Continue in my love" (15:9), which follows Christ's statement that he loves the disciples as the Father loves him.

There are some striking statements about the depth of Christ's love. Thus we are told right at the beginning of the upper-room narrative that "he loved his own[8] who were in the world" and that "he loved them utterly [or, to the end]" (13:1). The Greek is capable of either meaning, but it seems that the emphasis is on the greatness of Jesus' love rather than on its continuance.[9] But the most significant of such sayings is that in which Jesus says, "This is my commandment, that you love one another as I have loved you. No one has greater love than this, that one lay down his life for his friends. You are my friends if you do what I command you" (15:12-14). Love is always sacrificial, but there is no greater sacrifice than the sacrifice of the life. The words are perfectly general, but they are spoken in the shadow of the cross and within a few hours Jesus was to lay down his life for those friends to whom he was speaking. There can be no doubt that he is referring to the extent of his love for them. It was no conventional affection, but a deep and abiding love that was ready to give all and did give all. There is no greater love than this.

Sometimes there are specific references to individuals whom Jesus loved. There is, of course, the unnamed "beloved disciple" over whom so much controversy has raged. Here it is not our business to try to identify him but simply to notice that it is said repeatedly that Jesus loved him (13:23; 19:26; 20:2; 21:7, 20; in 20:2 the verb is *phileō* but in all the other places *agapaō*). Jesus loved Lazarus (11:3), a fact to which the people who saw him weep when he was invited to see the tomb bore witness (11:36). John also tells us that Jesus "loved Martha and her sister and Lazarus" (11:5) where the separate listing of each of the three seems to indicate a love for each individual person rather than a general benevolence toward the family.

But as in the case of the Father, not only the passages that use one or other of the words for love are important. What, for example, are we to make of the saying of John the Baptist that Jesus is "the Lamb of God who takes away the sin of the world" (1:29)? Some scholars doubt the authenticity of the saying on the lips of John the Baptist,[10] but that is not our immediate concern. The point is that the author of the Gospel has included the words, and he plainly regards them as telling us something important about the work Jesus came to do. In his capacity as "the Lamb of God" he would die to take away the world's sin. This points to a deep concern for the world's need, a readiness to die so that the sin which the world could not take away should be effectively dealt with.

This concern runs through the whole of the opening section of the Gospel as we read of the testimony of the Baptist to Jesus (1:19, etc.) and of the bringing of the early disciples to Jesus (Andrew and his friend, 1:35ff.; Peter, 1:40ff.; Philip, whom Jesus found for himself, 1:43; and Nathanael, whom Philip brought, 1:45). That they should be brought to Jesus shows something of his concern for them and also for those who would in due course be reached through the service that they would render. Coming to Jesus means life (5:40), so we should not downgrade these enlistings of disciples. The motif continues to the end of Jesus' public ministry with the incident in which some Greeks asked Philip that they might see Jesus. Philip hesitated, but after he had consulted Andrew the two brought them to the Lord (12:20ff.). We are surely meant to see in this the truth that not only Palestinian Jews might come to Jesus but Greeks as well. His horizon and his love extended to the whole world.[11] This is specifically recognized by the Samaritans, who refer to him as "the Saviour of the world" (4:42), to which we should perhaps add the reference to his being "the light of the world" (8:12). And Jesus speaks of drawing "all men" to himself (12:32).

Jesus' first miracle at the wedding in Cana of Galilee demonstrates his concern for people who were evidently poor and unimportant in themselves. But they were in need and that was all that mattered. Jesus helped them. A similar comment might be made about each of the miracles recorded in this Gospel. In each case there was need and in each case Jesus met it. Sometimes the recipients were not exactly worthy, like the lame man in John 5. He did not know who his Healer was but, when he found out, he immediately told the opposition, thus initiating a persecution of Jesus (5:15f.). It cannot be said that Jesus healed the man because he had a deep faith (he did not even know that it was Jesus who was talking to him) or because he was an attractive person (he was nothing of the sort). He was in need and that was enough. The love of Jesus did not ask questions but acted. There is no point in working our way steadily through all the miracle stories. Jesus' compassion is evident in all of them and they all form part of the evidence that Jesus had a love for all people.

When we move into chapter 3 we find Jesus taking time to talk to Nicodemus, and in chapter 4 to the unnamed Samaritan woman he met at the well. It might be held that Nicodemus was an important person and one who deserved a hearing, but neither could be said about the woman. In both cases the overriding consideration was surely need. Jesus cared about people and he gave himself to the meeting of their need. This kind of thing abounds in this Gospel, and it may fairly be said that, as John depicts it, the whole ministry and mission of Jesus are an expression of the divine love for sinners. God's compassion on those who had gone astray is to be discerned throughout Jesus' whole life.

Expression is given to it in the incident of the washing of the disciples' feet. This was no glamorous task but menial service, the lot of the lowliest slave. John introduces this lowly act by saying, "knowing that the Father had given all things into his hands, and that he had come out from God and was going to God, he rose from supper . . ." (13:3f.). There is here Jesus' full consciousness of his high dignity and his certainty also that he would soon be reunited with the Father. And in the light of this and of the near approach of the cross Jesus laid aside his garments, took the water and the towel, and washed the feet of the disciples. This is a striking lesson in humility, but it is more than that. It is a setting forth in action of the principle of lowly service that we see on the cross. There Jesus would cleanse sinners (which is the point of his dialogue with Peter).[12] The incident is a compelling demonstration of Jesus' love and concern for those for whom he was about to die.

Sometimes we read that Jesus came to give life. He is "the bread of God" who "comes down from heaven and gives life to the world" (6:33). He came "that they may have life and have it abundantly" (10:10). This is not a gift that comes with effortless ease, for Jesus says that it is necessary to eat his flesh and drink his blood (6:53ff.). His life must be offered in sacrifice and appropriated by believers. He is the Good Shepherd who gives his life for the sheep (10:11, 15, 17f.). It is impossible to understand this aspect of John's Gospel without seeing that Jesus' whole life, and especially its culmination in the death on the cross, is an outpouring of his love for sinners and of his passion to redeem them.

Human Love

John makes it clear that that which should characterize Jesus' disciples above all else is their love. He reports Jesus as saying, "A new commandment I give you, that you love one another, as I have loved you." He goes on, "By this will all men know that you are my disciples, if you have love for one another" (13:34f.).[13] It is interesting to find the requirement of love called "new," for the commandment to love is as old as Lev. 19:18. The novelty appears to arise from the fact that it is to be practiced in a brotherhood created by the outworking of the love of Christ. There had never been a community redeemed in this way, and to have been saved by a sacrificial love means that one is brought into a situation where love is the all-important thing. There is radical novelty here, just as there is a repetition of something that is old. Jesus repeats the command, which shows that it is urgent, while the fact that their love is to be like the love he has for them, the love we see on the cross, shows that the love Jesus requires is no weak and tepid thing. This love, moreover, is not to be treasured up in secret. It is to be practiced in such a way that it will be obvious to all, to those outside the brotherhood as well as to those inside it, for it is by this love that the world is to know that the disciples belong to Jesus. And whatever may have been the shortcomings of Christ's church throughout the ages, there was a time when the heathen were constrained to say, "See how they love one another."[14] The command to love is repeated (15:12, 17),[15] and there is every indication that it was meant to be taken with the utmost serious-ness. Above all, the followers of Jesus must be loving persons. Ladd sees in this the central thing: "It is not too much to say that Jesus' whole ethic in John is summed up in love."[16]

Sometimes it is thought that there is a problem in the command to love, for love is not something we perform to order. Bultmann reminds us that this must be understood in conjunction with the whole Christian experience. It is not that non-Christians are bidden to add love to their various other activities. Jesus is addressing people who are liberated from their bondage to sin through what he has done for them, and the command to love is the outworking of the redemption that is operative in them.[17] The command shows that Jesus is not speaking about a natural emotion, nor about an affection kindled by the attractiveness of those loved. There is an emphasis on the will. The loving person is one who sets himself to respond to what God has done for him in Christ, and who wills to do what that means in practice. The test of practice is one the New Testament often makes. Fine words are no substitute for fine deeds. But we ought not to go to the other extreme, and see love as no more than the performance of certain deeds. The Good Samaritan did what was required of him in the situation. But he was also moved by compas-sion (Luke 10:33).

These days those who stress "situation ethics" often put an an-tithesis between love and obeying a set of regulations. They point out that Christians have all too often seen the living out of their faith as a matter of doing certain things and abstaining from others. Believers have often been more conspicuous for the things they do not do than for anything positive. So it is said that the one important thing is love. Keeping the commandments is of no consequence alongside this and, indeed, may be set aside, depending on the answer we give to the question, "What would love do in this situation?" I do not wish to deny the element of truth in this position, but simply to point out that it is not shared by John. Over and over he records words of Jesus that insist on the importance of doing what he says if we really love him. "If you love me you will keep my commandments" (14:15) is the simplest way of putting it. Real love for Jesus is not possible if we ignore the things he said. So our Lord went on to say, "He who has my commandments and keeps them, he it is who loves me" (14:21), and again, "If you keep my commandments, you will abide in my love, as I have kept my Father's commandments and abide in his love" (15:10).[18] Jesus is not asking his followers to do anything that he himself did not do first. He knows what it is to obey as a proof of love. He did it himself, and he asks the same of his followers.

Sometimes there is a reference to Jesus' "word" or "words," both of which seem to mean much the same. "If anyone loves me he will keep my word," while by contrast, "he who does not love me does not keep my words" (14:23, 24). Jesus' "word" stands for his whole message, and there does not seem to be a significant difference between the singular and the plural (just as there seems to be little difference between his "teaching" and his "teachings"). In this slightly different form Jesus is saying that his followers must be careful to do what he commands them. This does not mean that being a Christian means memorizing a set of rules and meticulously carrying them out. It means that the response of love to love is to do the things that are pleasing to the beloved. Christ's people are those who have been purchased at great cost, the cost of a perfect life laid down in perfect love. The love he has shown calls forth an answering love, and that love is shown in an eagerness to do the things Christ has prescribed. John is telling us that love is always costly. It cost Christ his life at Calvary, and it costs us our lives in surrender to him. Living carelessly is not an option for those who have been died for.

Now and then the disciples' love is connected with Jesus' heavenly state. Thus in the upper room he responded to their perplexity and consternation at the news that he was going to leave them by saying, "If you loved me, you would rejoice, because I go to the Father" (14:28). They did not understand enough about him to understand that his going to the Father was something wonderful. Their love was lacking. Had it been that deep and wonderful thing that a right response to his love is they would have been happy at what he told them.[19] It meant loss to them, of course (though that loss would be speedily cancelled out by events like the resurrection and the sending of the Spirit). But it meant gain to him, and true love would have rejoiced at that. Their love is seen in a somewhat more favorable light a little later when Jesus says, "you have loved me and have believed that I came forth from the Father" (16:27). Their love is connected with a faith about Jesus' heavenly origin. All the more reason accordingly for expecting them to rejoice at the news that he was to return to the Father.

Finally we should notice the scene by the sea when Jesus three times asked Peter, "Do you love me?" Three times Peter affirmed his love, and on each occasion he was commissioned to feed Christ's flock (21:15ff.). There can be no doubt that this is a way in which Jesus publicly put back into his position of leadership that disciple who had three times publicly denied him. The interesting thing for our present purpose is that the commissioning took the form of Peter's confessing his love. Jesus does not ask about Peter's faith nor whether he has learned anything from his failure. He does not interrogate him about his courage or his determination or his qualities of leadership or anything of the sort. He asks about his love. That is the one thing that matters. Love is the critical thing for the follower of Jesus.[20]

John uses the love terminology to show how and why some people go wrong. Thus he can say, "This is the condemnation, that light has come into the world, and men loved the darkness rather than the light, because their deeds were evil" (3:19). With this we should take some words of Jesus to Jews who rejected him, "You do not have the love of God in you" (5:42). The Greek here might refer to "God's love for you" or "your love for God." The probabilities are with the latter, though the former may not be out of sight. It is the consistent Christian idea that God's love is the primary thing. It was this that sent the Christ into the world to die for sinful people and bring about their salvation. Any love that they have is a response to that great love of God. Jesus is saying, then, that his hearers have failed to respond to God's love with an answering love, they did not find within them a resting place for that love of God. This is really the same thing as to say that they loved the darkness rather than the light. Love for God is demanding, and they preferred their comfortable sinful ways. In that is their condemnation.

There is something similar in the other references to love. "If God were your Father," Jesus said to the Jews who turned from him, "you would have loved me, for I came forth from God" (8:42). Their failure to respond to God's love put them outside the heavenly family and meant that they did not respond with love to the Son of that family when he came. Their values were wrong. They "loved the praise of men rather than the praise of God" (12:43). But then it is characteristic of the world to love its own (15:19). The world has never learned the lesson of the reckless self-giving of love nor the converse that "he who loves his life loses it, whereas he who hates his life in this world will keep it in life eternal" (12:25).

Love for Those Outside

So far we have seen that love is consistently demanded in the Fourth Gospel. But the passages that explicitly speak of love mostly refer to love for those in the fellowship, love for one's fellow-Christians. We have not noticed very much in the way of explicit demands for love for those outside. The emphasis on love within the brotherhood was important, given the circumstances of the early church. Surrounded by enemies, liable to persecution at any time, and with no mighty organization to keep dissidents in line and opponents at bay, it was necessary that the bonds that held the little group together be as strong as they could well be.[21] A further factor was the profound conviction that man's greatest need is the salvation Jesus died to win. It was accordingly more important to bring them the gospel than anything else. This made for a concentration on evangelism rather than on what we would call deeds of love. But we should not overlook the fact that for the early church the most important deed of love that could possibly be performed was evangelism.

John's concern for evangelism is enough to show that he is not concerned only with love for believers. And there is nothing in this Gospel to match the demand by the men of Qumran that members of the community "hate all the sons of darkness."[22] Indeed, the whole thrust of the Gospel is otherwise, for John stresses the great love of God, and the love he looks for in men and women is an answering love, not some meritorious achievement of the believer. But God's love is explicitly said to be for the world (3:16), so it is impossible to think that the love looked for in the servant of God is a narrow love within the household.[23] This is implied also in the condemnation of the world's attitude (15:19). The world knows love indeed, but it is an exclusive love, a love for its own which includes a hatred for Christ and Christ's disciples. The counter to this is not a corresponding exclusiveness, but a universal love, a love like that of the Father.[24]

Much in the Gospel bears this out. For example, Jesus had a long conversation with the woman at the well and the immediate result was that she displayed an interest in the well-being of others. She told the men of her village about Jesus and led them to him (4:28ff.). During the same incident Jesus had a conversation with the disciples in which he spoke of the importance of the harvest (v. 35) and went on to tell them that others had labored and they entered into those labors (v. 38). It is difficult to see what these labors could be if they were not labors for those outside the fellowship. Jesus is directing their endeavors outward. They are to be concerned for the needs of others than their own band, for people like the despised Samaritans whom their Master was in the process of serving.

That the believer is to be outgoing seems to be the meaning of the difficult passage about the Spirit in John 7:38. Many exegetes think that this refers to Christ, but it seems on inadequate grounds. It is better to see the passage as teaching that the believer becomes a source of blessing to others. In other words the coming of the Spirit into the life of a person turns his attention outward. He becomes deeply concerned about bringing others the blessing they need, which is another way of saying that his love is directed toward them.

And what else are we to make of Jesus' words, "If you continue in my word, you are truly my disciples, and you will know the truth, and the truth will set you free" (8:31f.)? Jesus is certainly not speaking as a philosopher and claiming that a knowledge of the truth of things will set people free from the bondage of error and superstition. He is speaking as a religious teacher and pointing them to that truth which will liberate them from sin. And what does that mean if not that they will no longer be in bondage to selfishness? There are other forms of sin, but this subtle one is certainly included. And to cease to be self-centered is to see the importance of other people. In other words the passage implies that those who come to know Jesus enter into something of his experience of love for the world. The self-centered life is condemned also in the words about him who loves his life losing it (12:25). The way to life eternal is by hating the life, which is surely a graphic way of saying that Christ's follower does not cling to life at all costs. Indeed, compared with the love he has for God his affection for life is but hatred. This puts him in the position of being more concerned with the interests of other people than he is for his own. This is so because he has come to believe in Christ and as a consequence does not walk in darkness (12:46).

I have already referred to the incident of the feetwashing and pointed out that it is a parable of humble service and that it graphically sets forth the principle of service we see so wonderfully displayed in the cross. We should bear in mind that Judas was among those whose feet Jesus washed and further that Jesus said, "you, too, ought to wash one another's feet; for I have given you an example, that as I have acted, you should act too" (13:14f.). We do not reflect often enough on the significance of these words in the light of the presence of Judas. Jesus is not saying that his followers must have a concern to serve others within the brotherhood. He is saying that they must have a concern to serve others. The inclusion of the traitor makes it clear that the words refer to others than the deserving. While we have Judas in mind it may perhaps be worth pointing out that that apostle's complaint that the perfume poured out over Jesus' feet might have been sold for more than three hundred denarii and given to the poor indicates that the apostolic band might have been expected to favor the giving of such a munificent sum to others (12:5; cf. 13:29). This does not look like self-centeredness.

Jesus made a staggering assertion when he told the disciples that they would do greater works than he did (14:12). What works were these? We should not fix our eyes on miracles as though the Lord was interested in the spectacular. His whole ministry cries out against such a view. Surely we cannot do justice to this saying without considering the outgoing, unselfish nature of his entire ministry, culminating in his self-sacrifice on the cross. "Greater works than these" (14:12) can scarcely be understood of anything inward-looking and self-centered. Whatever else the words mean, they must include a great effort on behalf of people outside the fellowship.

Throughout this Gospel there is a concern for evangelism, and John tells us that he wrote his book that people might believe (20:31). Why? It is not possible to see the Fourth Gospel as a book written in order to build up the numbers in the first-century church. Its splendor forbids any such thought. The reason for evangelism is not the aggrandizement of the church or the building up of the egos of its evangelists. It is rather that the unevangelized need the gospel. The reason is in their need, not in that of believers. The church of God may not always have evangelized from the right motives, but there is no doubting the intention of the Fourth Gospel.

From a variety of directions then we see that this Gospel is one which insists on love. The primary thing is the great love of God, a love we see in the whole ministry of Christ but more especially in his death on the cross for our salvation. That great love awakens an answering love in those who believe and that love, while obviously to be manifested among those in the household of faith, is not to be confined to them. The thrust of this book is outward, and those who have absorbed its message must be filled with love, not only to those in the family, but to those at large.

NOTES TO CHAPTER 2

1. Hugh Montefiore thinks so. He sees in the synoptics "the love that gives to anyone in need without hope of reward." By contrast, "In the Johannine litera-ture it is forbidden to love anyone outside the closed circle of the Christian community; the 'new commandment' is for reciprocal love within the Christian fellowship" (*Awkward Questions on Christian Love* [Philadelphia: Westminster Press, 1964], p. 107). So also John Knox, "There is in the Fourth Gospel no sign of interest in those outside of the community"; in John, "*Agape* is brotherly love, not neighborly love. 'The world' is given up and disregarded" (*The Ethic of Jesus in the Teaching of the Church* [London: Epworth Press, 1962], pp. 93, 94).

2. Cf. R. Bultmann, "one might equally well say that he surrenders his life because the Father loves him. What is being said here is that in his sacrifice the Father's love for him is truly present, and that this sacrifice is therefore a revelation of the Father's love" (*The Gospel of John*, trans. by G. Beasley-Murray [Philadelphia: Westminster Press, 1971], p. 384).

3. *Homilies on the Gospel of John*, CII.5; cited from *Nicene and Post-Nicene Fathers*, First Series (New York: The Christian Literature Company, 1888), VII, 391.

4. V. F. Furnish, referring to John 14:21, 23; 16:27, says, "It is important to observe, however, that the contexts from which these texts are drawn speak about

the promised *return* of Jesus as the Paraclete, God's Spirit, and thus about the *continuing* love of God and the Son for those who belong to them. Such statements in no way contradict the fundamental declaration of the Gospel that God's Son *has already been sent* in love to men and that their seeing, believing, obeying—and 'abiding in love'—is absolutely dependent upon the prior bestowal of light, life, and love" (*The Love Command in the New Testament* [Nashville: Abingdon Press, 1972], p. 146).

5. R. Bultmann, *op. cit.*, p. 521.

6. E. Käsemann dismisses this as "a traditional primitive Christian formula which the Evangelist employed" and he sees its "sole purpose in John" as stressing "the glory of Jesus' mission, that is to say the miracle of the incarnation" (*The Testament of Jesus according to John 17* [Philadelphia: Fortress Press, 1968], p. 60). But even if this is a traditional formula (which may be legitimately doubted), John would not have used it unless he accepted it. It stands as part of his writing and we have no knowledge of it apart from this. In contrast to Käsemann, C. H. Dodd says, "The statement in iii.16 is quite fundamental to our author's position, and the reader is intended to bear it in mind during the following discussions" (*The Interpretation of the Fourth Gospel* [Cambridge: Cambridge University Press, 1953], p. 307). Cf. R. Schnackenburg, who sees a reference to "God's immense love" and to the world as "the object of God's infinite love and mercy" (*The Gospel according to St John* [London: Burns & Oates, 1968], I, 399).

7. Raymond E. Brown translates, "filled with enduring love" (*The Gospel according to John*, in *AB* [Garden City: Doubleday, 1966], I, 4).

8. Bultmann reminds us that we should not see a contradiction with the Father's love for the world (John 3:16). "Of course the love of the Son, like that of the Father, is directed towards the whole world, to win everyone to itself; but this love becomes a reality only when men open themselves to it" (*op. cit.*, p. 488). Hugh Montefiore overlooks this in his curious comment, "Jesus does not pray for the world (John xiii 9) and it is to be presumed that he does not love the world, but only his disciples" (for which he cites John 13:1; *NovT*, 5 [1962], 164). Montefiore selects a few passages to support his view, but overlooks the bulk of Johannine teaching, and specifically he makes no mention of passages pointing in the other direction.

9. The Greek is *eis telos*. John often uses expressions that may be understood in more ways than one and it seems that he wants his readers to accept both meanings at least on occasion. This is not improbable here. But the aorist *ēgapēsen* seems to show that the emphasis is not on continuity, so that we should see the words as pointing primarily to the depth of Christ's great love (though it is of course true also that he did love his disciples right to the end).

10. On this point see the discussion in Leon Morris, *The Gospel according to John* (Grand Rapids: Wm. B. Eerdmans, 1971), pp. 149f.

11. Elsewhere I have written, "In this Gospel we see Jesus as the world's Saviour, and evidently John means us to understand that this contact with the Greeks ushered in the climax. The fact that the Greeks had reached the point of wanting to meet Jesus showed that the time had come for Him to die for the world" (Leon Morris, *op. cit.*, p. 590).

12. Cf. J. C. Fenton, "the cleansing of which he speaks is cleansing from everything that contradicts love" (*The Gospel according to John in The Revised Standard Version* [Oxford: Clarendon Press, 1970], p. 140).

13. C. K. Barrett comments, "John, however, more than any other writer, develops the conception of love as the nature of God himself and as the means by which the divine life, the relation of the Father and the Son, is perpetuated and demonstrated within the community (13.35)" (*The Gospel according to St John* [London, S.P.C.K., 1955], p. 180).

14. Tertullian, *Apology,* 39 (cited from *Ante-Nicene Christian Library* [Edinburgh: T. & T. Clark, 1869], XI, 119).

15. The command to love in John 15:12 is followed by "greater love has no one than this, that one lay down his life for his friends," a clear reference to Jesus' death for his own. Raymond E. Brown points out that this is an incentive to self-sacrifice which "has left a greater mark on subsequent behavior than, for example, a similar sentence in Plato (*Symposium* 179B): 'Only those who love wish to die for others' " (*op. cit.* [1970], II, 664).

16. George Eldon Ladd, *A Theology of the New Testament* (Grand Rapids: Wm. B. Eerdmans, 1974), p. 279.

17. Cf. R. Bultmann, "the care for oneself is changed into a care for one's neighbour. But since it is precisely this becoming free from the past and from oneself that is subjected to the imperative, the future that is grasped as command coincides with the future that is promised for loyalty of faith; for it was freedom from the past and from oneself that was promised to the believer. Thus the imperative is itself a gift, and this can be because it receives its significance and its possibility of realisation from the past, experienced as the love of the Revealer" (*op. cit.*, p. 525). I would take issue with him in the last word quoted: it is the love of the Redeemer, not the Revealer, that is the significant thing.

18. Sir Edwyn Hoskyns comments, "to this love is annexed obedience—indissolubly; for the fidelity of love is proved and shown forth in obedience." He goes on to affirm that "To abide in His love" and "to keep His commandments" are "but two modes of saying the same thing" (*The Fourth Gospel*, ed. by F. N. Davey [London: Faber & Faber, 1940], p. 563).

19. Raymond E. Brown thinks that the conditional construction "is meant not to deny that the disciples love him, but to indicate that their love is possessive instead of generous" (*op. cit.*, II, 654).

20. I have discussed the question of whether or not there is a difference of meaning in the two words for love used in John 21 and have come to the conclusion that there is not. See Leon Morris, *op. cit.*, pp. 871ff.

21. Cf. Hugh Montefiore, "the primitive communities would have been lost unless they had built up their own loyalties and concentrated on the strengthening of the Christian group" (*op. cit.*, p. 110).

22. Cited from G. Vermes, *The Dead Sea Scrolls in English* (Victoria, Australia: Penguin, 1962), p. 72. Raymond E. Brown seems to me to miss the thrust of John's teaching on love when he writes, "In this stress John is not far from the thought of Qumran" (*op. cit.*, II, 613). F. C. Fensham points out that love of the brothers was "a general characteristic of Jewish thought in those days," and he finds it in the Apocrypha and Pseudepigrapha or, more specifically, in *The Testaments of the Twelve Patriarchs* (*Neotestamentica*, 6 [1972], 75). As it is in the common background, too much ought not to be made of the fact that it is found in John and Qumran. We are not justified in reading into John statements about hate found only in the Qumran writings.

23. V. F. Furnish points out that the command to love one another "need not be regarded in itself as *excluding* love for 'neighbours' and 'enemies.' In fact it is hard to fit such terms into the framework of this writer's theology" (*op. cit.*, p. 148). Cf. W. F. Howard, "If man's love to man is determined by God's love to man, then, as that is universal in its scope, so also will the limitless claims of human need enlarge yet more and more the scope of this inspired activity of love" (*Christianity according to St. John* [London: Gerald Duckworth & Co., 1943], p. 170).

24. Cf. J. Painter, *John: Witness and Theologian* (London: S.P.C.K., 1975), p. 94.

3: *The Son of God and the Children of God in the Fourth Gospel**

MARINUS DE JONGE

In the Fourth Gospel, the reinterpretation of Jesus' kingship is given in terms of divine Sonship, understood in a typically Johannine way. Jesus is prophet and king because he is the Son sent by the Father, and only as the Son of the Father. The real heart of Johannine Christology is found in a typically Johannine emphasis on the unique relationship between Father and Son. At the same time this innermost secret of Jesus is revealed only to a small group of insiders. Only the children of God, those who were born from God (*ek theou egennēthēsan,* John 1:12, 13; 1 John 3:1, 2, 10; 5:2), are able to understand and follow the unique Son of God.

This leads us to some further remarks on Jesus' divine Sonship, and to an investigation of the relation between the Son of God and the children of God. I shall concentrate on the connection of ideas within the framework of the present Gospel, against the background of a number of stimulating studies in which the relation between God and Jesus is viewed in the light of general Oriental and Hellenistic ideas as well as particular Jewish ideas of agency.[1] The concept of agency covers a whole range of messengers and representatives (including the son of the house) and has juridical aspects (very important in the Fourth Gospel) as well. In the case of commissioning by God it includes prophets, angels, personified Wisdom, and the Son.

---

*This article is an expanded version of two connected lectures given December 10 and 17, 1975, in the "Theologische Etherleergang" of the N.C.R.V. (Dutch Christian Broadcasting Association); these lectures appeared in Dutch as "Gods Zoon en Gods Kinderen," *Rondom het Woord,* 18 (1976), 57-73. This article also appears in English in M. de Jonge, *Jesus, Stranger from Heaven and Son of God: Jesus Christ and the Christians in Johannine Perspective*, trans. and ed. by John E. Steely (Missoula, Montana: Scholars' Press, 1977); henceforth cited as M. de Jonge, *Jesus.*

Before we analyze the expression "the Father who sent me," which is central against this background, we shall do well to discuss a number of related terms that illustrate aspects of Jesus' mission that are essential to John's argument.

Whence?

In the disputes between Jesus and the Jews in John 7[2] the question "Whence?" is first posed with respect to Jesus' teaching and then with respect to Jesus himself. "Where did he get this?" is connected with "Where does he himself come from?" Jesus' very being and origin are discussed in the light of what he says and does. In 7:16 Jesus states: "What I am teaching you I do not have of myself, but it comes from him who sent me. He who wishes to do what God wills shall be able to discern whether my teaching comes from God or from myself." In vv. 27-29, referring to the Jewish position that "When the Messiah comes, no one will know whence he is" and the comment of the bystanders that they know very well whence Jesus comes, Jesus says: "So you know me, and you know whence I come? Yet I have not come on my own initiative; I am sent by him who is the true one; you do not know him. I know him, for I come from him. He has sent me."

Thus we see that the question "Whence?" is answered with terms such as "not from myself," "from the Father," and "sent." We find the same kind of response in 8:13-19 and 9:24-34. Anyone who does not know whence Jesus comes, such as his Jewish opponents, cannot recognize his authority. Pilate too is groping in the dark. After the Jewish accusation that Jesus has made himself God's Son (19:7), he asks the accused, "Whence do you come?" That he still must ask proves that he does not know, and indeed he never will know. That had already earlier become evident, in the conversation set forth in 18:33-38. Jesus' kingdom is not of this world (or, to put it in another way, is not from here); therefore his servants do not fight, and Jesus goes to the cross. Jesus' task is to witness to the truth; to this end he was born and has come into the world. And just as 7:16 declares that in order to understand Jesus one must will to do what God wills, so 18:37 states that "everyone who is of the truth listens to my voice." Then Pilate asks, "What is truth?" thus betraying his own ignorance. And yet it may be said of him, "You would have no power over me at all if God had not given it to you" (19:11).

Thus the question "Whence?" is the question of the source and authorization of what Jesus says and does.[3]

"Not on My Own Authority" and Related Expressions

In 7:17 "I speak on my own authority"[4] is set over against "the teaching given by God." The following verse says, speaking not merely of Jesus but in general: "Anyone who speaks on his own authority is seeking his own glory. But anyone who seeks the glory of the one who sent him is trustworthy." "Not on one's own authority" then signifies utter obedience to the one who sends, even *the* Sender. "Not coming of my own accord" (v. 28) also stands in parallel here with "not speaking on my own authority" (v. 17). This latter is again connected with "doing nothing on my own authority"; 8:28-29 offers a good example of this. There Jesus asserts that the Jews will see later "that I am he, and that I do nothing on my own authority, but I *speak* just as the Father has taught me. He who sent me is with me. He has not forsaken me, because I always do what he wills."[5]

Jesus as the true sent one is conscious of being one with his Sender; he is guided by what the Sender, his Father, has taught him as Son, and he continues to live in and by the power of the Father's nearness. There is a unity of willing, speaking, and acting between Son and Father.

Comparable passages are 12:49, 14:10,[6] and, above all, even earlier in the Gospel, the fundamental exposition in 5:19-30, a direct working-out of Jesus' word in v. 17, "So long as my Father works, I too am working," that prompts the Jewish adversaries to strive to put Jesus to death because he makes himself equal with God. I shall return to this shortly, but here I wish to point further to Jesus' utterance in 10:17 and 18, which forms a striking but sensible contrast with what has been related just previously. "The Father loves me, because I give my life, in order to take it again. No one takes it from me, but I lay it down of my own accord. I have power to lay it down and to take it up again. This is the charge that I have received from my Father." Precisely he who comes from the Father and acts in keeping with the Father's will has the authority to do something of his own accord—not under compulsion from others.[7]

"From Above"—"From Heaven"—"From God." We turn now to a complex of expressions which with some variation (and the variation is even greater in the Greek than it is in English: *anōthen, ek tōn avō, ouk enteuthen, ek / apo ouranou, apo / ek / para tou theou*[8] actually indicate the same thing: "from above"—"from heaven"—"from [or: out of] God." They serve to indicate the contrast between Jesus and his adversaries. In 8:23 Jesus says to the Jews: "You are from below, I am from

above." In this respect believers stand on Jesus' side: "If the world hates you, remember that they have already hated me. If you were of the world, the world would love its own; but because you are not of the world, but I have chosen you out of the world, therefore the world hates you" (15:18, 19; cf. 17:6, 14-16, 18). Parallel expressions also are used for the Son and the children of God. Thus Jesus says of himself, in 8:23, "I am from above," and in 8:42, "I proceeded and came forth from God," while in 8:47 he refers to the believer as "he who is of God." The point concerning Jesus and believers is their origin, their source that determines their entire being, and marks not merely their being, but all their speaking and acting. There is also a difference—we shall speak about that later—but as over against the outsiders they belong together.

In the series of expressions that concern us here, the point is, in the first place, (again) the fact of being sent and authorized by God. John the Baptist, an extremely important witness to Jesus in this Gospel, is called "a man sent from God" (1:6). Nicodemus, who does not grasp the real mystery of Jesus,[9] says to him: "Rabbi, we are convinced that you have come from God as a teacher." He is thinking in terms of a prophet or teacher like Moses. The Pharisees speak in the same terms when they say to the blind man who had been healed: "This man does not come from God, for he does not keep the sabbath" (9:16; cf. v. 29). The expressions used here are not incorrect; yet there is a fundamental difference between Jesus' coming from God and being sent by God on the one hand, and that of men like John the Baptist on the other hand. To indicate the unique character of Jesus' coming, the "from God" must be made more precise as "from heaven," "from above." This is done, then, in Jesus' answer to Nicodemus in 3:11-21, and in the parallel detached passage in 3:31-36, where the relationship between Father and Son is unavoidably brought into the matter.[10]

What is involved here is a genuine, reliable revelation of God which in God's name is brought by the Son, who is one with the Father, into a world that has no ear for it and hence is unbelieving. This is the point of 3:31, 32: "He comes from heaven and is above all. He who comes from this earth still belongs to the earth and speaks an earthly language. But he comes from heaven and is above all. He testifies to what he has heard and seen, and his testimony is not accepted." "From above" and "from heaven" are expressions for what is radically different about God; they also serve to ground the authority of Jesus who is speaking here by indicating his origin. Hence we read in v. 34: "He whom God has sent utters God's words," and this then is connected with the fact that God has given the Spirit fully to this one whom he has sent. Anyone who thus speaks and acts from God can only be identified with the name of "Son."

Vv. 35-36, then, also point out that the Father loves the Son and has given all things into his hands. It is in relation to him that the decision is made for belief or unbelief, life or death.

When the related expression, "I have come forth from God," is used in 8:42, this again is intended to underscore the unique authority of Jesus' words. Parallel to it are the expressions "I have not come of my own accord" and "He has sent me." Just before that (in v. 40) Jesus says: ". . . you seek to kill me, because I have proclaimed to you the truth that I have heard from God." The opposition that Jesus experiences ultimately goes back to the devil, as the following verses indicate (vv. 41-47). In contrast to that, it is only "he who is from God," the believer, who can accept Jesus' words as "words that are from God" (v. 47). The same thing is said very plainly in Jesus' last words to his disciples in chapters 13-17, where the expression "have come from God" (along with others) appears several times (13:3; 16:27-30; and 17:8). Only believers have the correct insight into Jesus' origin and therefore they also believe in his words: "Now they know that all that thou hast given me comes from thee. I have given them the words that I have heard from thee, and they have received them and know truly that I have come from thee. They have believed that thou hast sent me" (17:7, 8).

Believers know not only whence Jesus has come, but also whither he is going. Jesus' coming into the world presupposes a return: "I have come from the Father into the world. But now I leave the world and return to the Father" (16:28).[11] What this implies for Jesus and believers is to be considered later.

"The Father Who Has Sent Me"

As we have already stated several times in the preceding paragraphs, the divine origin and authorization of Jesus' words and deeds is very often expressed with a form of the verb "to send." An emissary is not simply someone who is sent, but also an envoy, a plenipotentiary: he speaks and acts in the name of the one who has sent him.[12] The perfect emissary identifies himself entirely with his sender. The expressions "he who has sent me" or, in the third person, "he who has sent him" appear in the Gospel no fewer than eighteen times,[13] and along with these we find the fuller reference to "the Father who has sent me [him]" six times.[14] No other single christological expression appears so often in the Fourth Gospel, and it is worthy of note that this actually is a theological term. Equally noteworthy is the fact that an active participle (from the Greek verb *pempō*) is used. Nowhere is the passive participle "sent" connected with Jesus.[15] When the author wants to say something about Jesus, he uses the expression ". . . whom God [or: he] has sent."[16] Thus once again an active form of the verb is used, this time of the Greek verb *apostellō*. The same verb appears even more often with God as the subject and Jesus as the object. Thus here also the emphasis is placed upon the sending activity of God, in which the unity of speaking, willing, and acting between God and Jesus, Father and Son, is grounded.[17]

My own exposition of the Johannine concept of *ergon* (*Jesus*, chap. 5) is also directly relevant here, especially my comments there about continuous cooperation. Jesus did not merely receive his commission and instruction once and for all; he continues to work in constant dependence upon the Father: *kathōs akouō krinō* (5:30; see also vv. 17, 19, and 20, and cf. 11:41-42). This is the Johannine variation of the Old Testament and Jewish idea that God is with the one whom he has sent (see, e.g., Jer. 1:4-10, 19, and the utterance of Nicodemus in 3:3!).[18] Jesus also uses the term *met' emou* for his relationship with the Father (8:29; cf. v. 16; 16:32). One notes again and again that the writer of the Fourth Gospel exhibits a close affinity with all sorts of Jewish conceptions and theories about prophets, angels, and especially Moses,[19] but that still at the critical moment more is said than can be expressed in categories of sending. That the Son is the perfect and, as such, unique emissary simply can no longer be expressed with the word "prophet," and the term "sent one" is just as far from being adequate.[20] To be sure, according to Jewish perspective also the son of the sender can function as the most fully qualified envoy, but what is said, with the help of many other expressions, about the Johannine Son goes even beyond this category (see, e.g., 5:17-30!).

". . . Making Himself Equal to God" (5:18). In 5:17-30 it also becomes evident that, in the opinion of the evangelist, according to Jewish views anyone who calls God his Father makes himself equal to God. In 5:18 we read how the Jews determined all the more to kill Jesus "because he not only subverted the sabbath, but moreover called God his own Father and made himself equal with God." Their motivation recurs in 10:33 as a direct accusation: *hoti sy anthrōpos ōn poieis seauton theon* (cf. 19:7: *hoti huion theou heauton epoiēsen*).

These objections also are used by the evangelist in order further to undergird his own Christian viewpoint. In 5:17-30 (and in 10:22-38) he undoubtedly is attempting to provide the members of the Johannine communities with arguments with which they can defend themselves in the debate with the synagogue and to enable them within their own circles to think through the implications of the position they have adopted.[21] In his article "The Divine Agent and his Counterfeit in Philo and the Fourth Gospel," Meeks has shown that here the Jews reproach Jesus with the same charge that Philo makes against Caligula. He, a man, is making himself God. What the Christian community says in defense against that charge is directly linked to what Philo and others remark about the relationship of Moses and the prophets to God. About chapter 5 Meeks says: "The dependence of the messenger on the sender is a leading motif in the Jewish conception of the apostolic prophet. . . . Further the notion that some messengers of God could be commissioned to perform tasks that are ordinarily God's works (raising the dead; executing judgment, vss. 21-22) appears in a number of Haggadic traditions and is at least implicit in Philo's account of Moses' miracles."[22] He points further to the midrash-like argumentation in 10:34-36. However, he correctly concludes that even here the Jewish traditions are used in such a way that the Jews themselves must, according to the experience and the perspective of the Johannine communities, reject this usage as absurd and blasphemous. As he puts it: "From the Jewish side, the Christian development of the 'envoy of God' notion has reached the point of blasphemy, and anyone who makes that kind of claim about Jesus has to be expelled."[23]

The Fourth Gospel identifies Jesus as God, and indeed at very significant points: at the outset, in 1:1 and 1:18, and at the end in 20:28.[24] The entire intervening testimony attempts to make clear that here we are not dealing with a man who has elevated himself to God, but with the Son, who at a crucial point in world history was sent by God, and who so fulfilled his mission that he became totally "transparent" to the Father, who spoke and worked in him (12:45; 14:7-11).

Some Supplementary Observations

Having arrived at this point, we shall do well to offer some further elucidation of the relationship of Father and Son by referring briefly to two points:

1. In speaking about "from above," "from heaven," there is presupposed a picture of the world in which God's heaven is exalted high above the world of men. Thus one can say that the author is speaking "mythologically" and can inquire what is the meaning of this mythic way of speaking.[25] In doing this it will be wise to note that neither the descent of the Son nor his return to the Father is described anywhere in the Gospel or the Epistles. The expressions we are discussing appear only in the

discourses of Jesus and not in the narrative portions of the Gospel. The "how" is not at all important, but the "that," expressed in *these* words, is essential. Evidently the Fourth Gospel cannot in any other way express how unique is the bond between Jesus and God and how alien is the world to God and to Jesus. How remarkable it is that the Son however, speaking and acting on God's initiation, has revealed God in the world; and how remarkable it is that men, in exceptional cases, have accepted this revelation, to live by it.

2. In recent years there has been frequent discussion of a "Christology of function" as contrasted with a "Christology of natures."[26] The objection then is raised against the early Christian dogma that, as it is said, places too much emphasis on the nature of God and the nature of Christ—one may think of such terms as "trinity" and "the two natures." What is important is not the "nature" but the "action" and "speaking" of God and of Jesus. The issue here is not whether the early Christian dogma is thus rightly interpreted; in the case of the Fourth Gospel we must be careful with the distinction that is being made here. Of course with John also, as was made clear above, all the emphasis is placed on the Son's acting and speaking in the name of the Father. But it was also made clear that in order to say something about what is distinctive in this acting and speaking, John had to go back to the origin of the one who here spoke and acted; it does not make sense to play acting and being, function and nature, off against each other. In its "mythical" discourse the Fourth Gospel is also dealing with the nature of the Son, in his relationship with the Father.

The Children of God

The Son of God enters the world as an alien, and is neither comprehended nor accepted. Those who do accept him are also themselves aliens in a hostile world. In the history of the Son the children of God recognize their own history. The communities in which the Fourth Gospel and the Epistles arose and were read were conscious of being threatened by a hostile outpost. To quote W. A. Meeks again: "The story describes the progressive alienation of Jesus from the Jews. But something else is happening, for there are some few who do respond to Jesus' signs and words, and these, while they also frequently 'misunderstand,' are progressively enlightened and drawn into intense intimacy with Jesus, until they, like him, are not 'of this world.' Now their becoming detached from the world is, in the Gospel, identical with their being detached from Judaism." [27]

Let us first work out, in somewhat more detail, three aspects of being a child of God: the origin of believers; their relationship to Jesus; and their relationship to the world.

The Origin of Believers. In the prologue the children of God are called "begotten of God" (1:12, 13); here "of God" is set in contrast to "of blood," "of the will of the flesh," and "of the will of man." That which is divinely new stands over against that which is typically finite and human. In 3:3-8 new expressions are added: "to be born/begotten anew" (in the Johannine perspective that is "to be begotten from above"); "of water and Spirit" (a reference to baptism); and "of the Spirit" (that is, not "of flesh"). Believers are begotten from above; God takes the initiative through the Spirit (of whom man does not know "whence he comes and whither he goes," no more than in the case of Jesus himself).

Hence 8:47 calls the believer "he who is from God"; in the First Epistle also, in 3:9-10, we find the expressions "begotten of God," "children of God," and "from God" parallel to each other. The First Epistle, which speaks often of being "begotten of God" (2:29; 3:9; 4:7; 5:1, 4, 18), in one passage (5:18) also connects this expression with Jesus: "We know that everyone who is begotten of God does not sin [this refers to the believer], because he who was begotten of God [that is, the Son] keeps him."[28] Here the participle used for the Son is different from the one used for the believer; with all the similarity, there is a distinction. This is evident also in the use of the words "children" and "Son." Believers are always called "children" (1:12; 11:52; 1 John 3:1, 2, 10; 5:2), never "sons" (a word that one does find in this connection in Paul; see Rom. 8:14, 19; 2 Cor. 6:8; Gal. 4:6, 7); they are distinguished from the Son *par excellence.* Yet they are related to him, for they are the ones who have said "yes" to the Son when God sent him into the hostile world. They too may call God "Father," although a distinction still remains: "I go to my Father, who is also your Father, to my God, who is also your God," is the message of the risen Jesus who is about to return to his Father, a message that Mary Magdalene must take to his "brethren" (20:17). It is only thanks to the Son that the children belong to the great family of God.

Believers and Jesus. Thus one does not become a child of God apart from the Son.[29] Sometimes the dependence is clearly expressed, as in the texts about the sending of believers by the Son, who himself is sent. Here we can refer to 4:38, 17:18, and especially 20:21, where after the resurrection Jesus addresses the assembled disciples: "As the Father has sent me, so also I send you forth." Here the crucial word is "as." It not only indicates a similarity, but also a difference; the "as" is at the same time "because." When Jesus says in 17:18: "As thou hast sent me into the world, so also I send them into the world," reference is made to the similarity between Jesus and those who are his, but that *their* being sent in based on *his* being sent is also indicated. In the last analysis, everyone is dependent upon "the Father who has sent *him*." One may also think of the many other utterances where the little word "as" is used. As an example I mention 6:57: "As the living Father has sent me and I live through him, so also shall the one who eats me live through me." The terminology is borrowed from the Supper; it is clearly stated how the believer is dependent upon Jesus, and how Jesus is dependent upon the Father.[30]

In 1:12, 13, "begotten of God" is connected with "receive him" (that is, in this context, the Word), and "believe in his name," in such a way that the human decision is mentioned first, and then God's initiative. Yet faith is a response to, and not a pre-condition of, that initiative. This is evident in the Nicodemus story in chapter 3, where Jesus declares that one must first be begotten/born from above/anew before one can enter the kingdom of God, and where Nicodemus does not comprehend this and thus is unable to understand Jesus at the deepest level.

We find something of the same sort in 7:17: only one who wills to do what God wills recognizes what Jesus teaches as something that comes from God. Only those who are "of the truth" listen to Jesus when he comes into the world as a witness to the truth (18:37). But how can you know what is God's will and what is truth without first knowing and accepting Jesus? John does not solve this problem; he does underscore the point that only within the relationship of trust among Father, Son, and children is justice actually done to God's intention. We would like to know what is first and what comes later, and we like to think in terms of cause and effect, but the Fourth Gospel and the First Epistle also simply put things side-by-side, and they attribute all that is good, and all that is willed and given by God, to his initiative. Thus, very fittingly, in 3:21, where the author speaks of the divine light that is kindled in the darkness in Jesus: "He who does the truth seeks out the light, for there it is evident that it is God who is at work in all his deeds."

Believers and the World. It is precisely the children of God who recognize and confess the Son of God, and therefore they stand together with the Son over against a hostile world. This is made clear particularly in the farewell discourses. Reference is first made in 15:18ff., in the passage that begins with "If the world hates you, remember that it has already hated me," and that then, especially in 16:1-4, speaks very specifically of "putting you out of the synagogue" and "killing you." In chapter 17 also we read that believers as aliens in the world and as disciples of the Stranger from Heaven remain behind in the world with their commission (vv. 14-18). There yawns a great gulf of misunderstanding, unbelief, and enmity between "the world," often represented by "the Jews," on one side and Jesus with his disciples on the other side. The prayer in chapter 17 ends with the words: "Righteous Father, the world does not know you, but I know you, and those whom you have entrusted to me know that you have sent me. I have taught them who you are, and I continue to do this, for the love with which you have loved me must dwell in them, and I myself also must dwell in them" (vv. 25-26).

God, the Son, and the World. It is not improbable that in this strong emphasis on the distinction between believers and the world, and in the concentration on believers, as it is found among other places in 17:25, 26, the concrete circumstances of the Johannine communities are reflected; these people were exposed to suspicion and persecution, from the side of those whom they identified as "the Jews,"[31] and likewise from all sorts of other forces and groups in the world.

But the question must be posed whether in this concentration on the children of God one has not lost sight of the world. Why is it said, in this Gospel also, and precisely here, that God so loves *the world* that he sent his Son? Is God concerned with the world, or with the group of believers?

To the World, into the World. The one who is sent by God and comes from God comes into the world. Whenever in the use of verbs of "sending" or "coming" attention is not directed simply to the "whence," or whenever we do not have simply a statement of the fact of the sending or coming, "the world" is given as the destination of that sending or coming.

After the feeding of the five thousand the people of Galilee accept Jesus as "the prophet who should come into the world" (6:14). Martha reaches a profounder level when she confesses Jesus as "the Christ, the Son of God, who should come into the world" (11:27).[32] Various times we hear that God has sent his Son into the world (3:17, along with "he gave" in v. 16; 10:36; 1 John 4:9). Then it is said of him that he speaks to the world what he has heard from his Father (8:26). He has come into the world for judgment (9:39): "I was born and came into the world to be a witness to the truth," Jesus says to Pilate (18:39), and just before that he answers the high priest that he has always spoken "to the world" openly and without hiding anything (18:20).

Jesus has come into the world as a light (12:46; cf. 1:9; 3:19). He then also calls himself the light of the world (8:12; 9:5), just as in 4:42 and 1 John 4:14 he is called the Savior of the world and in 1:29 "the Lamb of God, who takes away the sin of the world" (cf. 1 John 2:2). He who comes into the world from God is also sent to the world. God is not interested in the condemnation but in the saving of the world (3:17; 12:47). The discourse about the bread from heaven states plainly that this bread of life is intended for the world (6:33, 51).

The world can gain insight. Jesus is going to the Father, via the cross, because "the world must know that I love the Father and do all that he has commanded me" (14:31). Obviously then the world also *can* know this and thus has no excuse, as is clearly indicated in 15:22-24 (cf. 10:37, 38): "If I had not come and spoken to them . . ." and: "If I had not done in their presence what no one else ever had done, then there would be nothing to reproach them for. But now they have seen that, and yet they will to know nothing of me and of my Father." In 8:28 Jesus makes this prediction about the time after the crucifixion: "When you [the Jews] have lifted up the Son of man, then you will see that I am he, and that I do nothing of myself, but proclaim what my Father has taught me."

Here the reference is to the time when the disciples will act as representatives of the Son. They too are sent into the world (17:18) and live there without actually belonging to this world (17:11)! If they proclaim the word, then others will come to believe in Jesus through that word (17:20). These believers must all be one because of the unity between Father and Son and the "reciprocal indwelling" of Father and Son in believers. "Then the world will know," Jesus says to the Father, "that you have sent me and have loved them just as you have loved me" (17:23; cf. v. 21).

Thus the world can gain insight and come to repentance; that is also God's intention in the sending of the Son. And yet what the Johannine writings say about the world is primarily negative.

The Reaction of the World. In a recent study of the use of the word *kosmos* in the Gospel and the Epistles of John, N. H. Cassem comes to a number of interesting conclusions.[33] When we distinguish the positive and negative use of the term, the division is 18 to 9 in the first twelve chapters of the Gospel, and 7 to 30 in chapters 13 through 18. For the First Epistle the ratio is 3 to 19. The second part of the Gospel and the First Epistle are concerned with the situation of the community in the world after Jesus' departure; all the emphasis clearly falls on the actual response of the world to the message of Jesus and of his disciples after him; this response is negative, and equally negative is the judgment upon this response. In the first half of the Gospel more emphasis is placed upon God's attitude toward the world; this is quite clearly positive.

A second conclusion is that there is a clear distinction made in the meaning of "world" dependent on the various prepositions used in connection with the word. As mentioned above, "to/into the world" appears particularly in connection with words of "sending" and "coming." Thus it stands in the context of God's orientation to the world. Of the fifteen times that the expression "out of the world" appears, it occurs ten times in connection with "being of the world," and that is clearly a negatively regarded state. "Being in the world" is a negatively or neutrally regarded condition.

God is concerned with the world; this is why Jesus came and why the disciples also are sent forth into the world. But in the concrete confrontation with Jesus it becomes evident that he brings about a division. Many people say No; those who say Yes are the exception: thus quite clearly in 3:19-21, which declares that the coming of the light signifies a separation, because men love darkness rather than light. This is the way they are, this is the way the world is, and the outcome is obvious: everyone who does evil things has an aversion to the light, because he is afraid that his deeds will be brought to light. God's Son comes to save, not to condemn, but the judgment brings irrevocable separation (3:16-18). In the story of the healing of the young blind man in chapter 9 it is made clear that men *may* see because their eyes are opened. It appears also that men who think that they see in essence are stone blind. "I have come into this world," says Jesus, "to bring the decision [the judgment]: the blind begin to see and those who see become blind" (9:39).

The rejection by the world is declared, not explained. It is just as great a mystery as the faith of believers. In some texts, however, the devil is brought into the picture. Just as faith and good deeds are ultimately traced to their divine origin, unbelief and evil works are traced to their devilish origin. When in chapter 8 (vv. 39-47) the debate between Jesus and his Jewish adversaries becomes intense, and the Jews appeal to their having descended from Abraham, Jesus makes it clear that Abraham is on his side and not on theirs. In their hatred against Jesus and their efforts to kill him they are behaving just like their father, the devil: "You are of the devil; he is your father, and his desires are your intention also. He is a murderer from the very beginning" (v. 44). Jesus' adversaries simply do not have the right to say, "God is our Father, God alone" (v. 41).

This idea is further worked out in 1 John 3:4-12, where the children of the devil stand over against the children of God and where Cain is branded as "of the evil one" because he killed his brother. Evil works and evil men are literally of the evil one.[34] A couple of times something is said also about the "prince of this world." In Jesus' elevation/ glorification it becomes evident that the reign of that prince is coming to an end (12:31; 16:11). He has no power over Jesus (14:30). Therefore the disciples, who now suffer oppression in the world, may be of good courage: "I have overcome the world" (16:33; cf. 1 John 5:4, 5); or, as it is said in different words in 1 John 2:13, 14, but likewise for encouragement: "You have overcome the devil."

Whence the "prince of this world" comes and where he gets his power is not clear. Moreover, it is nowhere stated that man can shift the responsibility off on him. He is there, and he is at work, as is evident even within the circle of the disciples in the case of Judas (13:2, 27; 6:70). The Johannine theology is strongly dualistic, and that dualism comes to a focus in speaking and acting; but at the same time the question of origin is constantly being posed, and then everything that is not of God is ultimately of the evil one. But the existence of evil and of the evil one is not explained, and in the last analysis the Word, which is related to God in a unique way, is the power that has created even the world (1:3, 9).

The Father has given all power into the hands of the Son (3:34; 5:20; 10:17; 13:3; 17:2), and Jesus gains a victory over the hostile powers in the world, but only those who accept him have received what God intended to give them. In the beginning of the prayer in chapter 17 we read: "Thou hast made him lord and master over all men and hast given him power to bestow eternal life upon every one whom thou hast entrusted to him." Hence the farewell discourses begin in 13:1 with the remark that Jesus has remained faithful to the end to those who belong to him in the world. And hence the evangelist says in 11:52 that Jesus died "to gather together again God's children who are scattered abroad over the whole world."[35] This concerns not only the children of God in Israel, but also those among the Gentiles (cf. 10:16; 12:19, 20; and especially 12:32).[36] God's intention for the world is realized in the church as the community of those who have accepted and kept the word of Jesus.

The World as a Temporary Dwelling-Place. The story of the children of God in a hostile world is not yet finished. The Son does not remain in the world but has returned to the Father; those who belong to him will follow him at the time that is destined for them. Now a few remarks about this, which must be brief because Jesus' return to the Father is only one facet of what John calls Jesus' exaltation or glorification—a typical Johannine complex of ideas that in grand fashion takes Good Friday, Easter, Ascension, and Pentecost together and interprets them together.[37] We can concern ourselves only with the four or five Greek words used to indicate

Jesus' return to the Father[38] and ask what this departure signifies for the community that is left behind.

Here also the outsiders comprehend nothing. When Jesus during the disputes in Jerusalem related in John 7 says: "I shall not be with you long, for I am returning to him who has sent me" (v. 33), his adversaries think that he will go to the Jews in the Dispersion (vv. 35, 36).[39] In v. 34 and in a later stage of the discussion (in 8:21, 22) it is underscored that the Jews will not be able to come where Jesus is going, because "You are from here below, I am from above; you belong to this world, I do not belong to this world" (v. 23).

In the farewell discourses of Jesus the disciples are prepared for this departure.[40] In the utterances about this we can distinguish various trains of thought. In 13:31-38 we hear first that the same thing holds true for the disciples as for the outsiders: "Dear children, I shall not be with you much longer. Now I say to you the same thing I said to the Jews: You shall seek me, but where I am going you cannot come." But that is not the final word. To his question, "Lord, where then are you going?" Peter receives the answer, "Where I am going you cannot follow me now, but later you will follow me." Here (see also vv. 37-38) and elsewhere (12:25, 26; 21:19, 20) "follow" clearly also has the overtone of "follow in the footsteps, imitate" with all the consequences implied.[41] In vv. 34-35 the commandment is given for the interim that people must love each other.

In 17:24, almost at the end of the prayer that concludes the farewell discourses, Jesus asks of God: "Father, this I desire, that all those whom thou hast entrusted to me shall be where I am, and that they shall see the glory that thou hast given to me, for thou didst love me before the foundations of the world were laid." The Son in his journey travels from the Father to the world, and back to the Father, from glory to glory. Ultimately, all those whom God has entrusted to Jesus, liberated from their troubled existence in this world, shall see that glory and share in it.

In 14:1-3 the idea of Jesus' going away is connected with "preparing a place" and returning to fetch believers, "for," Jesus says, "you shall be where I am." In 14:4-6 the announcement of the departure evokes the question as to the way. This question is answered with the well-known words: "I am the way, the truth, and the life. No one comes to the Father except through me."

Much more might be said here; anyone who studies the farewell discourses carefully will note how Jesus therein offers encouragement and admonition to believers for the time between his departure and their departure. For John also the community lives in an interim period.

There is, however, still another word that indicates the return to the Father and hence demands our attention. It is the word "ascend," which appears three times (3:13; 6:62; 20:17; cf. 13:1) and which corresponds to "descend," used in 3:13 and particularly in chapter 6 in the discourse about the bread from heaven, with which Jesus identifies himself (vv. 33, 38, 41, 42, 50, 51, 58). Still more clearly than the other terms discussed in this closing section, these words indicate that in connection with going to the Father people thought in spatial categories, and that they actually could not help speaking "mythically." But just as in the use of "descend" in chapter 6 the point is not at all the spatial idea itself but rather doing the will of the Father (vv. 38, 44-46) and the bestowal of life that by virtue of its source conquers all death, so also in the case of the contrasting "ascend" the point is not a relocation. In 6:62 and 20:17 it indicates the conclusion of the period of the descent. In his return the one who descended shows that he truly came from God; the one who was sent returns to the one who sent him; he has completed his work.[42] At the same time the ascension, as an element in Jesus' exaltation, introduces a new phase in the process of revelation (20:19-23).

NOTES TO CHAPTER 3

1. See P. Borgen, *Bread from Heaven*, in *NovTSup*, 10 (Leiden: E. J. Brill, 1965), pp. 158-164; his "God's Agent in the Fourth Gospel," in *Religions in Antiquity: Essays in Memory of E. R. Goodenough*, ed. by J. Neusner (Leiden: E. J. Brill, 1968), pp. 137-148; and his "Some Jewish Exegetical Traditions as Background for Son of Man Sayings in John's Gospel (John 3:13-14 and context)," in *L'Evangile de Jean: Sources, Rédaction, Théologie*, ed. by M. de Jonge (Gembloux [Belgique]: Duculot, 1977); see also M. de Jonge, *Jesus*, chap. 8. Important also are W. A. Meeks' publications. Besides his *The Prophet-King: Moses' Traditions and the Johannine Christology*, in *NovTSup*, 14 (Leiden: E. J. Brill, 1967), pp. 301-306, and his "Moses as God and King," in *Religions in Antiquity* (see above), pp. 354-371, we should mention here his important paper, "The Man from Heaven in Johannine Sectarianism," *JBL*, 91 (1972), 44-72, in which he also points to the parallelism between Jesus the Revealer and the recipients of the revelation. A more recent contribution to the subject is his "The Divine Agent and his Counterfeit in Philo and the Fourth Gospel," in *Aspects of Religious Propaganda in Judaism and Early Christianity*, ed. by E. S. Fiorenza (Notre Dame: University of Notre Dame Press, 1976), pp. 43-67. J. P. Miranda's dissertation, *Der Vater, der mich gesandt hat: Religionsgeschichtliche Untersuchungen zu den johanneischen Sendungsformeln; zugleich ein Beitrag zur johanneischen Christologie und Ekklesiologie*, in *EH*, XXIII, 7 (Bern/Frankfurt: Lang, 1972), gives interesting material, but is not very clear in its conclusions. His last chapter deals with the concept of the prophet. I have also had access to a not yet published study by J. A. Bühner, "Prophet und Engel: Abstieg und Aufstieg Jesu nach dem Vierten Evangelium im Licht der jüdischen Religionsgeschichte," which is important particularly for the author's patient search for and interesting analysis of further Jewish parallels to the Johannine ideas of agency. Interesting

also is K. Berger's treatment of the Amen-sayings in the Fourth Gospel, on pp. 95-117 of his *Die Amen-Worte Jesu: Eine Untersuchung zum Problem der Legitimation in apokalyptischer Rede* in *BZNW*, 39 (Berlin: de Gruyter, 1970). His conclusion is: "Because Amen-sayings are only testimonies to what Jesus has heard from the Father, they are set entirely in the context of Jesus' having been sent by God and similarly in the context of the disciples' being sent by Jesus. If one assumes a prophetic figure derivable from Deutero-Isaiah, Jesus appears here as a prophet" (p. 116). See also Berger's "Zum traditionsgeschichtlichen Hintergrund christologischer Hoheitstitel," *NTS*, 17 (1970-71), 391-425, and "Die königlichen Messiastraditionen des Neuen Testaments," *NTS*, 20 (1973-74), 1-44.

2. On this see M. de Jonge, "Onbegrip in Jeruzalem: Jesus en 'de Joden' in Johannes 7," *Rondom het Woord*, 15 (1973), 61-80. On 7:14-24 see also M. de Jonge, *Jesus*, chap. 3.

3. One may defend the thesis that the evangelist hints at a deeper meaning in all other instances where *pothen* is used (1:48; 2:9; 3:8; 4:11; 6:5). See, e.g., B. Olsson, *Structure and Meaning in the Fourth Gospel*, in *ConB*, NT Series, 6 (Lund: Gleerup, 1974), p. 59.

4. On the "prophetic" background of this term see R. Bultmann, *The Gospel of John*, trans. by G. R. Beasley-Murray (Oxford: Blackwell, 1971), pp. 249-250. To the Old Testament parallels mentioned by him one may add also Jub. 6:35.

5. See also 8:40, 42-43.

6. In 5:43 Jesus says that he comes in the name of the Father (cf. 10:25); he contrasts himself with those who appear in their own name—a clearly related expression. Caiaphas (11:51) and the Spirit of truth (16:13-15) also speak "not of themselves." Cf. also the use of this expression in 15:4 and 18:34.

7. See J. Blank, *Krisis: Untersuchungen zur johanneischen Christologie und Eschatologie* (Freiburg: Lambertus-Verlag, 1964), p. 113: "Because Jesus' activity issues entirely from God and is grounded in God, he has full authority for and freedom in action. Thereby the being and action *ouk aph heautou* confirm the fact that Jesus is the Son, the eschatological emissary of God, who fulfills the divine will in all that he does." An interesting parallel to 10:17-18 is found in Hermas, *Mand.* 11:5.

8. On the use of *para, apo,* and *ek* in these contexts, see C. H. Dodd, *The Interpretation of the Fourth Gospel* (Cambridge: Cambridge University Press, 1952), p. 259, and T. E. Pollard, "The Father-Son and God-Believer Relationships according to St. John: a Brief Study of John's Use of Prepositions," in M. de Jonge, *et al.*, *L'Evangile de Jean* (see n. 1). One should not stress the differences (between the prepositions, and in the use of these prepositions in connection with different persons), but rather note the combinations of expressions using different prepositions.

9. On this see M. de Jonge, *Jesus*, chap. 20.

10. See *idem.*

11. See also 13:3.

12. See, e.g., K. H. Rengstorf, *apostellō*, *TDNT*, I, 398-406, and the literature mentioned in n. 1 above.

13. 4:34; 5:24, 30; 6:38, 39; 7:16, 28, 33; 8:16(?), 26, 29; 9:4; 12:44, 45; 13:20; 15:21; 16:5. Cf. 7:18; 13:16.

14. 5:23, 37; 6:44; 8:16(?), 18; 12:49; 14:24.

15. *Apestalmenos* occurs twice in connection with John the Baptist (1:6; 3:28) and once with people sent by the Pharisees (1:24). In addition, it is used once as the translation of the name Siloam in 9:7, clearly referring to Jesus' mission in the world. See also J. P. Miranda, *op. cit.*, p. 9, n. 3. *Apostolos* occurs only once in a general statement in 13:16, where *apostolos* versus *ho pempsas auton* stands parallel to *doulos* versus *kyrios*.

16. 3:34; 5:38; 6:29; 10:36; 17:3.

17. J. P. Miranda, *op. cit.*, p. 29, rightly says concerning the use of the two verbs for sending: "In the Johannine usage . . . a certain consistency can be discerned, which however does not suffice for a conceptual differentiation." This contra K. H. Rengstorf (see above, n. 10), p. 404; J. Blank, *op. cit.*, p. 70, n. 61; and many others, among them J. Seynaeve, "Les verbes *apostellō* et *pempō* dans le vocabulaire théologique de Saint Jean," in M. de Jonge, *et al.*, *L'Evangile de Jean* (see n. 1).

18. For further parallels see R. Schnackenburg, *The Gospel according to John* (London: Burns & Oates, 1968), I, 366, n. 61.

19. See particularly J. A. Bühner's study (see above, n. 1) also on the points raised in this section.

20. Here one should, of course, also take into account the use of the terms Son of God, the Son, etc., in other early Christian writings, in their relations in conceptions of prophecy and agency; see the articles by K. Berger mentioned in n. 1 above, and J. Hengel, *Son of God* (Philadelphia: Fortress Press, 1976). An interesting case, where prophethood and sonship are distinguished and connected, is found in Mark 12:1-8, coming after 11:27-33. See M. de Jonge, "The Use of *Christos* in the Passion Narratives," in *Jésus aux origines de la christologie*, ed. by J. Dupont, in *BETL*, 40 (Gembloux: Duculot, 1975), pp. 169-192, esp. p. 180.

21. Cf. M. de Jonge, *Jesus*, chap. 5, in discussion with others. See esp. J. L. Martyn, *History and Theology in the Fourth Gospel* (New York/Evanston: Harper & Row, 1968); "Source Criticism and Religionsgeschichte in the Fourth Gospel," in *Jesus and Man's Hope*, ed. by D. G. Buttrick (Pittsburgh: Pittsburgh Theological Seminary, 1970), I, 247-273; and "Glimpses into the History of the Johannine Community," in M. de Jonge, *et al.*, *L'Evangile de Jean* (see n. 1 above).

22. W. A. Meeks, "The Divine Agent" (see above, n. 1), p. 55.

23. *Ibid.*, p. 59.

24. See B. A. Mastin, "A Neglected Feature of the Christology of the Fourth Gospel," *NTS*, 22 (1975-76), 32-51.

25. On this point see W. A. Meeks, "The Man from Heaven" (see n. 1 above).

26. See, e.g., O. Cullmann, *The Christology of the New Testament* (Philadelphia: Westminster Press, 1959), esp. chap. 9, sec. 3 (pp. 258-269), and pp. 297-303. See p. 300: "A oneness of essence exists because there is a complete oneness of will." J. Blank, *op. cit.* (see above, n. 7), pp. 112-113, speaks "not only with respect to mind and will, but ontological and essential [unity]." R. E. Brown, *The Gospel according to John*, in *AB* (Garden City: Doubleday, 1966), I, 408 (on 10:37): ". . . although the Johannine description and acceptance of the divinity of Jesus has ontological implications (as Nicaea recognized in confessing that Jesus Christ, the Son of God, is himself true God), in itself this description remains primarily functional and not too far removed from the Pauline formulation that 'God was in

Christ reconciling the world to Himself (II Cor v 19).' " See now also the study by T. E. Pollard mentioned in n. 8 above, in which he returns to some earlier statements on moral and ontological aspects of the Sonship of Jesus in his *Johannine Christology and the Early Church*, in *SNTSMS*, 13 (Cambridge: Cambridge University Press, 1970).

27. "The Man from Heaven" (see n. 1 above), p. 69.

28. See M. de Jonge, *De Brieven van Johannes* (Nijkerk: G. F. Callenbach, 1973), pp. 228-230; cf. C. Haas, M. de Jonge, and J. L. Swellengrebel, *A Translator's Handbook on the Letters of John* (London: United Bible Societies, 1972), p. 128.

29. W. A. Meeks, "The Man from Heaven" (see n. 1 above), p. 68, rightly points out that ". . . the Fourth Gospel never provides us with the myth which explains how some men could be from below and others from above." The status of those who are *ek tou theou* "is a *conferred* one, not an ontological one."

30. See, e.g., 6:57; 10:15; 13:15, 34; 15:9, 10, 12; 17:11, 14, 16, 21, 22, 23.

31. On the use of "the Jews" in this Gospel see the recent studies of T. L. Schram, "The Use of *Ioudaios* in the Fourth Gospel" (Diss. Utrecht, 1974), and R. Leistner, *Antijudaismus im Johannesevangelium?* (Bern/Frankfurt: Lang, 1974). Also important is W. A. Meeks, "Am I a Jew? Johannine Christianity and Judaism," in *Christianity, Judaism, and Other Greco-Roman Cults*, ed. by J. Neusner (Leiden: E. J. Brill, 1975), I, 163-186.

32. On the coming of the Messiah/Christ without any more explicit reference to place see 4:25; 7:27, 31; cf. 12:13, 15. See also 1:15, 27, 30 (par. to John the Baptist, 1:31); 10:10 (as over against those who came before Jesus). In 1 John it is emphatically stated that the coming of Jesus Christ occurred "in the flesh" (4:2; 5:7; and 2 John 7). Also spoken of is the coming of the Antichrist (2:18) and of his spirit (4:3); it is revealed in the emergence of false prophets in the world (4:1). See also M. de Jonge, *Jesus*, chap. 8.

33. N. H. Cassem, "A Grammatical and Contextual Inventory of the Use of *kosmos* in the Johannine Corpus with Some Implications for a Johannine Cosmic Theology," in *NTS*, 19 (1972-73), 81-91.

34. In 17:15 and in 1 John 5:19 one should translate "the Evil One" and not "evil."

35. Jesus had the charge not to allow to be lost any of those whom the Father had given him (6:39; 10:28, 29; 17:12; 18:9). Judas is the great exception (17:12; cf. 6:64, 70).

36. See, particularly, Excursus III, "Mission in John," in B. Olsson, *op. cit.* (see n. 3 above), pp. 241-248.

37. See W. Thüsing, *Die Erhöhung und Verherrlichung Jesu im Johannesevangelium*, 2nd ed. (Münster: Aschendorff, 1970).

38. *poreuomai, hypagō, erchomai, proserchomai, aperchomai, anabainō.*

39. A typical bit of Johannine irony, incidentally; see "Onbegrip in Jeruzalem" (see n. 2 above), pp. 68-69.

40. On John 13-17 see also M. de Jonge, *Jesus*, chap. 7. Cf. W. A. Meeks, "The Man from Heaven" (see n. 1 above), pp. 61-66.

41. See also 1 John 2:6, 29; 3:16; 4:17 for expressions about the *imitatio Christi*.

42. On this see also P. Borgen, "God's Agent in the Fourth Gospel," in *Religions in Antiquity* (see n. 1 above), pp. 137-148, and J. A. Bühner, *op. cit.* (see n. 1 above). Much has been written lately on 3:13; see P. Borgen's article in *L'Evangile de Jean* (see n. 1 above) and J. A. Bühner's study. The most likely interpretation, in my opinion, is still the one that sees here a denial that anyone (Moses, prophets, apocalypticists) ever ascended to heaven to receive revelation and to see God; the One who descended from heaven gives revelation and life.

4: *The Transfiguration Motif in the Gospel of John*

VERNON H. KOOY

The Fourth Gospel is replete with problems and may be said to be the most difficult of the Gospels to interpret. One comes away from its study with a certain dissatisfaction, a feeling of inadequacy and restlessness.[1] Not only is there difficulty in finding a satisfactory outline to the Gospel,[2] but one must adjust to a totally different portrayal of Jesus himself. Whether due to the sources upon which the evangelist drew, his theological and missionary interest, or the editor of the work, the Christ of the Fourth Gospel openly acknowledges his messiahship,[3] performs no exorcisms,[4] is argumentative and aggressive whenever he confronts the Jews,[5] indulges in long discourses, and conducts his ministry chiefly in Jerusalem. No satisfactory explanation has yet been given to account for this difference in presentation.[6] It certainly cannot be due totally to the sources upon which the author drew,[7] nor yet to his whim and fancy. There are other causes suggested, such as a theological, liturgical, sacramental, evangelistic, kerygmatic, or apologetic concern of the evangelist, but all explanations falter to some extent and one is left with a feeling of perplexity.

While it may be true, as Dodd, Brown, and others have said, that John's Gospel is composed of a book of signs and a book of passion (glory), both of which are more complex than appears on the surface, there is a motif of the passion story lying behind the totality of the writing.[8] It may be mere coincidence that he begins and ends with a week of activity, but it would suggest some liturgical pattern.[9] Can it be that John took the messianic portrait of Jesus in the traditional presentation of the "passion week" story[10] and extended it over the whole of the account of Jesus' life and work? One notes in the synoptic portrayal at this point an open declaration of messiahship, a militancy and antagonism on the part of Jesus in confronting the religious practitioners of the day, an aggressiveness in debate and controversy, and a final conclave with his disciples prior to the arrest, trial, and crucifixion. All of this is evident in the Fourth Gospel. Jesus is openly the Messiah.[11] There is an initial disclosure of his messianic glory (2:1-11). He is militant and aggressive as he cleanses the temple (2:15f.) and engages in a series of controversies,[12] all of which take place in Jerusalem and end in an attempt to arrest him and put him to death.[13] Jesus has a final word with his disciples (chaps. 13-17) and then follows the story of the cross and resurrection. This pattern[14] is only a general outline and some of it is already a part of the tradition of Jesus' ministry,[15] but nowhere is this portrayal of Jesus so consistent and so sustained as in the Fourth Gospel. Such a suggestion does much to account for the emphasis on Jerusalem, open messiahship, and the aggressiveness of Jesus in this Gospel. If there is some plausibility to the above, it would appear that John has woven a passion pattern into his sources as a prelude to the passion story itself.[16]

I

It is noteworthy that at the climactic point[17] of the synoptic portrayal of Jesus' ministry[18] and as a prelude to the passion story stands the transfiguration narrative (Mark 9:2-11; Matt. 17:1-13; Luke 9:28-36). From this point on Jesus turns his attention away from the crowds and concentrates on teaching his disciples;[19] from this point on he sets his face toward Jerusalem.[20] The transfiguration marks a bridge between the works of Jesus, climaxed in the confession of Peter at Caesarea Philippi, and the ministry and passion at Jerusalem. It confirms the confession of Peter (Mark 8:27-30; Matt. 16:13-20; Luke 9:22-27) and the disclosure of the coming passion in the passion announcements (Mark 8:31-9:1; cf. Matt. 16:21-28; Luke 9:22-27) and looks forward to the passion itself and the *parousia*.[21] It presents Jesus as the Son who brings the word of God to which men are to give heed. It authenticates the suffering servant concept of Messiah which Jesus has voiced in the passion announcement, and is the means by which the messiahship of Jesus, evidenced by his mighty works[22] and the passion, are brought into harmony and unity.[23] The whole marks a moment in which the glory of Jesus is set forth, his relationship with the Father is disclosed, and his mission is attested as part of the program of God. In this light the subsequent story of the passion is to be read.

Nowhere are these themes elaborated upon so well, and made so much a part of the whole story of Jesus' life and ministry, as in the Fourth Gospel. This would suggest that behind the Gospel of John lies not only a passion motif but a transfiguration motif as well which elucidates the glory and messiahship of Jesus. John's purpose, like that of

Mark, is to present the reader with the fact that Jesus, the crucified, is the Messiah. Mark's descriptive account is a gradual unveiling of the Messiah. During the sweep of the story Jesus is Messiah in secret, not to be made known until after the resurrection (8:30; 9:9).[24] John, in similar fashion, writes a post-resurrection theological account, stressing that Jesus is Messiah from the beginning. He did not become Messiah through the resurrection or ascension. He was always the Messiah, the Word which became flesh, and manifested the glory of God in his works or signs. It is this glory of God present in Jesus, both in the works performed through the power of God and in the radiance that emanated from his personality, that evidences his messiahship. Yet there is a certain hiddenness about this messiahship. Jesus speaks the words of God and performs the works of God but the people fail to recognize him or believe in him.[25] While Jesus' glory was there to see in his works and words, it was visible only to those who had eyes of faith. The writer seeks to disclose in all of Jesus' ministry the hidden glory of Jesus[26] so that those who have not witnessed his ministry, who "have not seen" (John 20:29), may yet believe.

II

The transfiguration pericope in the synoptics is a theophanic vision disclosing Jesus' glory. The story, with its features of a mountain in the north,[27] radiance, heavenly messengers, word about tabernacles, cloud, and voice, gathers up into itself many themes. It has been shown that the details of the story find a counterpart in the Sinai tradition,[28] and would perhaps add the prophet-Moses Christology to that of Son and suffering servant in the pericope. If the story is composed, as Cope suggests,[29] on the model of the Sinai stories, the feature of glory becomes all the more dominant.

The essential elements of the story are nearly the same.[30] The radiant light that surrounds Jesus, making his clothes glisten (Mark 9:3) and his face shine (Matt. 17:2), gives a momentary glimpse of the glory surrounding Jesus (Luke 9:32).[31] Here, reminiscent of the theophanic presence or the *Shekinah* of the Targumists[32] (cf., e.g., Exod. 24:16; 34:29-35), it shows that Jesus shares the glory of God and that God is present with him, if not in him. The appearance of Moses and Elijah has been variously interpreted.[33] Above all, these figures mark the dawn of the messianic age, and focus attention on the word of Jesus, the future event of the cross, and perhaps the *parousia* itself. The cloud represents the presence and power of God, though veiling it, and the divine voice (*Bath Qol*) confirms Jesus as the Son[34] and his word[35] as the word of God to which the disciples are to hearken.[36] There remains the enigmatic and impulsive word of Peter, "Master, it is well that we are here; let us make three booths . . ." (Mark 9:5; cf. Matt. 17:4; Luke 9:33). However the imagery is understood, it suggests the Feast of Tabernacles and perhaps marks the eschatological significance of the scene.[37]

These elements in one form or another are found in all the synoptic accounts, yet each evangelist uses them to stress his particular emphasis. Mark has a "biographically descriptive presentation"[38] stressing the suffering servant theme and looking forward to the *parousia*.[39] The vision glimpses Jesus in parousian glory[40] while the *Bath Qol* points to the word of Jesus that the Son of man must suffer (8:31). Matthew stresses more the likeness to Moses with the glistening of Jesus' face, and the theophanic nature of the experience.[41] The whole is reminiscent of the Sinai experience[42] if not actually based upon that account. The climactic element is the voice from the cloud at which Jesus is confirmed as the spokesman of God.[43] Luke draws the parallel with Moses in another direction. The ascent to the mount is to pray (9:28). It is during prayer that Jesus is transfigured. Moses and Elijah appear in glory[44] and discuss with Jesus the exodus he is to accomplish at Jerusalem (9:31f.), symbolizing perhaps the cross as the means of leading the new people of God out of sin to new life.[45]

Allowing for the individual interests of the evangelists, the tradition as a whole stresses the Sonship of Jesus who is the bearer of the word. As such he shares the glory of the Father, a glimpse of which is given, and the cross becomes the *via gloriae*.

These themes are stressed in the tradition at the point of Jesus' baptism, at which the concepts of Son and suffering servant are joined together; the confession, where Son and messiahship are joined, messiahship being interpreted immediately in terms of suffering and the cross; and the garden scene, where Son and suffering are again joined together.[46]

These emphases receive elaboration in John's Gospel[47] and form the motif lying behind the totality of the presentation of the life and ministry of Jesus.[48] John takes Jesus from the mountaintop and sets him in the valley where men live and here he sets up his tent. It is in this tent of flesh where the glory of God appears and where it can be seen with the eyes of faith.

III

That the transfiguration theme lies behind John's book is suggested already by the prologue. At the climax of the poem stands the central affirmation of the writer and the theme of the Gospel as a whole: "The word became flesh and tented among us, and we beheld his glory . . ." (1:14).[49] The emphasis here is that the Word, which was in the beginning with God and in some sense was God (1:1), became flesh. It identified itself not only with man, but with flesh,[50] the very stuff out of which man was created with all its weaknesses and limitations, thus veiling the divine in the human. Further, the Word made flesh tented among men. This tenting probably alludes to the tabernacling presence of God and suggests that the new tabernacle of God is not some building but Jesus.[51] Again, the writer attests that it is in the flesh that the Word manifested his glory and that some, of whom he is one, beheld this glory, as of an only Son.[52] In the accompanying story the writer is going to reveal that glory just as the Son reveals the Father (1:18). In so writing he points to a glory hidden, yet seen.[53] Moreover, as the *Bath Qol* at the transfiguration testifies (Mark 9:7; cf. Matt. 17:5; Luke 9:35), this glory is that of a Son whose word is to be received and believed.[54] The "we" of the passage may represent the author's identification with the church[55] that here witnesses to seeing the divine glory in Jesus which the writer intends the reader also to behold through the events to be recorded. The beatitude at the conclusion of the Gospel (20:29), about not seeing and believing,[56] would indicate more than some spiritual disclosure of the glory of God in Jesus and might well reflect the transfiguration tradition, even as 2 Pet. 1:16 reflects this tradition with a more precise reference.

While there can be no certainty, the words of the Word becoming flesh, the tabernacling of the Word,[57] and the concluding words of the prologue, "No one has ever seen God; the only Son, who is in the bosom of the Father, he has made him known" (1:18)[58] make it at least possible that the fourth evangelist alludes to the transfiguration tradition. If so, then, since the prologue sets forth the themes of the Gospel, it would seem reasonable to suggest that for the evangelist the entire Gospel is a transfiguration story, each individual incident of which reflects that glory which, according to tradition, the favored disciples saw on the holy mountain.

Thus, at the very outset, the writer or editor sets forth the themes of his writing and the way in which he intends it to be read. The story is about the divine Word that became flesh, whose glory has been seen and is now to be disclosed in the ensuing account of the life and death of Jesus.[59] It is this Word which came from God, goes to God, and will come again, thus joining together incarnation, cross-resurrection, and *parousia*.

The prologue has always been viewed as setting forth the symphonic theme that runs through the entire Gospel. Besides performing this function, it also serves as an introduction to the book of signs. The glory of the Word made flesh is now to be disclosed in the works which manifest it. If the "passion week" theme outlined above is plausible, it would mean that the ministry of the Baptist (1:19-34), the call of the disciples (1:35-51), or the Cana miracle (2:1-11),[60] if not all three together, take the place of the entry into Jerusalem in the tradition. It is noteworthy that in these stories the messiahship of Jesus is openly declared and the reader prepared for the mission and work of the Messiah.

IV

This transfiguration theme comes to the fore in the three parts of this Gospel where the terms "glory" and "glorify" appear when related to Jesus:[61] (1) at the first (2:11) and last (11:4, 40) signs, as an interpretation of how they are to be viewed; (2) at the climactic point of the Gospel (12:20-47); and (3) at the prelude to the passion, the upper-room discourse (13-17).

At the beginning and end of the book of signs it is declared that they manifest the glory of Jesus.[62] Like the *Shekinah* of the Targumists the signs manifest the presence and power of God active in Jesus.[63] While a reference to glory does not appear[64] in each of the six major signs,[65] yet what is made explicit concerning the first and last signs as manifestations of Jesus' glory[66] might be said of all of them. One notes that Num. 14:22 also characterizes the signs of Moses as manifestations of the glory of God, binding together his words and works.[67] The Cana miracle (2:1-11) shows Jesus as the giver of the new wine of life which brings joy, that provision for man's cleansing more efficacious than the purifying rites of the Jews. The healing of the official's son (4:46-54) discloses that Jesus speaks the word that makes alive, the power inherent both in God and in him (5:21, 26). In the incident of the lame man at the pool of Bethesda (5:1-18) Jesus communicates spiritual life,[68] a work done on the sabbath.[69] The feeding incident (6:1-15) interprets Jesus as giving the bread of life; in healing the blind man (9:1-41) Jesus gives spiritual sight (cf. 9:37f.);[70] and in the raising of Lazarus (11:1-44) Jesus discloses his ability to give eternal life. All of these show Jesus communicating the gifts of God and give evidence of the power and presence of God at work in him, which is a way of manifesting his glory, the theme of the transfiguration. In John all these are works that the Father does (cf. 5:19ff.; 10:25, 37), even as Jesus' word is the word of God (7:16; 8:28; 12:49f.).

The second section in which *doxa* appears is 12:20-43, which serves as a transition[71] between the book of signs and the book of passion,[72] and also serves as an introduction to the latter. It immediately follows the entry into Jerusalem (12:12-19) and occupies the place of the cleansing story in the synoptic accounts.[73] The cleansing of the temple in the synoptics provides the motivation for the Jews to put Jesus to death (cf. Mark 11:18) which John attributes to the last and greatest of signs (11:47-53; cf. 12:10) as the climax of all of them. The story here confirms the decision of the priests as the will of God.[74]

Some Greeks come and seek Jesus.[75] This invitation, or temptation, elicits from Jesus a word about the necessity of his death in order to bear fruit (12:24), or the necessity of the cross as a prelude to the gentile mission.[76] The hour has now come for the Son of man to be glorified (12:23). The gentile world is ripe for the gospel. It is time for the cross and Jesus' glorification (12:24). This is Jesus' way of saying, or John's way of emphasizing, that the cross is a necessity and the way of glory. The words following about loving life and losing it (12:25f.), reminiscent of the passion announcements of the synoptics,[77] reflect the response of Jesus to the Caesarea Philippi confession (Mark 8:34f.; Matt. 16:24f.; Luke 9:23f.) which immediately precedes the transfiguration event in the synoptics.

Here the evangelist adds words suggestive of the agony of the garden and Jesus' prayer for release: "Now is my soul troubled. And what shall I say? 'Father, save me from this hour?' No, for this purpose I have come to this hour. Father, glorify thy name" (12:27, 28a).[78] This utterance reemphasizes that the hour of glorification is the hour of crucifixion and that it is necessary for the Messiah to suffer and die. At this point John records a saying giving the response of a heavenly voice, "I have glorified it and I will glorify it again" (12:28), reflecting the voice at the transfiguration[79] but with a different message. The subsequent misunderstanding of the *Bath Qol* by the people, some of whom thought it thundered (12:29) and others that an angel had spoken to him (12:29), and Jesus' response that the voice came for their sakes (12:30) show that the message was intended to be intelligible to the multitude and they should have understood it.

Even as in the transfiguration story where confession, transfiguration, and garden events are drawn together by the theme of glorification, so also here in John. Elements from the story of the confession (12:25f.), the transfiguration (12:23, 28), and the garden scene (12:27), all anticipating the cross event (12:24, 27, 32), are drawn together and interpreted under the theme of the glorification of Jesus.

The transfiguration is used by the synoptics to show that the *via crucis* is the *via gloriae*. So also John draws together these themes with the same intent, making explicit what is implicit in the synoptic tradition. The passage then stands as a bridge between the deeds of Jesus and the passion, between the book of signs and the book of glory, introducing the latter, even though following the pericope of the entry. It thus more fittingly introduces the private teaching of Jesus.

By far the majority of passages in which "glory" or "glorify" appear,[80] with one exception,[81] are to be found in Jesus' farewell discourses[82] to his disciples (13-17). If the preceding discourse reflects the transfiguration, and the words of the *Bath Qol* in that event were familiar in the church, one would expect at this point a series of private teachings,[83] which is what occurs. As noted above, the transfiguration comes at a point in the gospel accounts where Jesus turns from the crowds to his disciples. So also here. Interestingly enough, it is this section (13-17) more than others which identifies Jesus' hour of glorification with the cross. In this section there are three references to "glory": (1) a reference to Jesus' pre-existent glory (17:5, perhaps also 17:24); (2) a reference to the glory Jesus evidently possessed during his lifetime which he passed on to his disciples, a gift from God (17:22); and (3) the glory Jesus possessed in his oneness with the Father, which he possessed before the Word became flesh and which will be restored through the cross-resurrection event (17:24). All these noticeably are found in chapter 17.

Of the uses of "glorify," three speak of Jesus being glorified in the near future, undoubtedly referring to the cross and its sequel (13:31, 32 [2x]).[84] Three declare that God is glorified or will be glorified in Jesus, two referring to the coming cross (13:31, 32) and the third (14:13) as a reference to God being glorified through Jesus' response to future apostolic prayers. Two declare that Jesus glorifies God, one by the cross (17:1) and the other by his work on earth (17:4). One reference speaks of the Holy Spirit glorifying Christ in declaring what belongs to Christ to the disciples in the future (16:14). And one remaining reference speaks of God being glorified through the missionary activity of the disciples (15:8).

This brief survey shows a close correlation between the glorification of Jesus and the glorification of God, not only on the cross, which is the special hour of glorification, as the sayings on being "lifted up"[85] also attest, but also during his earthly ministry and in his future ministry through the Holy Spirit and his disciples. As in the transfiguration event it is disclosed that Jesus shares the glory of God, so it is made plain to the disciples in this collection of sayings under the guise of Jesus' farewell discourse. Here again themes of glory, cross, Sonship, and future exaltation are drawn together as the cross is viewed as a return to the Father.[86] John makes explicit, thus, in the whole life and ministry of Jesus, in his works[87] and in his cross, what is implicit in the tradition underlying the other Gospels. Jesus is the Son who glorifies God by his works and by his cross, and who, following the completion of his mission, returns to his Father in glory.

It would appear that the transfiguration story is more than a record of an event in the life of Jesus or an element in the tradition underlying the accounts of the evangelists. It summarizes neatly in a single event what is basic to and underlies the whole story of Jesus; who he is and what he came to do. Whether or not John knew the incident, he certainly was aware of the motif it embodied. It is this motif, noted above as coming to the fore in the strategic events of baptism, confession, and passion, that John elaborated on and wove into the warp and woof of his tapestry. Assured that a disclosure of the glory of Christ would lead to faith even as in the case of the first disciples (2:11), he let the radiance of Christ shine forth in the events he records. It is the works of redemption and the radiance of the divine personality that draw men to Christ. Wherever these are present, even today, in the work of his church or in the lives of his disciples, they bear witness that Jesus is the Savior of the world and challenge men to believe in him.

Oscar Cullmann in *Christ and Time* has pointed to an important aspect of biblical thought by his "already" and "not yet" terminology. This marks the relationship of the earthly and the heavenly. The kingdom of God is already here but not yet consummated. Eternal life is already experienced but not yet realized. Death is already conquered but not yet banished. The glory of Christ is already manifest but not yet actualized. All of these anticipate something more to come; a new coming of Christ, a final transformation of all things, a grand and glorious *parousia*.

The perplexity of interpreting the Fourth Gospel is increased by the fact that many themes besides glory, such as light, life, faith, word, and Spirit, can be traced through the book. None of these by itself wholly discloses the full meaning of the author. Yet each of them gives some new insight and helps to plumb some of the mystery of the riches the author has hidden in it. It is in this light that this study on "glory" is submitted. It would be too much to claim that it unlocks the key to the whole book. Yet, by providing some new perspectives, it may perhaps further the understanding of a precious and complicated work.

NOTES TO CHAPTER 4

1. See Sir Edwin Hoskyns, *The Fourth Gospel*, ed. by F. N. Davey (London: Faber & Faber, 1947), p. 20.

2. Due to a variety of materials intermingled: a series of signs (1:1-11; 4:46-54; 5:1-9; 6:1-15; 6:16-20; 9:1-7; 11:1-44); a festival cycle (Passover, 2:13; an unnamed feast—Sabbath? or Pentecost?—5:1; Passover or, perhaps better, Unleavened Bread, 6:4; Tabernacles, 7:2; Dedication, 10:22; Passover again, 12:1, 12); a series of narratives (Jesus and Nicodemus, 3:1-21; Jesus and John, 3:22-30; Jesus and the woman of Sychar, 4:1-27; Jesus and the Samaritans, 4:28-41, omitting the pericope of the adulteress, 7:53-8:11); a certain rearrangement of material; and some possible dislocations.

3. There is no command to silence or hiding of his identity.

4. The victory over the powers of darkness is on the cross.

5. Cf., e.g., 5:37f., 42-47; 6:53; 7:19, 28f.; 8:15, 19, 23f., 37-47; 8:55; 10:25f.

6. This may, of course, reflect the controversies between the church and the synagogue, but to read this back into the story and so alter the personality of Jesus seems unreal.

7. There appears to be a basic common tradition behind all the Gospels, somewhat differently reported to be sure, yet recognizable and perhaps due to an accepted pattern of early preaching.

8. Even as in the case of Mark. Cf. here C. W. Smith, "Tabernacles in the Fourth Gospel and Mark," *NTS*, 9 (1962), 133: "The Gospel of John is not a chronological account of Jesus' ministry (in either fact or intent) but a discussion of and meditation upon the Passion." Vs. E. Käsemann, who sees the passion coming into view only at the very end as John could not fit it organically into his work (*The Testament of Jesus according to John 17* [Philadelphia: Fortress Press, 1968], p. 7).

9. Cf. Oscar Cullmann, who feels John is concerned to show the connection between contemporary worship and the historical life of Jesus; *Early Christian Worship* (London: SCM Press, 1953).

10. Of the Gospels, only in Mark and John can the final events of Jesus' life be set in the framework of a week. How early a "passion week" scheme rose in the early church is difficult to say, but the rudiments are already to be found in these Gospels.

11. Most, if not all, of the messianic titles are attributed to Jesus by his first disciples: "the Messiah," 1:41; "him of whom Moses in the law and also the prophets wrote," 1:45; "Son of God," 1:49; "King of Israel," 1:49; cf. "Son of Man," 1:51; and "Lamb of God," 1:29, 35. See also n. 3.

12. He cleanses the temple with a whip (2:15); distinguishes the children of God from the children of the devil (8:9, 39-49, a passage in which the Jews claim to be the children of Abraham); differentiates between the sons of light and the sons of darkness (9:39-41); and is truly the coming one with a winnowing fork in his hand (cf. Matt. 3:12; Luke 3:18). The Christ of John lives up much more to the expectation of John the Baptist in Matthew and Luke than does the Christ of those Gospels.

13. Cf. 5:16-18; 7:19, 25, 30, 44; 8:37, 40, 59; 10:31, 39. See also 8:20, 49; 9:22, 34; 11:50-57.

14. Which may account in part for his placing the summary conclusion to the book of signs (12:37-43) after the entry (12:2-19) since it takes the place of the cleansing in the other Gospels.

15. E.g., Mark's series of controversies ending in a decision to put Jesus to death (2:1-3:6) and the irritableness of Jesus in Luke 13:31f. and perhaps Mark 7:1-13 (Matt. 15:1-9). See also Matthew 23.

16. John is at one here with all the Gospels, which in one way or another are explanations as to why the Messiah had to die.

17. Cf. A. M. Ramsey, "The transfiguration of Jesus on the holy mount has for the first three evangelists the place of a watershed in the scene of the mission of Jesus. Behind it is the ministry of preaching and healing, and the confession of St. Peter at Caesarea Philippi; in front of it is the journey to Jerusalem and the passion"; "The Transfiguration in Scripture and Tradition," *Eastern Churches Review*, 1 (1967), 216.

18. Which probably owes its pattern to apostolic preaching rather than any oral or written collection of tradition.

19. Cf. Mark 9:30.

20. Cf. Luke 9:51. Only in Matthew is there little suggestion of any interruption or change in activity except a change of locale (19:1). The journey to Jerusalem is first encountered at 20:17.

21. So G. H. Boobyer, *Mark and the Transfiguration Story* (Edinburgh: T. & T. Clark, 1942). See also P. Riga, "Signs of Glory" in *Interpretation*, 17 (1973), 414.

22. See, e.g., Matt. 11:2-15, a passage in which John the Baptist is equated with Elijah even as in the sequel to the transfiguration account (Mark 9:11-13; Matt. 17:10-13).

23. Note the scandal of a crucified messiah, the Son of man who is the suffering servant, is offset by the Son of man in glory, an image taken from the *parousia*.

24. While the demons recognized him and later the disciples, these were enjoined to silence.

25. Cf. John 12:37-43.

26. Which for him was an authentication of Jesus' messiahship.

27. On the significance of the mountain in the north see John Bright, *Jeremiah*, in *AB* (Garden City: Doubleday, 1965), p. 192, and Roland de Vaux, *Ancient Israel* (London: Darton, Longman & Todd, 1962), p. 279. The mythical abode of the gods was on a high mountain in the north. The Ras Shamra poems call it Saphon, where the gods meet and Baal has his throne. The Hebrews also had sacred mountains in the north, Tabor, Hermon, and Carmel. Ps. 48:2 seems to identify Zion with the mythical abode of the gods. Thus it becomes quite appropriate for a theophanic vision to take place on a northern mountain such as Tabor or Hermon.

28. See O. Lamar Cope, *Matthew: a Scribe Trained for the Kingdom of Heaven*, in *CBQMS*, 5 (Washington: The Catholic Biblical Association of America, 1976), p. 99, and W. D. Davies, *The Setting of the Sermon on the Mount* (Cambridge: University Press, 1964), p. 50. See also Jacob Enz, who feels there is a deliberate literary pattern in the Gospel of John in which the career and place of Jesus are interpreted in the light of the ministry of Moses ("The Book of Exodus as a Literary Type for the Gospel of John," *JBL*, 76 [1957], 208-215).

29. See n. 28.

30. Whether each element has some particular significance or whether it is the story as a whole that is important may be debated.

31. Ramsey, *op. cit.*, p. 217, designates the glory as that in which the Son of man is to appear at the *parousia*.

32. See Boobyer, *op. cit.*, p. 80.

33. Joseph Klausner remarks that the presence of the two Old Testament figures simply would suggest to a Galilean Jew that Jesus was the Messiah who was to come and promulgate "the law of Moses throughout the world by the aid of miracles, like to the deeds of Elijah" (*Jesus of Nazareth* [New York: Macmillan, 1925], p. 303), although Moses also substantiated his word as the word of God through signs. Boobyer suggests that Moses and Elijah, instead of representing the law and the prophets or the presence of the messianic age come in Jesus, may represent the living saints who are with God in glory and with whom the people of God anticipate sitting at banquet together. Here Jesus is seen already in glory, anticipating the *parousia* and showing that the *via crucis* is the *via gloriae (op. cit.*, pp. 72-74).

Many have understood them as representing the law and the prophets now fulfilled in Jesus and his coming passion or the dawn of the messianic age. Cf. A. M. Ramsey, *op. cit.*, p. 217.

Others suggest that Moses and Elijah of all the prophets were especially bearers of the word, which now is fulfilled in and spoken by Jesus, if indeed he was not that word. F. R. McCurley notes that Moses and Elijah were the only ones God spoke to on Mount Sinai ("And After Six Days," *JBL*, 93 [1974], 80).

34. McCurley, *op. cit.*, p. 78, sees in "This is my Son, the Beloved" a reference to Isaac.

35. Perhaps his word about the cross and the coming passion.

36. Cope suggests that Jesus is commissioned here as a teacher of disciples (*op. cit.*, p. 100). It is interesting to see that Matthew follows the incident with a bloc of teaching (chap. 18).

37. Cf. Ramsey. The three tabernacles of Peter reflect that "God would, as of old, tabernacle with his people, whether in poetic imagery (Tobit xiii. 10) or in a literal tabernacle in the wilderness again (Josephus, *Ant.* xx. 167, 188) or in a link between the feast of tabernacles and the messianic age (Zech. xiv. 16-19). . . . Peter's remark on the mount shewed a glimpse of the eschatological significance of the scene which he was witnessing" (*op. cit.*, p. 217). R. H. Lightfoot notes that Tabernacles was a foreshadowing of the day of the Lord, or the messianic age (*St. John's Gospel* [Oxford: Clarendon Press, 1956], p. 182).

38. So H. Riesenfeld, *The Gospel Tradition* (Philadelphia: Fortress Press, 1970), p. 58.

39. See Boobyer, *op. cit.*, p. 57.

40. Cf. Mark 8:38; 10:37; 13:26.

41. Note the theophanic words, "Fear not" (17:7) and the words *mēdeni eipēte to horama* (17:9). One notes that the disciples fall down at the divine voice (as at Sinai) and are raised by Jesus (17:7).

42. See n. 28.

43. And perhaps the teacher of disciples. See n. 36.

44. Peter and those with him are evidently sleeping, for upon waking they see Jesus in glory and the two messengers from beyond. One notes there is no charge to keep silence in Luke.

45. On the Exodus and deliverance see G. B. Caird, "The Transfiguration," *ET*, 67 (1956), 191b.

46. See here A. M. Ramsey, *The Glory of God and the Transfiguration of Christ* (London: Longmans, Green and Co., 1949), p. 101.

47. While the baptism, confession, and garden scenes are missing or transformed in John's Gospel, these themes appear also at the beginning, climax, and close of the story.

48. Berkouwer, Caird, Davey, Feuillet, H. Kittel, Howard, A. M. Ramsey, Riga, Sanders and Mastin, C. W. Smith, T. C. Smith, Thornton, and others all call attention to the glory theme as extending over the entire story of Jesus in John's Gospel.

49. Translation mine. On 1:14 as the theme of the Gospel see Ernst Käsemann, *op. cit.*, pp. 6, 10, who sees the statement "the Word became flesh" overshadowed by the confession "we beheld his glory" so that it receives its meaning from it.

50. On "flesh" see R. Bultmann, *The Gospel of John*, trans. by G. Beasley-Murray (Oxford: Basil Blackwell, 1971), p. 70.

51. Jesus here is set in place of the tabernacle. He brings what no tabernacle can, the presence of God. See Adolf Schlatter, *Der Evangelist Johannes* (Stuttgart: Calwer Verlag, 1960), p. 23. Riga, *op. cit.*, p. 410, calls attention to the fact that ideas of the tent and glory are tied up with the notion of heaven. This seems to be alluded to in the enigmatic word of John 1:51 which implies that Jesus is the new means of access to God.

52. *Monogenēs*, Son in a unique sense or "only son," which, according to semitic custom, shared all the prestige, honor, and position of his Father. John also reserves *huios*, "son," for Jesus while using *teknon*, "child," for others, thus also setting Jesus apart as uniquely the Son of God. On *monogenēs* see D. Moody, "God's Only Son: The Translation of John 3:16 in The Revised Standard Version," *JBL*, 72 (1953), 213-219.

53. As in the transfiguration story where for a moment what is hidden becomes visible, that is, to those who have faith.

54. To "hear" (Mark 9:7) carries with it the implication "to obey" in semitic thought.

55. 2 Pet. 1:16-18 likewise testifies to having witnessed the divine glory, making a plain reference to the transfiguration; this "we" being the Christian community, or an eyewitness of the events and the transfiguration (so Morris). This would be in line with the passage from 2 Peter. Of course, the "we" might refer to the church, going back to the apostles, which carried within its tradition a remembrance of the event. The plural in John 1:16 and the use of "we" in John 3:11 might suggest this.

56. On "seeing and believing" see Cullmann, *op. cit.*, p. 239.

57. Suggestive both of the tabernacling presence of God as seen in the cloud, in the sanctuary, or on the mount, and the suggestion of Peter to build three tabernacles in the transfiguration account (Mark 9:5, *treis skēnas*; cf. Matt. 17:4; Luke 9:33).

58. Which may reflect the concluding word of the transfiguration story, "This is my beloved Son; listen to him" (Mark 9:7; cf. Matt. 17:5, adding "in whom I am

well pleased"; Luke 9:35, "my Son the Chosen," using the reading of θ as a variant).

59. The chief emphasis of the Gospel of John is, of course, that the glory of Jesus is seen preeminently in the cross-resurrection event. He overcomes the problem of extending it over the whole life of Jesus by making the whole story a passion story and a transfiguration experience.

60. It is interesting to note that the baptism of Jesus and the Cana miracle are traditional lectionary readings for Epiphany, the manifestation of Christ to the world. This theme is akin to that of the entry into Jerusalem.

61. Some passages speak of receiving praise and honor (*doxa*) from man, while Jesus receives his from God. Cf. 5:44; 7:18; 8:50, 54. There would seem to be a slight difference between the use of "glory" when referring to Jesus' works and cross and the use of glorify. "Glory" seems to relate more to the majestic radiance of God associated with light and fire, that *mysterium tremendum* and *mysterium fascinans* of Otto. This Jesus shares with God. "Glorify" signifies more a special honor or praise given to God or Christ through his activity and death.

62. John 2:11; 11:4, 40. In Hebrew writing beginning and end have a common theme which is elaborated in what occurs in between. See also 12:37, 41.

63. See Raymond Brown, *New Testament Essays* (Garden City: Doubleday, 1968), p. 245.

64. As the emphasis of faith does, e.g., which occurs repeatedly.

65. The walking on the water, 6:16-21, seems to be an event attached to the feeding story in the tradition (cf. Mark 6:45-53; Matt. 14:22-34a) and does not appear to be specially set apart by John. It was perhaps so closely related to the feeding incident in the tradition as to appear part of a single event or the sequel to it (cf. Mark 6:52). One notes its absence at this point in Luke, however, who goes directly from the feeding to the confession of Peter (9:18-20), which John somewhat parallels. But the story lacks the character of hyperbole attached to the others, unless one considers the immediate arrival at their destination such. All other signs are extraordinary ones the likes of which no other had ever performed (see, e.g., 9:32).

66. Or God's glory (John 11:4, 40).

67. See Brown, *op. cit.*, p. 239.

68. *Ibid.*, p. 241.

69. Disclosing God creatively at work in him (cf. 5:17). God's sabbath rest is broken by his recreative activity.

70. Brown, *op. cit.*, p. 41.

71. Of course the pericope 12:20-35 may be placed here, as Bultmann holds (*op. cit.*, p. 419), simply as an illustration of 12:19, "the world has gone after him."

72. D. Moody Smith sees only John 12:37-42 performing this function ("The Setting and Shape of a Johannine Narrative Source," *JBL*, 95 [1976], 231-241). So also Bultmann (*op. cit.*, p. 419), who holds this passage originally was the conclusion to the first half of the Gospel.

73. Which John has recorded earlier, 2:12-22. Note that this account contains a prediction of the passion (2:19-22), a remnant perhaps of its original place in tradition.

74. On the one hand serving a function similar to the passion announcements which also interpret the death of Jesus as the will of God; see F. C. Grant, *The Earliest Gospel* (New York: Abingdon, 1943), pp. 73f.; and on the other hand akin to the transfiguration story that confirmed the passion announcements of Jesus as God's will.

75. Seemingly, for the author, to offer Jesus an opportunity to forsake the Jews and minister to them, thus escaping the cross. Otherwise why the word about the "grain of wheat" (12:24) and the subsequent disclosure of the cross as the purpose of his coming (12:27)?

76. Note also the emphasis in Matthew's Gospel that the mission to the gentile world must await the event of the cross; Matt. 10:5f.; 15:24; 23:13f.; 28:19.

77. Mark 8:31-9:1; 9:30-32; 10:32-34. Cf. Matt. 16:21-28; 17:22f.; 20:17-19 and Luke 9:22-27, 43b-45; 18:31-34.

78. An evident allusion to the garden prayer (Mark 14:34, 36; Matt. 26:38f.; Luke 22:42).

79. Cf. Mark 9:7 and parallels.

80. These passages are (omitting the five occurrences in chap. 12, vv. 16, 23, 28 [2x], 41): 13:31, 32 (2x); 14:13; 15:8; 16:14; 17:1 (2x), 4, 5, 10; 21:19.

81. 21:19, a reference to Peter's death as glorifying God.

82. Farewell discourse is a misnomer as the section is a composite comprising all the teachings given to the disciples in this Gospel.

83. Even as in Matthew: transfiguration, 17:1-13; teaching, 18:1-35.

84. Although cf. 7:39; 11:4; 12:16, 23 which also speak of Jesus' glorification as the event of cross-resurrection, perhaps also ascension-*parousia*.

85. John 3:14; 8:28; 12:33, 34.

86. See 13:1, 33, 36; 14:2, 3, 12, 20, 28 (2x); 15:26; 16:5, 7, 10, 17, 28; 17:11, 13.

87. The author refers to them as "signs" but Jesus consistently refers to the miracles as "works."

5: *Mark 8:15–A Misunderstood Warning*

ROBERT P. MEYE

The Pharisees came and began to argue with him, seeking from him a sign from heaven, to test him. And he sighed deeply in his spirit, and said, "Why does this generation seek for a sign? Truly, I say to you, no sign shall be given to this generation." And he left them, and getting into the boat again he departed to the other side.

Now they had forgotten to bring bread; and they had only one loaf with them in the boat. And he cautioned them, saying, "Take heed, beware of the leaven of the Pharisees and the leaven of Herod." And they discussed it with one another, saying, "We have no bread." And being aware of it, Jesus said to them, "Why do you discuss the fact that you have no bread? Do you not yet perceive or understand? Are your hearts hardened? Having eyes do you not see, and having ears do you not hear? And do you not remember? When I broke the five loaves for the five thousand, how many baskets full of broken pieces did you take up?" They said to him, "Twelve." "And the seven for the four thousand, how many baskets full of broken pieces did you take up?" And they said to him, "Seven." And he said to them, "Do you not yet understand?" (Mark 8:11-21)

I. Extended Introductory Comments

Throughout Mark's Gospel Jesus addresses his audiences in parables (see especially Mark 4:33-34), and throughout the Gospel Jesus is misunderstood. This is clearly true of Jesus' warning to the disciples, given in Mark 8:15, that they beware of the leaven of the Pharisees and the leaven of Herod. Unfortunately for later interpreters of Mark's Gospel, the meaning of Jesus' warning is not clear—with the result that the interpretations of this passage are legion. Differing radically as they do, they cannot all be right; many of them are in some measure misunderstandings of the *Marcan* meaning.

The present essay is based on the conviction that important Marcan clues have been neglected, and that it is possible to attach a meaning to Jesus' warning which does more justice to the text itself, as well as the entire narrative, than the interpretations typically offered in commentaries and other sources. The essay's thesis is that *Mark 8:15 is a warning by Jesus to the disciples to be wary, lest they become accomplices with the Pharisees and Herod in effecting his death.* As we shall see, recognition of the sharp focus reflected in the words "in effecting his death" adds meaning, power, and poignancy to the Gospel's message.

The essay is developed along the following lines. First, its place in the flow of Marcan interpretation is established through a brief review of some of the major commentaries and other contributions to the message of Mark's Gospel. The basic argument of the essay follows this review of the "received exegesis." There are two parts to the major argument itself. First there is a review of some of the accepted postulates in Marcan interpretation, upon which exegesis of the passage before us can build with some confidence. Following this, key points in the formulation of the specific hypothesis of the essay are given. It concludes with a consideration of the application of all of this in the Christian community that Mark addresses, as well as the church today.

The importance of the present study is emphasized by the broad consensus among students of Mark's Gospel that Mark 8:14-21 is a very difficult unit in the Marcan narrative.[1] The redaction-critical perspective is that it is a decisively *Marcan* unit in makeup and content.[2] If this is true, then the presumption is that Mark 8:15 participates in that reality. In their own way, even those perspectives which view 8:15 as a kind of surd element[3] in Mark bear tacit testimony to the possible importance of this saying. The study of Mark 8:15 is in fact, as we shall see, a classic illustration of the relationship between text and context, the part and the whole.

One preliminary remark may be offered at this point, for it suggests the spirit in which the present essay is written. The more one works with Mark's Gospel, as well as the other Gospels, the more one is impressed with the achievement of the evangelist. Consider the challenge he faced: it was necessary to tell the story of Jesus in relatively *brief* compass if it was to be most serviceable in the church of that time; manuscript and other considerations that are well known apply here. It was impossible to tell the *whole* story—even if the evangelist had been in possession of the fullest tradition about Jesus. From the perspective of faith, it was also imperative that the *divine* origin and meaning of the incarnate Jesus shine through the story as *historical* narrative. And finally, all of this had to achieve the goal of ministry to the church in Mark's time. The attention this Gospel receives today, as well as the meaning it has had for the church *as canon*, suggests that the purposes of the evangelist were achieved. The church rightly speaks of the inspiration of the Gospel. It is the shape of that inspiration which is so remarkable. For example, the very gaps in the story serve to impress upon the reader the divinity and the humanity of the narrative with which we have to do. We do not "control" this story. Not only is much of it unknown to us, but the explanation of the events and their interrelationships lie "beyond us." Thus, there is an aura of the numinous that surrounds the whole and the parts. At the same time, there is a concreteness and reality, a simplicity and directness, which instructs and inspires. Finally, there is a fruitful circularity evident in Gospel study (see Mark 4:23-25). The Christian reader approaches the story with the conviction that it does bear witness in truth and in depth to the incarnate Jesus who is the Lord of his people today. Approached in that conviction, the story unfolds with meaning and blessing. But not all hear and receive precisely the *same* message—and that makes every honest interpreter into a humble seeker of God's truth, in Mark's Gospel and in all things. It is the knowledge that the spirit here described is characteristic of the life and work of the one to whom this essay is dedicated that causes it to be offered with the hope that it will be received as a modest tribute to and thanks for a life given to the ministry of interpretation.[4]

II. Our Heritage: Interpretations of Mark 8:15 to Date

Because the history of interpretation of Mark 8:15 is so varied—even divergent—it is not only interesting but imperative that we take note of at least some more recent contributions to that history. What is offered here is perforce a broad sample of characteristic interpretations in more recent studies. This will both reveal possible approaches to the text, and also show in sharper profile the thrust of the present essay. The focus of our attention will be gathered up in two questions: (a) What is understood by the expression "the leaven of the Pharisees and the leaven of Herod"? (b) What is the relation of Mark 8:15 to the surrounding context?

We may begin with the influential contribution of Ernst Lohmeyer,[5] whose work has been mediated to English-speaking readers through the studies of R. H. Lightfoot.[6] Lohmeyer believes that "leaven" in Mark, unlike Luke, cannot be understood in an ethical or theological sense. For the thing that binds the Pharisees with Herod is "the national-political goal of a united Jewish people and state." The focus then is on the kingship in Israel and has to do with the politico-messianic question. The warning of Mark 8:15 is to be attached to Mark 8:10-13, and its Pharisaic demand for a sign, the means by which a political messiah would confirm himself to the people.[7] In a very influential commentary stemming from the same decade, Julius Schniewind[8] comments that leaven speaks of hypocrisy (here, see Luke 12:1), which sets man off from God. It is illustrated in Israel's hardness of heart, as described in Isa. 6:9. Jesus' reprimand shows that the disciples' attitude is really no different than that of the multitudes who follow after Jesus, and reincarnate the attitude of rebellious Israel.

The very important English commentary by Vincent Taylor[9] understands leaven as an "evil disposition." Taylor believes that v. 15 is ignored in 8:16f., where attention is rather focused upon the stupidity of the disciples. As is usual, Taylor provides many helpful comments upon individual elements in the text. C. E. B. Cranfield[10] sees the warning in a twofold sense, i.e., having reference to differentiated qualities in the Pharisees and in Herod: "It is apparently a warning against the godlessness of the man of the world, while the reference to the Pharisees is a warning against a false and inconsistent piety." Cranfield explains the apparent discontinuity between 8:15 and the following text as lying in the historical failure of the disciples to understand Jesus' warning. He concludes that Mark has located the saying in v. 15 in its rightful historical setting.

Still within the British scene, D. E. Nineham,[11] in line with the rabbis, views leaven as indicative of an evil tendency or inclination. With respect to the Pharisees, then, it would have reference to "false teaching and piety which made them enemies of Jesus and would make them equally hostile to his disciples." Nineham does not see v. 15 as an integral part of the Marcan context. Nonetheless, Nineham feels that Mark has had a stronger-than-usual role in molding the material in Mark 8:14-21. C. F. D. Moule[12] explains the leaven of the Pharisees from the preceding text, Mark 8:11-13, as being illustrated in the Pharisees' legalistic demands, missing the heart of religion understood as joyful acceptance of personal fellowship with God. He goes on to comment that the leaven of Herod could possibly refer to Jewish nationalist intrigues, and notes that the disciples solemnly (and mistakenly) understand Jesus' words literally.

We note finally two more recent commentaries that are bound to receive continued wide usage. Eduard Schweizer,[13] whose commentary replaces that of Julius Schniewind in the notable German series, *Das Neue Testament Deutsch*, comments only very briefly on the leaven here, noting that it symbolizes something evil for the rabbis, especially the evil desire of sin. Thus, it is possible that the Marcan meaning has to do with its infectious, and continuous, operation. Professor Schweizer believes that the Marcan text makes more sense if 8:15 is handled as a parenthesis. William Lane's more recent major commentary on Mark[14] interprets leaven against the backdrop of the "Jewish understanding of leaven as the evil will and its expression." In contrast to the evil disposition of the Pharisees which calls for a sign, the disciples are exhorted to "faith and understanding apart from signs." Lane comments quite specifically upon the relationship between 8:15 and the context: "The intimate connection between 8:14-21 and the preceding verses determines the context for the interpretation of verse 15."

The commentary of Leslie Mitton[15] well summarizes and represents the history of exegesis of Mark 8:15: "We cannot be sure what is meant by the phrase here." His continuing comment describes the situation in some commentaries: "Some apply it [i.e., leaven] loosely to the unholy alliance between the Pharisees and Herodians to get rid of Jesus (3:6), but the word *'leaven'* is not very suitable to the meaning." This is surely a mistaken position, as we shall see!

All sorts of perspectives emerge. Some believe that the disciples are warned because they could become objects of the physical violence originating in the Pharisees and Herod. Others see the warning as having to do with an attitude or disposition that is evil and infectious. Mark 8:15 is variously attached to its context; some interpretations are embarrassed by its presence. Others speak of an intimate connection. Whatever their perspective, the following section stands as a comment upon, and silent argument with, much of that history. At the same time, it is set forth with gratitude for the work of those who have labored to mediate a better understanding of Mark's Gospel to others.

III. Marcan Elements Essential in Understanding Mark 8:15

There is a set of Marcan data that should be kept in mind at all times as a framework in which Mark 8:15 is to be understood correctly. These data are noted here in seriatim fashion, with but brief comment.

A. Jesus is the strong Son of God, and reveals the Father in his person, word, and work.[16] Even when it is not so stated, all this is always to be understood. This throws into sharper contrast all failure to understand Jesus or resistance to Jesus. Failure to understand highlights the very glory of Jesus' revelation.[17]

B. When God's revelation comes (in Jesus), it is liable to opposition and rejection at every level. Thus, at the very outset of Jesus' ministry, he is subject to temptation by Satan (1:13). This "satanic" opposition is embodied throughout the narrative in almost every circle, including the disciples.[18]

C. Mark places a special focus upon Jesus' selection of and accompaniment by a circle of twelve disciples.[19] They are with him from the beginning to the end of his ministry, present in its high moments as well as in its moments of humiliation. The presupposition of Mark is that the disciples are always there—unless it is clearly stated that they are not.[20]

D. The opposition to Jesus already expressed (see B) manifests itself finally in the cross, the shadow of which falls over the entire narrative. Mark 8:27-10:52 is a discrete narrative unit preceding the passion narrative with a strong focus upon the way of the cross,[21] but it by no means exhausts the Marcan references to the fact. Such items as Jesus' baptism (1:9f.; cf. 10:38f.), the saying concerning the bridegroom (2:18f.), plots to seize and destroy Jesus (3:6; 12:12, 13), the death of John the Baptist (1:14; cf. 6:14ff.; 9:12-13), already appear early on in the story and give to Mark the quality of a passion story with extended introduction.[22]

E. There is an abruptness in the Marcan style which, though regularly recognized by Marcan scholars, nonetheless seems difficult for interpreters to accept in the actual process of interpretation. The Gospel plunges into the midst of things, ends abruptly (on any view), and constantly leaves the reader without clues regarding causal connections in the story line.[23] (Mark 8:15 is no exception to this rule!)

F. One must stress the importance of John the Baptist in Jesus' ministry. Several major Marcan studies have adequately laid out the data for us.[24] At the head of a sequence of redactional studies of Mark stands Willi Marxsen's initial essay in *Mark the Evangelist* on John as *the* forerunner of Jesus. John is much more than a temporal predecessor of Jesus; John is "true forerunner."[25] This is especially important with a view to John's death, that death being the trigger for the appearance of Jesus (Mark 1:14). Lane rightly and characteristically speaks of "two passion narratives," the first of which reports the imprisonment and death of John the Baptist.[26] The story of John's "passion" is included by Mark both to clarify the statements in chapter 6:14, 15 and to point forward to the suffering and death of Jesus.

G. We have already implied that Marcan scholars are now in a position to view Mark as "a piece," namely, a narrative with some kind of unity stemming from the vision and work of the evangelist, rather than a collection of traditional bits and fragments brought together with relatively little or no harmony.[27] This perception has never been entirely absent from the field of Gospel interpretation, but it is a mark of the so-called "critical" scholarship that it has returned to this perception, albeit from a different vantage-point. More particularly, much of the unity is viewed as the result of the evangelist's redactional (creative) work, rather than as a quality of the tradition that the evangelist received.

H. Accompanying the new redactional emphasis is a new willingness to speak of "structure" in the narrative.[28] Again, this is by no means a *novum* in the field of Gospel studies, but the perspective from which structure is seen is different.

IV. The Marcan Narrative Structure

We have noted that there is a new willingness in Gospel studies to view the evangelical narrative in terms of pattern and structures. For purposes of clarity and brevity, we note here at the outset a way of viewing the larger Marcan narrative context of Mark 8:15; we then go on to justify this way of interpreting the text.

Mark 4:1-34   The Revealing Word of Jesus
Mark 4:35-8:26 The Revealing Deed of Jesus
Mark 8:27-10:52 The Way of the Cross; Rejection of the Revealer, His Word, and His Deed

In the schema presented above, Mark 8:15 is in position near the end of one major Marcan section, standing at a major junction in the narrative. There is a broad consensus in Marcan scholarship that Mark 8:27-10:52 has integrity as a narrative piece, in which Jesus reveals the fact of his death and comments on its meaning, the disciples being the locus both of that revelation and its misunderstanding. The postulate that Mark 4:1-34 and 4:35-8:26 are two discrete narrative units is not common and needs some comment. Mark 4:1-34 has an obvious focus on the word of Jesus; the question is whether it is in fact a part of a larger unit, or somehow has its own integrity in the Marcan intention. The latter is the most usable hypothesis when one perceives Mark's singular concentration upon the *works* of Jesus in 4:35-8:26. All but two narrative units in the Huck-Lietzmann[29] division of the text have to do with the deeds of Jesus; the exceptions are Mark 6:17-29 and 7:1-23. Since it is doubtful that one can separate Mark 6:14-16 from Mark 6:17-29, there is really only one point in the whole narrative sequence of Mark 4:35-8:26 not readily amenable to the theme of "Jesus' works," that is, Mark 7:1-23, with its teaching on "what defiles a man" (Huck-Lietzmann).

But there is far more than a mere catenae of miracle stories and related material in Mark 4:35-8:26. In Mark's perspective, they are bound together in *a unity of meaning or purpose* as well as in the external unity of appearance. Mark 8:14-21 itself suggests the connection between the two (separated) episodes of feeding the multitudes (see Mark 8:17-21). And the evangelist earlier suggests a relationship of understanding that binds the multiplication of loaves in 6:34-44 with the miracle of deliverance at sea in 6:45-52 (see especially 6:52). There is a cumulative effect in the story—which makes any failure to understand the more reprehensible. Thus, Mark 8:21 aptly concludes with the reproach of Jesus, "Do you not yet understand?" In their failure to understand, the disciples are one with the Pharisees, who, like Satan (1:13), tempt Jesus (8:11) in spite of all that he has done. The judgment upon the Pharisees is that they are a generation whose hearts are hardened, and whose blindness leads to non-questions which are really satanic thrusts against Jesus.

The key question standing over the entire narrative unit from 4:35-8:26 appears in 4:41: "Who then is this, that even wind and sea obey him?" That this is a vital question in understanding the narrative direction is variously reflected. The implicit question of Jesus' identity is posed, when he returns to his own country, in the reduction of Jesus by his own folk to a mere carpenter, son of Mary, and brother of James and Joses and Judas and Simon, and their sisters (6:3f.). And the question remains alive in 6:14-16, where King Herod, the murderer of Jesus' forerunner John, also poses it. But, more important, it is Jesus himself who raises the question of his identity at the head of the following main narrative unit (8:27-10:52): "But who do you say that I am?" (8:29). That they answer correctly must be related to the focus on Jesus' identity in 4:35ff., and Jesus' reproach in 8:17-22. They *now* reflect (but only in terms of *bare identification*) the right understanding. The story of Jesus' two-stage healing of the blind man (Mark 8:22-26) is an illustrative, or parabolic, transitional unit in the narrative.[30] It is a judgment upon the misunderstanding of the disciples, who do not see even after two great miracles. It is also an affirmation of Jesus' power to effect sight by the humblest of means in those who truly seek to see.

These narrative and contextual perceptions are the framework and context for understanding Jesus' warning regarding the leaven of the Pharisees and the leaven of Herod.

V. Exegetical Data Supporting the Essay's Thesis

We are now ready to take into account the specific exegetical data which establish the thesis that the word of Jesus in Mark 8:15 is nothing less than a warning to Jesus' disciples against becoming accomplices in his death.

A. *Warnings in Mark's Gospel.* The warnings and prophecies of Jesus occupy an important place in Mark's narrative; *the evangelist is concerned to show how Jesus pointed out the way to his passion—and beyond.* The most notable example of Jesus' foretelling activity is the series of prophecies concerning his passion (8:31; 9:31; 10:32-34) in Mark 8:27-10:52 ("the way of the cross"). To these one may also attach Jesus' prophecies that one of the twelve would betray him (14:20-21), that all would forsake him when he was stricken (14:27), and that Peter would deny him three times (14:30). The prophecy of Jesus regarding his death also appears directly or indirectly in such places as 2:20; 8:34; 10:39; 14:8, 24. Other texts could be noted and added. The material is often specific, but sometimes figurative.

A second point needs to be made here: Just as Jesus' prophecies are true prophecies, i.e., they actually come to pass, so warnings can be real, rather than hypothetical. Jesus warns against that which he sees as certain; Mark 13:23 is a classic example of this. It employs the language of warning, *blepete* (see 13:5, 9, 33), stating "But take heed; I have told you all things beforehand." This one passage well embodies the tenor of Jesus' way to the cross.

B. *The Leaven of the Pharisees and the Leaven of Herod.*[31] More specifically, Jesus warns the disciples against the leaven of the Pharisees and the leaven of Herod. What is the meaning of the figure "leaven" here? Leaven was an utterly familiar material in Jesus' and Mark's world. In ancient times, rather than using yeast, a piece of dough was held out from each baking. It would continue to ferment, and then serve as a fermenting agent in the next batch of dough, causing it to rise in preparation for baking. The work of leaven could be likened to the process of infection (as in 1 Cor. 5:6). Although leaven could bear a neutral connotation, it came to have a bad or evil connotation. As a rabbinic metaphor, it symbolized the evil tendency in man; only rarely in the New Testament does it have a good or neutral connotation (see Matt. 13:33 par. Luke 13:21). That this dominant evil connotation governs Mark 8:15 is apparent (1) from the fact of the warning itself, (2) from the combined reference to the Pharisees and Herod, whose companying together in Mark has a decisively evil overtone (3:6; 12:12, 13), and (3) from the tone of Mark 8:16-21.

Can we gain any precision regarding the meaning of leaven beyond what we learn in Mark 3:6 and 12:12, 13 where the Pharisees and the entourage of Herod are Jesus' would-be destroyers? There is some help offered in Mark 4:35-8:26, with its focus on the deeds of Jesus. Here,

Herod appears as one who wickedly murders John the Baptist, even though he recognizes John to be a righteous and holy man. Jesus and John are linked in this same narrative context, when Herod perceives the power in Jesus as a sign that John, whom he had beheaded, was raised from the dead (6:16-17). For their part, the Pharisees pounce upon Jesus immediately after his mighty works to tempt him for a sign from heaven. They thus function in a satanic way, for it is Satan who approaches Jesus to tempt him at the outset of his ministry (Mark 1:13). The verb "seek" (Greek, *zēteō*) consistently has strongly negative overtones elsewhere in Mark (see 3:32; 11:18; 12:12; 14:1, 11, 55). In the Lucan parallel to Mark 8:15, leaven is defined as hypocrisy (12:1). The Old Testament and strong New Testament meaning of "hypocrisy" is characteristic of Herod and the Pharisees; in the Old Testament leaven stands for "radical opposition to God and the wickedness of the one so opposed."[32] John is the righteous and holy one; Jesus is the holy Son of God. Both are radically opposed; those who do so (the Pharisees and Herod/the Herodians) are exposed as radically evil by their actions. And now, in Mark 8:15, Jesus warns the disciples that they too can become accomplices in the radical opposition which plots his death, and which arises out of a hardened, evil heart (8:17-18). There is a lack of unity in the exegetical tradition relative to the direction of the danger. Some envision the disciples as the objects of actions from the outside. Others envision the disciples as the actors. In the latter case, their action is typically understood as the embodiment and radiation of some evil disposition. However, *blepete apo* is certainly to be understood in the meaning, "Beware of."[33] It clearly bears this meaning in Mark 1:38. Moreover, this perception best accords with the idea of leaven, which enters from the outside and permeates as in an infection.

But leaven, once entering an object, creates in that object a new and similar power. That is the property of leaven which forms the point of Jesus' figure, a point that is all too often missed. Thus, the danger facing the disciples is that they incarnate the way of those who are actively hostile to God. Understood in this way, Jesus' prophecy receives a multiple and complete fulfillment. Peter, almost immediately thereafter, shows his hostility to God's purposes in Jesus. That is why Jesus' rebuke of Peter's denial of the way of the cross (8:33) is so sharp: "Get behind me, Satan!" For Peter behaves just like the Pharisees who tempted Jesus to go in another than the God-ordained way (8:11). The warning is also fulfilled in that the disciples do become accomplices in Jesus' death. Of this, more in the following section.

C. *The (Evil) Leaven in Jesus' Disciples.* We have already seen (1) that Jesus' warnings are more real than hypothetical (A above), and (2) that the leaven warned against is an evil spirit that manifests itself in hostility to God's way and God's servant (B). This describes the way of the disciples in the aftermath of Jesus' warning. Although the disciples are by no means guiltless of *misunderstanding* Jesus prior to Mark 8:27ff., they now, for the first time, resist Jesus' plan. They manifest a spirit other than the spirit of Jesus, and are ultimately involved in his death through Judas the betrayer.

As noted above, it begins with Peter's resistance to Jesus' announcement of the way of the cross (8:33). Then, whereas Jesus walks in the way of the suffering servant (see especially 10:32ff.), the disciples argue about personal position and priority in the kingdom (10:35-45). They fail to watch and pray with him in his hour of distress (14:37ff.). They all forsake him when he is seized (14:50). Peter thrice denies that he has anything to do with Jesus, sealing his denial with a curse upon himself, and an oath (14:66ff.)—all this despite Jesus' warning and Peter's boasted strength. Although all of this demonstrates an evil spirit (testing Jesus, like the Pharisees—see 8:13), the worst has not been stated.

One of the twelve, Judas, becomes an accomplice in Jesus' death. It is extremely important to observe two strong Marcan notes regarding Judas. First, Judas is solidly placed within the community of twelve disciples. The catalog of disciples (3:16-19) already establishes him as one of the twelve. Even more important, in the passion narrative Judas is repeatedly identified (unlike any other disciple) as "one of the twelve" (14:10, 20, 43). (The student of Mark must not let familiarity with this phrase rob it of its Marcan meaning!) The second feature emphasized is that Judas is Jesus' betrayer. This fact is also noted first in connection with his naming in the catalog (Mark 3:19); the text speaks of "Judas Iscariot, who betrayed him." The fact of the betrayal is then stated no less than seven times in the passion narrative (14:10, 11, 18, 21, 41, 42, 44). It is not an exaggeration to say that the evangelist *dwells* on the fact. For our purposes it is not ultimately determinative whether Mark simply reports the tradition as he received it, or shapes it by his own hand to conform to what he understood. What he actually communicates is of first and decisive importance for Mark.

The radically evil nature of Judas' action needs underlining. Betrayal at the hand of a friend has always been viewed as a most heinous evil. Thus, it is emphasized that Judas *eats with* Jesus (14:20), and *kisses him* as friend (14:44, 45). All this is the prologue to shameful and evil betrayal. The certainty of this betrayal and the fact that the cross is a part of God's way does not make Judas' action less evil (Mark 14:21). Mark's description of Judas as "one of the twelve" may be viewed as the terminological expression of the frequently emphasized Hebrew concept of corporate solidarity. Within this framework, there is corporate identity of the one in the many, as well as a life of mutual responsibility flowing between the one and the many. Thus, in the Marcan narrative, the act of Judas is hardly solitary; it finds its setting within a solid sequence of "bad conduct" on the part of the company of twelve (see above). Too often commentators resolutely ignore Mark's emphasis that Judas is one *of the twelve*, and thus miss the complicity of the twelve *in Judas* in the fact of Jesus' death. When this is the case, Mark 8:15 is then seen as only a surd element in the narrative—when nothing could be further from the truth.

Marcan interpretation has also missed the way when it has driven an artificial, unbiblical, and unreal wedge between the attitude and the conduct of the disciples. Leaven does indeed characteristically describe an evil attitude in Mark 8:15, but the biblical and Marcan picture suggests that an attitude (such as a hard heart) always produces fruits in conduct (2:8; 3:5-6; 4:13-20; 4:40; 6:52; 7:21-23, etc.). It is an un-Marcan foreshortening of leaven to assign its meaning to the realm of "spirit" alone.

Marcan interpretation pays a high price for ignoring the Marcan clues. It is the pathetic picture of the chosen disciples, forewarned, yet unwitting accomplices in the way of the cross, which gives special dramatic power and poignancy to the narrative. Contrary to a recent emphasis in Marcan study, Mark does not *create* and sustain an *unrelieved negative* portrait of the twelve.[34] Nonetheless, this emphasis regarding the twelve in Mark's perspective does, in its own way, support the view of "the leaven of the Pharisees and the leaven of Herod" represented in the present essay.

D. *Mark 8:15 and the Meaning of Mark 8:16-21.* Although we have found solid ground for interpreting Mark 8:15 in its larger Marcan context, we have not as yet established a close relationship to the following passage, vv. 16-21. This was not, first of all, deliberate. Nor was it mistaken. For we have seen that the key to Mark 8:15 lies beyond the immediate context. Second, the quest was allowed to move in relation to this larger horizon simply because of the troubled interpretational waters swirling about Mark 8:16-21. However, we can by no means bypass these verses—if for no other reason than the simple fact that Mark binds them together in the narrative. Jesus' reprimand of the disciples is, after all, dependent upon their misinterpretation of his warning: They think "bread," but Jesus is speaking of leaven, and reprimands them for their talk about bread. What is the meaning of Jesus' reprimand?

Jesus' reprimand unfolds along two parallel lines. One is the "story line," and the other the "interpretation" of the story. The story line is carried in Jesus' questioning regarding the feeding of the five thousand

and the feeding of the four thousand. He asks them about the number of baskets of bread taken up—and the answer is "twelve" and "seven" respectively. Marcan interpretation has typically leaned heavily upon the actual numbers, and seen in them a eucharistic meaning,[35] or Mark's perspective upon the Christian mission (e.g., to the Jews and to the Gentiles).[36] But the numbers must be viewed in relation to Jesus' simple question: "Why do you discuss the fact that you have *no* bread?" (Mark 8:17). The point is that the disciples are foolishly involved in a discussion about not having bread in the presence of the One who twice fed a great multitude with a few loaves and fishes with an enormous quantity left over. It is the abundance and greatness of Jesus' work which is the point. Jesus' words in 8:16-21 are his own counterpart to what has been happening throughout the story previously; everyone is amazed at his great works. It is not accidental that Mark recorded shortly before, at the end of Jesus' restoration of speech and hearing to the deaf and dumb man (Mark 7:37), that: "He has done all things well; he even makes the deaf hear and the dumb speak." In the extended section on the deeds of Jesus (Mark 4:35-8:26), one can note a similar motif, directly or indirectly, in 4:40, 41; 5:20, 22, 28, 42; 6:14-16, 51, 56; 7:24. The disciples' discussion was academic; worse, they missed the meaning of Jesus' works, being hard of heart and dull in all their perceptions.

Mark never identifies in so many words the meaning—the second line of movement in the passage—which the disciples are supposed to perceive and see and hear and understand in the great deeds of Jesus. However, the thrust of the narrative, as has already been suggested above, imposes one perception above all others upon the reader. It is the identity of Jesus which has "not yet" been understood (see Mark 4:41; 6:14-16; 8:27ff.). There is no other issue of like magnitude in Mark's Gospel. Jesus' identity is given to the reader in the first line (1:1). Demons know it (1:23-25, 34; 3:11-12; 5:6-7; 9:20). Jesus offers it obliquely in a variety of ways where he speaks of the Son of man, the Christ, or Son (of God). Jesus' identity is initially in question when the hostility leading to his death first manifests itself (2:7), and it is his identity which is in question in the hour of trial and judgment (14:61; 15:2, 9, 12, 18, 26, 32, 39). At the end of the narrative the question of Jesus' identity is *the* question. But it is also *the* question posed by Jesus at Caesarea Philippi, immediately following Mark 8:16-21 and the healing of the blind man (8:22-26).

Jesus' call to discipleship, and the appointment of twelve, already embodies an implicit Christology, some perception of who Jesus is. But the disciples' questions along the way make it abundantly clear to the reader that, prior to Caesarea Philippi, they still did not understand the true dimensions of Jesus' person. They, like the Pharisees and Herod, could fail to perceive it in spite of all that Jesus had done. But failure to perceive it was really the fruit of a hard heart (8:17). And in their hardness of heart they showed themselves to be leavened with the same evil that leavened those who sought to destroy him (3:6; 12:12, 13). Just as Jesus' movement to the cross is based upon a christological foundation, so the opposition to Jesus which led to that cross is based on a perception hostile to Jesus' own understanding of his identity. It is against this leaven that Jesus warns his disciples in Mark 8:15.

VI. The Church Then and Now

It is notably difficult to reconstruct the historical background of Mark's Gospel. Nonetheless, the interpreter must give attention to the historical situation in and to which the evangelist ministered through the message of his Gospel. Although this essay is written in the conviction that the evangelist faithfully records the story of Jesus, it is also written in the belief that he effectively used that story as an instrument that could minister to the need(s) of the church in his day.

The findings of this essay (see especially section IV above) fit well the strong hypothesis that the Gospel is written to a church facing persecution.[37] Mark 13 (see also 8:34ff.; 10:29-30; 8:27-10:52) seems particularly well-suited to speak to those who suffer. Jesus suffers and prepares his own to face the same lot as a decisive fact of their existence. Mark in turn now shows (and warns) his church that it cannot expect a different lot than its Lord.

There are features in the thirteenth chapter that parallel our preceding analysis. There is an emphasis on Jesus' identity from the outset; the first warning is against those who lead Christians astray, saying "I am he" (13:5). The same matter of false identification with Jesus the Christ is posed again in 13:20ff. And the actual language of warning is repeated (13:23) in this latter instance. The work of these pseudo-Christs is to show wonders that lead the elect astray; this stands in contrast to Jesus, whose works were not done as ends in themselves (Jesus refused such signs, as in Mark 8:11-12), but as pointers to the truth—which hard hearts missed. Mark does not show his readers wherein these false Christs lead away from Jesus, but the context of both 13:5 and 13:21-22 suggests that they divert the community from the way of suffering, a way in which Jesus had already gone. Here one readily thinks of Peter's resistance to Jesus' way of suffering as the disciples' first response to that way, mirrored continually in their attitude along the way of the cross (8:27-10:52).

Mark's portrait of Jesus' ministry called the church in his own time to unwavering confession of Jesus as the messianic Son, and a willingness to suffer everything (Mark 8:34ff.) as disciples of the crucified and glorified Lord. Jesus' warning concerning the evil leaven in Mark 8:15 fits this perception. Where the evil leaven does its work, confession of Jesus is abandoned. However, when one rejected the name of Jesus and ceased to confess him (owing to the pressures of trial and tribulation), it might follow that other members of the family who maintained their confession would be betrayed. Mark may well be warning his readers against such dire consequences of rejected faith—and exhorting to steadfastness to the end, even if it meant the same death that Jesus died.

The church in the world today is in the midst of fiery trials in some places—and will no doubt be subjected to new and sterner trials in the future. Mark's Gospel both presents such a picture of the future—and warns against apostasy. That the disciples, in Judas, became accomplices in Jesus' death shows the awful consequences of not confessing the name of Jesus in its full (Gospel) dimensions. But Jesus' warning—and his resurrection—gives hope to the church in the hour of trial. Mark's message may be seen as an exhortation to the church to purge out the evil leaven (see 1 Cor. 5:7) and to confess Jesus Christ as Lord (Rom. 10:9). Upon this its very life depends.

NOTES TO CHAPTER 5

1. Cf. D. E. Nineham, *The Gospel of St. Mark*, in *PGC* (Baltimore: Penguin Books, 1963), pp. 214-215: "The passage is generally agreed to be 'an especially difficult one', and it would seem that St. Mark has here moulded his material in a symbolic interest to a greater degree than is his wont."

2. Cf. Eduard Schweizer, *The Good News According to Mark* (Richmond: John Knox Press, 1970), pp. 160-161; Etienne Trocmé, *The Formation of the Gospel According to Mark* (Philadelphia: Westminster Press, 1975), pp. 110-111.

3. Schweizer, *ibid.*, p. 160.

4. The present essay was first delivered in an earlier configuration to a seminary class audience at Western Theological Seminary. Its publication in the present context is both appropriate and fulfilling.

5. Ernst Lohmeyer, *Das Evangelium des Markus,* in *KKNT* (Göttingen: Vandenhoeck & Ruprecht, 1963).

6. R. H. Lightfoot, *Locality and Doctrine in the Gospels* (London: Hodder and Stoughton, 1938).

7. Lohmeyer, *op. cit.*, pp. 157-158.

8. Julius Schniewind, *Das Evangelium nach Markus*, in *NTD* (Göttingen: Vandenhoeck & Ruprecht, 1960), pp. 77-78.

9. Vincent Taylor, *The Gospel According to St. Mark*, in *MacNTC* (London: Macmillan, 1952), p. 365.

10. C. E. B. Cranfield, *The Gospel According to St. Mark*, in *CGT* (Cambridge: Cambridge University Press, 1963), pp. 259-261.

11. Nineham, *op. cit.*, pp. 213-215.

12. C. F. D. Moule, *The Gospel According to Mark*, in *CBCNEB* (Cambridge: Cambridge University Press, 1965), p. 62.

13. Schweizer, *op. cit.*, p. 161.

14. William Lane, *The Gospel According to Mark*, in *NICNT* (Grand Rapids: Wm. B. Eerdmans, 1974), pp. 280-281.

15. Leslie Mitton, *The Gospel According to St. Mark*, in *EPC* (London: Epworth Press, 1957), p. 61.

16. Cf. Vincent Taylor, *op. cit.*, p. 120: "Beyond question this title represents the most fundamental element in Mark's Christology."

17. H. J. Ebeling, *Das Messiasgeheimnis und die Botschaft des Marcus-Evangelisten*, in *BZNW*, 19 (Berlin: A. Töpelmann, 1939), pp. 146-179, esp. 178-179.

18. Cf. James M. Robinson, *The Problem of History in Mark*, in *StBTh*, no. 21 (London: SCM Press, 1957), pp. 43-53.

19. Cf. Robert P. Meye, *Jesus and the Twelve* (Grand Rapids: Wm. B. Eerdmans, 1968).

20. Cf. R. Bultmann, *The History of the Synoptic Tradition*, trans. by J. Marsh (Oxford: Basil Blackwell, 1963), p. 344.

21. Cf. Bultmann, *op. cit.*, p. 350.

22. Martin Kähler, *The So-Called Historical Jesus and the Historic, Biblical Christ* (Philadelphia: Fortress Press, 1964), p. 80, n. 11. Significant as his observation is, standing alone it is a misleading foreshortening of the Marcan perspective which also includes the resurrection.

23. Cf. R. P. Meye, "Mark 16:8—The Ending of Mark's Gospel," *Biblical Research*, 14 (1969), 1-11.

24. Ulrich Mauser, *Christ in the Wilderness*, in *StBTh*, no. 39 (Naperville: A. R. Allenson, 1963); Willi Marxsen, *Mark the Evangelist* (Nashville: Abingdon, 1969), pp. 30-53.

25. Marxsen, *ibid.*, p. 42.

26. Lane, *op. cit.*, p. 215.

27. Cf. Ralph Martin, *Mark: Evangelist and Theologian* (Exeter: Paternoster Press, 1972), pp. 46-50.

28. Cf. Norman Perrin, in *Christology and a Modern Pilgrimage: A Discussion with Norman Perrin*, ed. by Hans Dieter Betz (Claremont: New Testament Colloquium, 1971).

29. See *Gospel Parallels*, ed. by B. H. Throckmorton (New York: Thomas Nelson, 1957).

30. Cf. Schweizer, *op. cit.*, p. 161; Lane, *op. cit.*, pp. 286-287.

31. In the following discussion, Herod (Mark 8:15) is understood as a Marcan cognate to the Herodians in 3:6 and 12:13. Mark evidently understands the Herodians as the "entourage" of Herod—whether more loosely or more closely cannot be determined.

32. Cf. F. W. Young, "Hypocrisy," in *IDB*, 2 (New York: Abingdon, 1962), 668.

33. Cranfield, *op. cit.*, p. 260.

34. Cf. T. J. Weeden, *Mark: Traditions in Conflict* (Philadelphia: Fortress Press, 1971), for an example of extended and consistent application of the perspective here denied.

35. Cf. Quentin Quesnell, *The Mind of Mark* (Rome: Pontifical Biblical Institute, 1969), esp. pp. 257ff.

36. Cf. G. H. Boobyer, "The Eucharistic Interpretation of the Loaves in St. Mark's Gospel," *JTS*, 3 (1952), 161-171; *idem,* "The Miracles of the Loaves and the Gentiles in St. Mark's Gospel," *SJT,* 6 (1953), 77-87.

37. Cf. Lane, *op. cit.*, pp. 12-17; Martin, *op. cit.*, pp. 208-209.

6: Jesus, Simeon, and Anna
(Luke 2:21-40)

BO REICKE

The latter half of Luke 2 consists of two pericopes dealing with early visits of Jesus to the temple in Jerusalem.[1] It is the first of these pericopes, Luke 2:21-40, that will be investigated below. Jesus is here a little child who is brought from Bethlehem to Jerusalem by his parents, and the theme is his encounter with the prophets Simeon and Anna in the temple. In the second pericope, 2:41-52, Jesus, now a boy, journeys with his parents from Nazareth to Jerusalem and is later found in the temple conversing with the scribes.

After an introductory remark on circumcision and name-giving in Luke 2:21, the pericope in question describes three episodes: (1) the presentation of Jesus in the temple, 2:22-24; (2) his blessing by Simeon, 2:25-35; and (3) his meeting with Anna, 2:36-38. Then in 2:39-40 is added a short remark on the move of the family to Nazareth. In spite of the allusion to Bethlehem in 2:21 and the references to Nazareth in 2:39 and later in 2:51, the interest of those who told Luke the stories found in both pericopes was definitely to illustrate early visits of Jesus to the temple.

I

Luke 2:21 serves as introduction to the pericope 2:21-40. It concerns two ceremonies, the circumcision and naming of the child a week after its birth in Bethlehem. With these the reader is prepared to follow the parents and the child to Jerusalem.

V. 21 offers two examples of a *kai* used like a w^e in Hebrew or Aramaic; the second *kai* introduces the main clause in the sense of "then": "And when [the stipulation about] eight days (Lev. 12:3) had been fulfilled so that he was to be circumcised, then (*kai*) his name Jesus was proclaimed which had been announced by the angel . . ." (Luke 2:21).

Such a generous use of *kai* is found throughout the story about the infant Jesus in the temple. Every verse includes a *kai*, corresponding to the Hebrew and Aramaic habit of linking clauses by a *w^e*. Many other peculiarities may also be observed which prove the dependence of the story-tellers upon Semitic vernacular.

This strong preference for Semitisms is not characteristic of Luke in general. Whereas the prologue and most parts of the Third Gospel confirm his ambition to write in fairly good Hellenistic Greek, the narrative in question represents a popular style and was obviously based on traditions still dominated by Hebrew or Aramaic syntax, recalling the style of the Revelation of John. Luke cannot possibly have given the narrative such a Semiticizing character but must be assumed to have taken over the story without changing its main diction. The same is true of the preceding traditions about the births of John and Jesus, and of the subsequent narrative concerning the visit of the young boy to Jerusalem. Apart from an essential continuity of ideas, quite amazing differences of style emerge between the family stories in Luke 1:5-2:52 and the rest of the Gospel. This variation is generally acknowledged by modern expositors. But there is an inclination to ascribe the linguistic peculiarities in 1:5-2:52 either to (a) some Hebrew or Aramaic documents used by Luke or to (b) a stylistic adaptation carried through by him.[2] These literary theories are contradictory, and neither of them can explain the organic combination of Jewish diction and Christian thinking found in 1:5-2:52. Furthermore, regard is not paid to Luke's declaration that he endeavored to collect direct communications from servants of the gospel who had been active since the beginning (Luke 1:2). One has rather to conclude that Luke left oral traditions associated with the families of the Baptist and the Savior relatively unchanged because of a special respect for informants thought by him to represent living connections with the origins. He confirmed this expressly by assuring the reader twice of the fact that it was Mary who had kept in her memory the events reported (2:19, 51). Luke did not claim to have received direct information from Mary, but alluded to stories told in circles that had been in contact with her. In fact the author of the Third Gospel and the Book of Acts was able to receive such information from Jerusalem. He was directly or indirectly acquainted with a number of women who followed Jesus from Galilee to Jerusalem (Luke 8:2-3; 23:49; 24:10); and since he can be identified with the author of the "we" sections in Acts, Luke had also met Philip, James, and other members of the primitive church (Acts 21:8, 18).

According to Luke 2:21, two Jewish ceremonies took place in Bethlehem on the eighth day, or a week after the birth of the child: its circumcision according to 2:21a and its naming according to 2:21b.[3] Half a year earlier Zacharias and Elisabeth had taken John the Baptist to the temple in order that the same ceremonies might be performed (1:59). Luke wanted to show that the will of God as represented in the law had been fulfilled not only by the parents of the Baptist, but also by the parents of Jesus (2:22, *kata ton nomon*). As is evident from details found in the following verses, he also wanted to indicate that Jesus was placed under the law, a christological aspect given direct expression by Paul in his well-known formula, "born from a woman, born under the law" (Gal. 4:4). It was the continuity between the old covenant, the predecessor, and the new covenant that had to be demonstrated.

The relevant prescription of the old covenant was Lev. 12:1-4. It implied that a mother was regarded as unclean for seven days after the birth of a son (Lev. 12:2), but that on the eighth day the circumcision of the child was to be celebrated (12:3). The circumcision of John the Baptist had taken place in the presence of the family and neighbors (Luke 1:58), whereas no visitors are mentioned in connection with that of Jesus.

Although there is no early Jewish evidence of name-giving on the same occasion, Luke probably referred to a normal Jewish habit when he combined the circumcision of John and Jesus with this event (1:59; 2:21b). The only peculiarity was that since these children were born to live under the complete guidance of the Holy Spirit (1:15, 35), their names were not chosen by the parents, but proclaimed in accordance with the instructions that had been delivered previously by angels (1:15, 31). To be sure, John and Jesus were not given unusual names, but since the Baptist and the Savior were to be filled by the divine Spirit and since a substantial connection was thought to exist between a person's soul and his name, they had to receive their names from above.

The mother of a newborn male child was regarded as unclean not only for the seven days until his circumcision, but also for thirty-three days afterwards (Lev. 12:4). She had to stay at home, and was not allowed to touch anything holy nor to enter the sanctuary. These periods of seven and thirty-three days are still illustrated by the intervals between Christmas Day, the New Year, and Candlemas, insofar as these days are celebrated in remembrance of Christ's nativity, his naming a week later, and Mary's visit to the temple thirty-three days afterward.

Lev. 12:6-7 prescribed that when the seven plus thirty-three days were over, the uncleanness of the mother had to be removed in the temple by the burnt offering of a lamb and the sin offering of a dove. If a mother could not bring a lamb for the burnt offering, Lev. 12:8 allowed her to replace it by a second dove. According to Luke 2:22a and 24, the parents of Jesus used this privilege of the poor to replace the lamb and the dove by a couple of doves, which they easily could have bought in the temple (Matt. 12:12 with par.). But the emphasis is not on any special poverty of Joseph and Mary. It was only the fulfillment of the law that interested the evangelist (*kata ton nomon Mōüseōs,* 2:22a). On the other hand Luke understood this fulfillment in a messianic sense; the pious acts of Joseph and Mary in the temple did not take place for the sake of the law, but for the sake of the Lord. Several passages in the Third Gospel, including 2:22 and its context, demonstrate Luke's conviction that Moses and the prophets had dealt with the coming of the Messiah in the person of Jesus (Luke 1:17, 31, 55, 70; 2:22, 23, 24, 27, 29, 38, 39, 49; 3:4; 9:30-31; 16:19; 24:27, 44; cf. Acts 3:22-25). Luke also understood the visit of Mary to Jerusalem in 2:22a and 24 as fulfilling the law in this messianic sense. The relation between 2:22a and 2:22b shows that the mother's purification was only regarded as offering an opportunity to bring the child to Jerusalem and to present it to God in the temple, an event that brought about the subsequent messianic proclamations of Simeon and Anna. For the two halves of v. 22 must be seen in the following logical relation: "When the number of days was complete for their purification in accordance with the law of Moses, they used the opportunity to bring the child to Jerusalem to present it to the Lord."

Luke regarded this dedication of Jesus in the temple as the central purpose of the visit to Jerusalem, more important than Mary's purification. It was meant to fulfill an essential prescription of the law, namely, the consecration of a firstborn son according to Exod. 13:2. The evangelist did not confuse the rules concerning the purification of a mother and those concerning the presentation of a child, as has been asserted by several expositors.[4] He only indicated that in the present case the purification of the mother permitted the parents to enter the temple so that they could also present the child to the God of Israel. In a similar way Samuel had been dedicated to God at Shiloh (1 Sam. 1:11, 22, 28). Otherwise the fulfillment of the basic commandment in Exod. 13:2 by the parents of Jesus was unique. For according to Exod. 13:13, which implies a facilitation of Exod. 13:2, a ransom was in normal cases to be paid for a male child without any such presentation in the temple (cf. below).

As soon as the purification of the mother permitted it, the parents entered the temple and dedicated their son to the Lord in fulfillment of that fundamental commandment concerning the firstborn. Luke quoted this scripture in 2:23, emphasizing that Jesus was presented to God in exact accordance with "the law of the Lord."

Every reader familiar with the law and Jewish customs would have been able to find indications here of two important conditions:

(1) In the present case, the prescription concerning the firstborn in Exod. 13:2 was fulfilled literally, so that Jesus was really given to the Lord and not ransomed like other males in accordance with the instruction about substitute offerings added in Exod. 13:13. According to Num. 3:47 and 18:16, the ransom should amount to five temple shekels, which later corresponded to five Tyrian selas (Mishna *Bek.* 8:7). No such ransom was paid by the parents of Jesus; the sacrifice of two doves mentioned in Luke 2:24 was for the purification of the mother. The presentation even excluded any substitute offering, for the ransom had to be paid to a priest anywhere in the country (Num. 3:48, 51; *Mek.* Exod. 13:2; 22:29; *Sif.* Num. 18:15). Against the normal custom the child Jesus was thus dedicated to God, and remained his property.

(2) This exceptional obedience to God's will implied fulfilling the law on its messianic level, that is, the law understood as evidence of the Lord's dispensations for the salvation of his people. Luke meant in 2:23 that "the law of the Lord" was fulfilled in such a higher sense, and he repeated the expression in 2:24 and 39, in each case referring to what the parents did for the child. In 2:27 Luke said expressly that the instruction of the law about the dedication had been formulated with regard to Jesus.

The first episode is concluded in 2:24 with a notice concerning the sacrifice of two doves following Lev. 12:8. Luke here referred back to Mary's purification mentioned in 2:22. The evangelist did not at all confuse the doves with the substitute offering for a firstborn son which consisted of five Tyrian selas (see above). He only rounded off the story with another reference to Mary's purification to reiterate the framework of the child's presentation.

II

The dedication of Jesus led to Simeon's encounter with the child in the temple, and this is the topic of the second episode, Luke 2:25-35.

Simeon is said to have lived in Jerusalem and to have been renowned for his piety (2:25). The construction of the clause (*kai idou anthrōpos ēn en Ierousalēm . . . kai ho anthrōpos houtos dikaios kai eulabēs*) is another striking example of Semitic influence on the Greek text (there is a similar construction in 1 Sam. 25:2: *kai ēn anthrōpos en tēi Maōn, . . . kai ho anthrōpos megas sphodra*). Simeon is also reported to have waited eagerly for the consolation of Israel. The expression "consolation" (*paraklēsis*) indicated the fulfillment of well-known prophecies of salvation (Isa. 40:1f.; 61:2). As a prophet, Simeon was filled with the Holy Spirit. He had received a revelation about the coming of the Messiah before his death (2:26). Moreover, the Spirit gave him an impulse to enter the temple precisely at the right moment (2:27a), so that with biblical flourish he could give utterance concerning the salvation of Israel as well as the future of the child and his mother (2:27b-35). The picture of Simeon found in this story implies profound knowledge of the Scriptures, ardent expectations of the Messiah, and close relations to the temple where the old man was accustomed to prophesying in public.

Behind the story told by Luke were remembrances of historical facts, and what is reported about the appearance of Simeon was not a legend. Post-exilic Judaism was inclined to be cautious toward anyone who made prophetic claims (mainly because of the warnings in Zech. 13:3); but the population of Jerusalem was actually familiar with prophets in the temple during the years before and after the birth of Jesus. These prophets represented the movement of the Essenes, now fairly well known from the Qumran scrolls and the books of Josephus as well as from certain accounts of Philo and Pliny. By the population in general, and by the authorities, Essene prophets were held in great esteem (Jos., *Bell*. 1:78-80; 2:113, 159; *Ant*. 13:311-313; 15:371-379; 17:345-348). They based their apocalyptic predictions on profound studies of Holy Scripture (Dan. 12:4; Commentary on Hab. 7:1-5; Jos., *Bell*. 2:159), and these studies resulted in messianic expectations (Manual of Discipline 9:11; Damascus Document 12:23; 13:1; 14:19; 19:10-11; 20:1; Blessing of the Patriarchs 3-4; Florilegium 1:11, "the Branch of David"). Essene prophets were known to preach and prophesy in the temple (Jos., *Bell*. 1:78; *Ant*. 13:311), preferably inside an entrance called the Gate of the Essenes (Jos., *Bell*. 5:145). A famous Essene prophet was active in the temple around 104 B.C. where he taught students the art of prognostication (Jos., *Bell*. 1:78). He and other Essene prophets were also renowned as successful advisors of Hasmonean and Herodian princes (according to Josephus in the passages quoted above).

During the years surrounding the birth of Christ, there was a famous Essene prophet in Jerusalem by the name of Simon. People remembered that Herod's son Archelaus (Matt. 2:22), who governed Judea from 4 B.C. to A.D. 6, had asked Simon five months before he was deposed to explain an enigmatic dream, and that the prophet had correctly foreseen his dethronement (Jos., *Bell*. 2:113; *Ant*. 17:346).

A number of analogies can thus be established between the picture of Essene prophets given by Josephus and the portrait of the prophet Simeon given by Luke. There is a striking convergence of the place, time, and form of their activity. In particular, the prophet Simon mentioned by Josephus was active exactly at the same time as the prophet Simeon described by Luke. Simon prognosticated the fall of Archelaus in A.D. 6, shortly before Quirinius arranged the Roman taxation of Judea which, according to Luke 2:2, was the chronological background of Christ's birth and therefore also of Simeon's encounter with the child in the temple. Even if the passages 1:5 and 26 make it probable that Luke in fact, like Matthew, ascribed the birth of Jesus to Herod's time, there is still a remarkable chronological harmony between the reports on the prophets Simon and Simeon.

The difference between the names Simon and Simeon is of no importance, for in Hellenism the Jews replaced the Hebrew name *Shim'ōn* either by the authentic Greek name *Simōn* or by the Greek transcription *Symeōn,* and the oscillation is also found in connection with the same person. In the Maccabean family, the grandfather was called Simeon and the grandson Simon (1 Macc. 2:1, 3), but the latter was also called Simeon (2:65) although his usual name was Simon (13:1, etc.). Luke alternated in the same way between Simon and Simeon with regard to Peter (Luke 4:38; Acts 15:14). For this reason, the prophet Simeon referred to by Luke can very well have been the same person. The numerous other analogies between them will certainly justify their identification.

Without pressing Luke's accuracy in a mechanical way, two conclusions may be drawn from these observations. (1) Luke's portrait of Simeon in the temple was not a product of pious imagination, but in fact was based on people's remembrance of an historical person, a well-known temple prophet active in the years surrounding the birth of Christ. (2) This man was the venerated Essene prophet Simon, and so the story-tellers and Luke wanted their contemporaries to understand that Essene prophecy had confirmed the coming of the Lord in relative conformity with the proclamations of Zechariah and John the Baptist (Luke 1:76-79; 3:16-17).

According to Luke 2:27a, the prophet Simeon was driven by the Holy Spirit to enter the temple at the right moment so that he met Joseph and Mary when they came with Jesus. The syntax of 2:27b-28a also offers a characteristic example of a *kai* used in semitic manner to introduce a main clause: "And when the parents brought in the child Jesus in order to act in accordance with what had been settled [*eithismenon,* "made a norm"] by the law concerning him [the dedication of a firstborn son in Exod. 12:3, just quoted in Luke 2:23], then (*kai*) Simeon took him up in his arms." Here it is explicitly stated that Moses had written about the consecration of a firstborn son with regard to Jesus.

The meeting must be understood to have taken place in the most central part of the temple to which Mary had admission, that is, the Court of the Women. In this representative environment the prophet Simeon took up the child Jesus in his arms to demonstrate the connection between the prophecy of the old covenant and the firstling of the new covenant. His motive is confirmed by the song of praise called *Nunc Dimittis*, which follows in Luke 2:28b-34. It is completely based on allusions to Second Isaiah, the same prophet who was quoted in connection with preparing the way of the Lord by the Essenes (Manual of Discipline 8:14) and John the Baptist (Matt. 3:3/Mark 1:3/Luke 3:4-6; John 1:23). Simeon saw the fulfillment of Isaiah's prophecy in the child that would bring mankind salvation.

The ability to improvise a hymn of the Old Testament type was characteristic of the Essenes (examples are found in the *Hodayot* of Qumran and a description in Philo, *De vita contemplativa* 80). Luke ascribed the same ability to Mary and the father of the Baptist (1:46-55, 67-69). The present song of praise may be divided into two parts: (a) a thanksgiving in 2:29, and (b) several reasons for the thanksgiving in 2:30-32.

(a) To begin with, according to 2:29 Simeon thanked the Lord for being allowed to finish his life in peace. In 2:29a, the expression "now you let go" (*nyn apolyeis, nunc dimittis*) must have the meaning of "now you discharge," for since Simeon characterized himself as a servant (*doulos*) of the Lord, the point is that now his function as a prophet was over.[5] This is confirmed by v. 30 which emphasizes that Simeon had now seen the salvation in reality, so that prophecy was no longer necessary. But as Simeon had been told he would not die before seeing the Messiah (2:26), his discharge also refers to his approaching death in peace, which is then indicated in 2:29b.

According to 2:29b, Simeon understood his discharge in peace as the fulfillment of a word spoken by the Lord himself. The word of scripture he drew upon was Ps. 4:9 where the Hebrew text reads: "I shall now lie down in peace and sleep, for thou, O Lord, allowest me to dwell with security in a separate place." In the Greek translation of Ps. 4:9, the expression "with security" was understood as implying "with (a good) hope," and this rendering is also found in the Greek text of Ps. 15(16):9 which is quoted in Acts 2:26 with regard to Christ's death, his dwelling in hope, and subsequent resurrection. Luke's readers would comprehend that Simeon expressed a similar hope in the salvation of the elect people when he indicated the word of the Lord found in Ps. 4:9.

(b) To his great satisfaction, Simeon had now seen the expected salvation realized in the child Jesus (2:30). His enthusiasm echoed a prophecy of Second Isaiah, namely, the Greek text of Isa. 40:5. Every expression in the following verses of the hymn is in fact also based on Second Isaiah. The preparation of the way of the Lord had been announced especially by this prophet in 40:3, a passage quoted by the

Essenes and also cited in connection with John the Baptist (see above). According to Luke, Simeon's prophecy represented a prolongation of the same perspective.

In accordance with the above-mentioned quotation of Isa. 40:5 in the Greek text, Luke made Simeon exclaim in 2:30 that by meeting the child his eyes had seen God's "instrument of salvation" (*sōtērion*). To this Septuagint expression used in a christological sense there is a linguistic analogy in the remarkable term "instrument of reconciliation" (*hilastērion*) used by Paul for Christ (Rom. 3:25).

According to 2:31 Simeon, speaking to God, describes Christ as this instrument of salvation "which you have prepared" (*ho hētoimasas*). In a similar way, Paul said that God had appointed Christ (*proetheto*) as his instrument of reconciliation (Rom. 3:25). With a quotation of Isa. 52:10, Simeon then stresses the universality of this salvation: "before the eyes of all the nations." This further analogy to Paul (Rom. 3:23, *pantes*; 3:28, *ethnē*) is the first reference to universalism found in the Gospel of Luke, for the preceding stories and hymns are only concerned with the salvation of the Jewish nation. Luke's informants had conveyed a picture of Simeon that enabled the evangelist to understand the prophet as foreseeing the universal missionary program of the church, a program for which Luke worked together with Paul, and to which Luke gave expression in later parts of his Gospel and in Acts.

On the other hand, whereas 2:32a continues the universalism of 2:31, the parallel line 2:32b returns to nationalism. There is no contradiction in this. Both halves of the verse contain allusions to Second Isaiah, and the organic relation between universalism and nationalism was characteristic of this prophet (see, e.g., Isa. 49:6). Luke 2:32a is based on Isa. 42:6 and 49:6 (*eis phōs ethnōn*). The implication is that Christ is the servant of the Lord who reveals the light of salvation to all nations. V. 32b alludes to Isa. 46:13. Here the conclusion is that Christ's revelation among the Gentiles brings glory to God's people Israel.

According to 2:33, Jesus' parents were amazed by what Simeon said about him. In this context Luke had not forgotten that in his reports on the birth of the child, Mary had already been informed about his messianic future (1:32-33, 35, 42-43; 2:17, 19). What astonished Jesus' parents was not the messianic secret as such, but the universal perspective now given to it by Simeon, since all previous revelations had been about the salvation of Israel (1:32f.; cf. 1:54, 68, 77; 2:10-11).[6]

After his song of praise, Simeon blessed Jesus' parents (2:34a), but then according to 2:34b-35 told his mother that Jesus would cause dissension in Israel and even make Mary uncertain. Here the syntax requires that v. 35a, referring to a sword in Mary's heart, be understood as a parenthesis.[7] V. 34b represents the main clause: "He is to bring about the falling short and the standing upright of many in Israel, and to become a sign that will be contradicted." A symbolic use of "falling" and "standing" was characteristic of Essene traditions.[8] Later the main clause in v. 34b is continued by the final clause in v. 35b: "in order that the intentions of many hearts may be revealed." In the middle the warning prophecy of the main clause in v. 34b is enforced by the parenthesis in v. 35a: "and even through your [Mary's] own soul a broad sword (*romphaia*) will go." As the context refers to a difference between doubters and believers in Israel, the additional remark on a broad sword (*romphaia*) that will also (*kai*) cut through (*dia*) the soul of Mary was not meant to evoke the picture of a *mater dolorosa* but to indicate a division of her mind (cf. the expression *dipsychos* in James 1:8). There is an instructive analogy to this picture of a sword in the Sibylline Oracles 3:316: "For a broad sword (*romphaia*) will go through you," indicating a crisis and division in Ptolemaic Egypt. Origen understood Simeon's image of the sword in a similar way, thinking of Mary's despair under the cross.[9] But the reference is rather to a wider context, namely to Mary's temporary hesitation vis-à-vis the activity of Jesus, a fact still known by the early believers. Christian story-tellers, who had been in contact with Mary, had told Luke that Simeon had already foreseen Israel's divided attitude to Jesus in Galilee and Judea (e.g., Matt. 12:22-50/Mark 3:20-25/ Luke 11:14-12:1), and even Mary's occasional uncertainty and provisional abstention (Luke 2:48; 8:19-21; 11:27-28) until after the death of Jesus when she joined the apostles in Jerusalem (Acts. 1:14).[10] The final clause in Luke 2:35b explains why Jesus must become such a sign that will be contradicted: "in order that (*hopōs*) the intentions (*dialogismoi*) of many hearts may be revealed." Here the emphasis is on "many," and thus the spread of the light to all people (2:31-32a) is referred to again. The opposition to Jesus among several of his countrymen will bring about the conversion of many Gentiles (similar to what Paul experienced according to Acts 13:46; cf. Rom. 10:19; 11:11). When these people declare themselves ready to believe in Christ, the deepest intentions of their hearts or the secrets parts of their souls are laid bare (as Paul declared in 1 Cor. 14:25).

III

The third episode forms a short analogy to the second one. According to 2:36-38, a female representative of prophecy appeared in the temple and welcomed Jesus in the same way as Simeon. The scene must still be supposed to be the Court of the Women.

The prophetess was an aged widow named Anna (2:36a), and she is said to have been from the tribe of Asher, which had settled along the coast west of Galilee. Vv. 2:36b-37a contain references to her previous life and present age of eighty-four years, and they imply that she met Jesus in the important moment when she had completed twelve periods of seven years. Assuming that she had married at the normal age of fourteen years (2x7), she was twenty-one when she became a widow seven years later (3x7) and had now served in the temple for sixty-three years (9x7), which corresponds to her reported age of eighty-four (12x7). The reader should conclude that her life had reached its culmination when she met the messianic child. According to 2:37b, her activities in the temple had been fasting and prayer night and day. Contrary to what is found with regard to Simeon, contemporary Jewish parallels to such a widow serving in the temple are not described in the documents available. But the parable of Jesus about the widow and the judge (Luke 18:1-8) presupposes intercession for Israel day and night, especially by widows. Another religious function of Jewish widows consisted in their lamentation at funerals (Acts 9:39). There is also evidence of Christian widows being treated as a particular religious group in the early church of Jerusalem (Acts 6:1), and supposed to be occupied with prayer night and day in churches of the Diaspora (1 Tim. 5:5). Anna probably interested Luke's informants because she had been a predecessor of Christian widows, and Luke will have taken over some reminiscences of her from people connected with the widows of the Jerusalem church.

But her analogy to Simeon is especially to be observed. According to 2:38, she approached (*epistasa*, aorist) the little group at the very moment that Simeon was prophesying about the child. She also began to praise and to speak (*anthōmologeito, elalei*, inchoative imperfects) about Jesus "to all people waiting for the liberation of Jerusalem." The last phrase is a combination of allusions to Ps. 130:5-8 and Isa. 52:8-10 where the picture of watchers on Zion is used to illustrate the waiting of the pious for the Lord. Isa. 52:10 had also been quoted by Simeon in 2:31. The tradition used by Luke thus implied that Simeon and Anna were both watchers on Zion filled with joy upon seeing the child that would bring the redemption of Israel promised by the Old Testament.

According to 2:39a, Joseph and Mary had now fulfilled everything in accordance with the law of the Lord. It is obvious from 2:27b (see above) and from the whole context that Luke was referring to a messianic fulfillment of the law, being a prophecy concerning the Lord. The sanctification of the firstborn son mentioned in Exod. 13:2 had taken place in a way that consummated the proper meaning of this scripture.

Luke knew that Joseph and Mary had later moved to Nazareth

(2:39b). Further details about the childhood of Jesus were not available to him. The concluding remark in 2:40 on the growth of the child and his being filled with wisdom and grace was meant to prepare the reader for the subsequent narrative about the wisdom displayed by Jesus in the temple when he was approaching the age of a student (2:41-52).

Concerning the episodes in the early years of Jesus treated above, Luke had Jerusalem traditions at his disposal. His reports can suitably be traced back to men and women connected with the early church who lived in direct contact with the temple (Acts 1:4; 2:46; 3:3, 11, etc.). Paul called these Jewish Christians in Jerusalem the Holy Ones (Rom. 15:25). In their eyes the temple was of central importance, a fact that became very obvious when the author of the "we" narratives in Acts came with Paul to the Holy City in A.D. 58 (Acts 21:20-26). Luke may have become familiar with the stories of Simeon and Anna in this context.

For the evangelist Luke, the joy of those who received the good news was always of special interest.[11] He reported that during the night when the Savior and Messiah of Israel was born in the city of David, angels proclaimed a great joy that would be offered to the whole people (Luke 2:10). On the basis of Jewish-Christian recollections available to Luke, this joy of the elect people was understood to be anticipated by the Baptist in his mother's womb (1:44)[12] and by the two witnesses, Simeon and Anna, in the temple (2:28, 38).[13] Later this joy found concrete expression among the apostles, the mother of Jesus (Acts 1:14), and other believers who lived in Jerusalem near the temple and were filled by an overwhelming enthusiasm because of spiritual experiences confirming the promises given to Israel (Acts 2:39). These very first Jewish-Christians were said to have been occupied with intense prayer (1:14), with jubilation and glorification (*agalliasei, ainountes*, 2:46-47), and even with hymn-like thanksgiving (4:24-30). It seems only natural that recollections about the joy of Simeon and Anna arose in this environment and were forwarded to Luke by some of those who had been servants of the Word from the beginning (Luke 1:2).

NOTES TO CHAPTER 6

1. Bibliographical references are in R. Laurentin, *Structure et théologie de Luc I-II* (Paris: J. Gabalda, 1957), pp. 189-223; H. Schürmann, *Das Lukas-evangelium* (Freiburg: Herder, 1969), I, 18-19, 119-145.

2. The alternative may be illustrated by a few examples: (a) A background in Hebrew documents was assumed by H. Sahlin, *Der Messias und das Gottesvolk: Studien zur protolukanischen Theologie* (Uppsala: Almqvist-Wiksells, 1945), pp.

239-287, 306-308; Laurentin, *op. cit.* (n. 1), pp. 93-119; P. Winter, "The Cultural Background of the Narrative in Luke i and ii," *JQR*, 45 (1954), 159-167, 230-242, 287; *idem*, "Some Observations on the Language in the Birth and Infancy Stories of the Third Gospel," *NTS*, 1 (1954-55), 111-121. These and similar papers of Winter were discussed by R. McL. Wilson, "Some Recent Studies in the Lucan Infancy Narratives," *Texte und Untersuchungen*, 73 (1959), 235-253, and there is a list of Winter's numerous contributions to the discussion in the article of H. H. Oliver (p. 209, n. 4) quoted below. (b) The influence of Luke's language was more emphasized by N. Turner, "The Relation of Luke I and II to Hebraic Sources and to the Rest of Luke-Acts," *NTS*, 2 (1955-56), 100-109; the influence of his theology by H. H. Oliver, "The Lucan Birth Stories and the Purpose of Luke-Acts," *NTS*, 10 (1963-64), 202-226; W. Barnes Tatum, "The Epoch of Israel: Luke I - II and the Theological Plan of Luke-Acts," *NTS*, 13 (1966-67), 184-195.

3. E. Galbiati, "La circoncisione de Gesù, Luca 2:21," *Bibbia et oriente*, 8 (1966), 37-45.

4. Thus, for instance, the exposition of Luke 2:22 in E. Klostermann, *Das Lukasevangelium*, 2nd ed. (Tübingen: J. C. B. Mohr, 1929), p. 41.

5. N. Geldenhuys, *Commentary on the Gospel of Luke* (Grand Rapids: Wm. B. Eerdmans, 1951), p. 119.

6. K. H. Rengstorf, *Das Evangelium nach Lukas* (Göttingen: Vandenhoeck & Ruprecht, 1963), p. 47.

7. H. Schürmann, *op. cit.* (n. 1), p. 128.

8. W. Grundmann, "Stehen und Fallen im qumränschen und neutestamentlichen Schrifttum," in *Qumran-probleme*, ed. by H. Bardtke (Berlin: Akademie-Verlag, 1963), pp. 147-166.

9. "Homily 17 in Luke," *Die griechischen christlichen Schriftsteller der ersten drei Jahrhunderte* (Leipzig: J. C. Hinrichs, 1930), XXXV, 116-118.

10. J. Winandy, "La propétie du Syméon, Lc. II: 34-35," *RB*, 72 (1965), 321-351, prefers to think of "la contradiction dont elle sera victime" (p. 348).

11. B. Reicke, *The Gospel of Luke* (London: S.P.C.K., 1964), pp. 75-88; P. J. Bernadicou, "Programmatic Texts of Joy in Luke's Gospel," *The Bible Today*, 45 (1969), 3098-3105; *idem*, "Biblical Joy and the Lucan Eucharist," *ibid.*, 51 (1970), 162-171; *idem*, "The Lucan Theology of Joy," *Science et esprit*, 25 (1973), 75-98.

12. H. B. Beverly, "An Exposition of Luke 1:39-45," *Interpretation*, 30 (1976), 396-400 (esp. p. 398).

13. Simeon and Anna are rightly called Luke's prime witnesses by F. W. Danker, "The Shape of Luke's Gospel in Lectionaries," *Interpretation*, 30 (1976), 339-352 (esp. p. 342).

7: *Another Look at the Parable of the Good Samaritan*

BASTIAAN VAN ELDEREN

Perhaps no parable in the Gospels is more familiar than the parable of the Good Samaritan. The narrative has been acclaimed as a fine piece of literature and its dramatic effect hailed as unsurpassed. It has appealed to the imagination of children, inspired the idealism of the activists, and troubled the hearts of the indifferent and calloused. The simple story, the realism of the *dramatis personae*, the directness of the punch-line—all contribute to the beauty and dynamic of the story. However, the prevailing interpretation based upon this simplicity and directness will be challenged in this study—dedicated to a man deeply interested in New Testament scholarship and especially concerned with the study and interpretation of the parables of Jesus. It is a pleasure to participate in this *Festschrift* honoring a friend and scholar.

The popular use of this parable fails to deal with two significant features of a parable—its context and its literary structure. The former, although so self-evident in exegesis, is virtually ignored; the latter, a discipline emerging in Gospel studies, is opening exciting vistas in interpretation.[1] Both of these features will provide the framework for this present study.

The parable of the Good Samaritan is part of a dialogue in which Jesus effectively deals with a problem in Mosaic law and its interpretation. The parable functions as an effective teaching device, cleverly used by Jesus, to instruct a questioning lawyer—in fact, the lawyer actually teaches himself by the answers evoked from him by Jesus. Parables were not used by Jesus to conceal truth from the masses, but rather, as Filson rightly observes, "to illustrate, clarify, and enforce truth and lead men to right decision as they faced his Kingdom teaching."[2]

The popular interpretation of the parable of the Good Samaritan usually emphasizes that Jesus is teaching a kind of humanitarianism in this parable. Following the example of the Good Samaritan, one must show kindness to and concern for a person who is in trouble and need.

Consequently, the term "Good Samaritan" has become a byword in the English language to describe a compassionate and humane person who shows kindness and concern in unusual circumstances. Even hospitals and similar institutions are given the name "Good Samaritan." No one will deny that such an emphasis is consonant with the teachings of Jesus, and the Samaritan in the parable surely is a figure worthy of emulation. However, the analysis here presented not only questions the validity of this popular interpretation, but will also place the emphasis where it addresses the particular problem of the lawyer. He did not need a lesson in humanitarianism—almsgiving and care for the beggars and unfortunate were part of his culture and religious commitment (cf., e.g., Matt. 6:2; Luke 11:41; 18:12; Acts 3:2; 10:2).

A further problem with this popular interpretation is the identity of the victim and the benefactor. Jesus would have taught the lawyer, a Jew, humanitarianism and compassion much more effectively if the parable pictured a Jew helping a Samaritan, whom he utterly despised. However, the *dramatis personae* are in the sequence they are in order to teach a more relevant and needed lesson to the lawyer.[3]

The Context

The parable of the Good Samaritan is found in the first half of the central section of the Gospel of Luke (9:51-18:14), usually referred to as The Great Insertion or Travel Narrative.[4] This section of Luke's Gospel has been subjected to numerous studies by scholars in an attempt to find an underlying theme or structure. None has advanced a satisfactory solution. Although this problem lies outside the scope of this present study, the attractive literary structure proposed by Bailey which involves a basic chiastic framework appears to provide an excellent approach and possible solution.[5] He feels that "90 percent of the material in the Travel Narrative of Luke has a carefully constructed inverted outline" (p. 79) and that this structure, consisting of a ten-unit section in the first part which is reversed in the ten-unit section in the second part, "is neither historical nor exclusively theological but rather literary" (p. 85). Luke 10:25-41 is Section 3 in the first part (p. 80):

   3. WHAT SHALL I DO TO INHERIT ETERNAL LIFE? 10:25-42
      (a) Dialog on the law 25-28
      (b) Love the neighbor—the Good Samaritan 29-37
      (c) Love the Lord—the story of Mary and Martha 38-42

This is balanced by Section 3' in the second part (p. 82):

3′ WHAT SHALL I DO TO INHERIT ETERNAL LIFE? 18:18-30
(a) Dialog on the law 18-21
(b) Love for neighbor—"Give to the poor" 22-28
(c) Love for the Lord—"We have left our homes and followed you" 28-30

Bailey has made a valuable and useful contribution to the study of the central section of Luke's Gospel.[6] The recognition that the first half is counter-balanced inversely in the second half juxtaposes the above pericopes in a meaningful way. Bailey's structural analysis provides a useful framework for the further study of the parable of the Good Samaritan.

The intent of parallelism is to reiterate in the second member the same basic theme with the possible addition of a special emphasis or nuance. The key thought in the two parallel units identified by Bailey is the inheritance of eternal life and the function of the law in that regard. Both inquirers, one identified as a lawyer (*nomikos*) and the other as a ruler (*archōn*),[7] know the law and, although in their judgment they are keeping it, are troubled regarding its application. The ruler's riches make him unaware of the poor; the lawyer's definition of "neighbor" makes him uneasy. How the latter responded to the definition proffered by Jesus is not indicated; the ruler, however, was not pleased with the advice of Jesus. The dominant place of the Old Testament law in both dialogues clearly identifies the inquirers as Jews, immersed in the teachings of first-century Judaism. Apparently, the lawyer was an expert in the Mosaic law.[8]

The question with which the lawyer opens the dialogue (10:25) is identical with the question of the ruler (18:18) except for the word of address: *didaskale, ti poiēsas zōēn aiōnion klēronomēsō*? (the ruler adds *agathe* in the address).[9] The structure of the question provides an insight into the questioners. Their concept of inheritance as a reward for a good deed poses serious difficulties, especially vis-à-vis the teachings of Jesus. Furthermore, the tense of the participle (*poiēsas*) used is aorist—focussing on a single act or good deed: "doing what specific deed?" It seems the questioners had a major act of benevolence, pilgrimage, or some act of devotion in mind. By performing it, they would be assured of eternal life. This misdirected concept of eternal life and good works is corrected by Jesus in the ensuing dialogue. Strikingly, when Jesus uses the verb *poieō* in responding to the lawyer, he employs the present tense of the imperative: *poiei* (10:28, 37), exhorting him to perform these acts of love repeatedly and continually—"keep on doing these things."

It must be noted that the law functions significantly in the answer(s) given by Jesus. However, the interpretation and application are conditioned by the attitude and motivation taught and emphasized by Jesus. Pride and conceit motivated the lawyer to misinterpret the law. His definition of "neighbor" was blurred and delimited because his pride had given him a conceited self-appraisal which virtually negated the humanness of a segment of his society—hence, such persons as publicans, Samaritans, Romans could not be his "neighbors."[10] Therefore, he desired a check-list so that he could assuredly ascertain for himself the reality of his eternal life (*thelōn dikaiōsai heauton* [10:29]). This seeking of security by such means is characteristic of all non-Christian religions, whereas for the Christian that assurance comes by the humble acceptance in faith of the gracious act of God in Christ Jesus. In dealing with this lawyer, Jesus had to break down his pride and conceit, rather than to teach him to be kind, helpful, humanitarian, and benevolent. The lawyer did not need a lesson in helping someone in need; rather, he needed a lesson in what it means to be human within the framework of the grace (and the law) of God.

Another interesting insight into the lawyer's thinking is the locus of his problem with the law. He had no difficulty in keeping the first commandment—in his judgment his love for God was adequately demonstrated in the performance of the ritual and other religious exercises.[11] However, the second commandment gave him difficulty. For this commandment he wanted a fixed regulation and routine, just as he had established for the first commandment. This wrongheaded approach, stemming from his conceited self-appraisal by which he made himself both the subject and object of his love, vitiated any demonstration of love on his part.

Luke reports that the lawyer in the initial question was seeking to test Jesus (*ekpeirazōn auton*). This questionable motive is somewhat qualified in the second question in which the lawyer sought to justify himself (*thelōn dikaiōsai heauton*). Apparently, the response of Jesus to his first question threatened him and consequently put him on the defensive in the second question. This psychological reaction must be observed in order to assess properly the dynamic and function of the parable in the dialogue between Jesus and the lawyer.

Literary Structure of the Dialogue

This dialogue in Luke 10:25-37 involves a double use of the Socratic method. The lawyer apparently wanted to use this method to test Jesus; however, Jesus in turn uses the same method to refute and instruct the lawyer. Twice Jesus responds to the lawyer's question with a question.

And the lawyer's answer to Jesus' question in reality becomes the answer to his own original question. Not only does the lawyer end up teaching himself by answering his own questions, but he also puts himself to the test (which he intended to do to Jesus) and censures himself rather than Jesus! Luke 10:25-37 is a literary piece whose dramatic effect is unparalleled. Unfortunately, most discussions regarding the literary quality of the pericope focus on the parable proper, but the total dialogue (including the parable) constitutes a literary unit of unusual dimensions.

Bailey in passing notes that the dialogue between Jesus and the lawyer is carefully structured and is an illustration of the use of the inversion principle:

> *Round One*
> Lawyer—Question 1 "*What* must *I do* to inherit *eternal life*?"
>   Jesus—Question 2 "What about the law?"
>   Lawyer—Answer 2 "Love God and your neighbor."
> Jesus—Answer 1 "*Do this* and *live.*"
>
> *Round Two*
> Lawyer—Question 1 "Who is my neighbor?"
>   Jesus—The parable of the Good Samaritan
>   Question 2 "Which of these three became a neighbor?"
>   Lawyer—Answer 2 "The one who showed mercy on him."
> Jesus—Answer 1 "Do and keep on doing this."[12]

This division of the dialogue into two parts places the emphasis on the answers of Jesus concluding both parts. These answers are very similar:

> *First answer: touto poiei kai zēsēi.*
> *Second answer: poreuou kai sy poiei homoiōs.*

The importance of these answers is further indicated by their imperatival form—these are the only positive instructions and exhortations found in the dialogue. Furthermore, many popular interpretations which emphasize the exemplary character of the Good Samaritan suggest that Jesus is instructing the lawyer to do as the Samaritan (*homoiōs*). However, the parallelism of the two answers requires that the second be interpreted as reiterating and underscoring the first. There is no direct object expressed for *poiei* in the second answer and the direct object in the first answer clearly refers to "love for God and neighbor." The focus in the second part of the dialogue is on "neighbor," and therefore Jesus is exhorting the lawyer to love his "neighbor" in this way (*homoiōs*). The adverb *homoiōs* relates directly to the answer of the lawyer in which by circumlocution he identified the Samaritan. The lawyer must love his neighbor (*touto poiei* in the first answer) who is (or can be) a Samaritan, just as he reluctantly identified him (*poiei homoiōs* in the second answer).

The lawyer is not instructed by Jesus primarily to do as the Samaritan did (i.e., help someone in need), but rather to fulfill the commandment of love for his neighbor who, he must recognize, can be a Samaritan—the very person his pride refused to accept.

This interpretation of the parable of the Good Samaritan which attacks the lawyer's pride and teaches him a telling lesson in humility is frequently overlooked because the parable is divorced from the immediately preceding context. This also destroys the structural balance of the two parts of the dialogue as discussed above. Furthermore, within each part there is a structural balance between the lawyer's question and Jesus' answer. In the first part the lawyer asked about a deed (*poiēsas*— aorist participle) to have life (*zōē*); Jesus answers by referring to a continuing activity (*poiei*—present imperative) and life (*zēsei*—future indicative of *zaō*). Similarly, in the second part there is a structural balance: the lawyer wants a definition of "neighbor"; Jesus answers by referring to a continuing activity (*poiei*—present imperative) with respect to the Samaritan whom the lawyer had identified. It is also at this point that the popular interpretation of the parable encounters difficulty. Did Jesus in fact answer the lawyer's question, "Who is my neighbor?" Hardly, if one places the stress on the importance of helping one in need and thus identifying one's neighbor, since the Samaritan whom the lawyer identified was not one in need!

R. Funk observes that the "discrepancy between the formulation of the question ('Who is my neighbor?' Lk. 10:29) and the question answered by the parable ('Which of these three proved neighbor?' Lk. 10:36) is regularly noted."[13] Later he refers to this disjunction between question and answer, but, in contrast to those who consider this inimical to the parable, in his interpretation he considers it necessary to the point.[14] Jeremias attempts to resolve the difficulty by noting the lawyer's concern for the object of the love and Jesus' concern for the subject of the love and by emphasizing the reciprocal relation in the word *rea'*, the *Vorlage* of the Greek *plēsion*. The parable then becomes a lesson in the boundless nature of love, i.e., no human being is beyond the range of one's charity.[15] These and other interpretations discuss important facets of the nature of love (*agapē*), but invariably the interpreter must engage in semantic maneuvers to derive such an emphasis from the parable. However, all of this becomes unnecessary if one notes the literary structure and balance of the pericope. Not only is this a well-structured and balanced narrative, but the parable with its commentary directly and logically answers the question of the lawyer and it is not necessary to refer to a discrepancy or disjunction in the narrative. Jesus is not sidestepping the issue as raised by the lawyer or introducing a new concept;

rather, he is meeting the lawyer "head-on" and addressing the issue squarely. He does define "neighbor" in the context of the lawyer's theology and practice.

The lawyer's question to Jesus was: *kai tis estin mou plēsion?* (Luke 10:29). At the conclusion of the parable Jesus asks the lawyer: *tis toutōn tōn triōn plēsion dokei soi gegonenai tou empesontos eis tous leistas?* (10:36). There is an amazing similarity in the components of these two questions, which can be seen in the following formulations:

> Lawyer: *tis   estin   mou   plēsion?*
> Jesus: *tis   gegonei tou empesontos plēsion?*

Structurally the question of Jesus is identical to that of the lawyer. By means of the parable and its interpretation, Jesus intended to answer directly the question of the lawyer. The above formulations place in direct relationship the lawyer and the victim.

The "Principle of Identification"

A useful and significant principle in parable interpretation is the "principle of identification." Part of the technique for effective story-telling is to involve the hearer or reader in the narrative by his identifying himself with someone in the episode. With whom would the lawyer identify himself in the parable of the Good Samaritan? In no wise with the Samaritan whom he despised and hated. Hardly with the priest or Levite whose conduct is scarcely commendable. Undoubtedly with the victim, who would surely have been a Jew travelling to Jericho. Such an identification by the lawyer of himself with the victim makes meaningful the questions asked by the lawyer and Jesus, as formulated above. Jesus then directly applies the lawyer's question to the parable. This becomes clearly evident when the similar components of the two questions are recognized: "Who is my neighbor?" / "Who is the victim's neighbor?"

The lawyer's answer to Jesus is, by circumlocution, the Samaritan.[16] The victim's neighbor is the Samaritan.[17] *Mutatis mutandis,* the answer to the lawyer's question identifies his neighbor as the Samaritan. By means of this parable and added question, Jesus not only forced the lawyer to answer his own question, but also taught him to recognize and identify the Samaritan as his neighbor. For the lawyer to respond in this way must have been an immensely humiliating experience. He could not escape the inevitable conclusion—the victim's neighbor was a Samaritan. This Jew had to learn that even a Samaritan, one to whom least of all he would want to be indebted, could be his neighbor. The pride and conceit with which the lawyer had written off the Samaritan have been devastatingly crushed by this dialogue. This lawyer had to learn a lesson in humility—and Jesus taught it effectively and without reservation. The Samaritan is the neighbor who must be the recipient of the lawyer's love. The victim must respond to the Samaritan who is the neighbor. The neighbor is not the victim—i.e., in this episode someone in trouble and need. Rather, the neighbor is the Samaritan whom the victim (and by the "principle of identification," the lawyer) on the basis of his theology and pride refused to love and respect. That is the lesson the lawyer had to learn—not a lesson in humanitarianism and benevolence by which one helps someone in need and distress. The barrier to keeping the love commandment was the lawyer's pride and conceit. This was love as taught and demonstrated by Jesus which the lawyer's theology could not tolerate. However, Jesus compelled the lawyer both to question and negate this theology when he identified the Samaritan as a neighbor.

Norman Perrin, in a discussion about the parable of the Good Samaritan, asserts that "to speak of Jesus as teaching the necessity of response to the neighbour's need as the crucial aspect of human relationships is misleading, unless it is clearly understood that this is an imitation of God's response to one's need."[18] He notes that Jesus "proclaimed a radically new concept of the forgiveness of God . . . the showing of mercy is a response to being shown mercy."[19] This draws a telling parallel between God's merciful act to the sinner and the Samaritan's merciful act to the victim. However, Perrin still functions with the Samaritan's action as being the exemplary one—the act of showing mercy, although he has correctly criticized the traditional emphasis and rightly recognized that there is more involved here than the concept of neighborliness.[20] Rather, just as the sinner's response to God must be love (the first commandment), the victim's response to the Samaritan must be love (the second commandment). And that was a dimension of forgiveness and mercy the lawyer did not realize—his pride prevented him from identifying a Samaritan as his neighbor.

Literary Structure of the Parable Proper

In his discussion about the types of literary structures in the New Testament, Bailey classifies the parables in Luke as generally following a form which he calls *Parabolic Ballad*.[21] Usually the parable is structured in three-line stanzas in a step parallelism or an inverted parallelism. He has analyzed the parable of the Good Samaritan into seven three-line stanzas (the first three counter-balanced by the last three where the Samaritan reverses the actions of the first three stanzas). Although one could quarrel about some details (which Bailey recognizes), nevertheless the basic pattern is convincing and places the focus on the fourth stanza (Luke 10:33):

"And a certain Samaritan, traveling, came to him
and when he saw him
he had compassion on him."

This climactic center, as Bailey calls it, makes clear the turning point of the passage and provides the clue to matching components in the two parts of the parable. The mistreatment of the victim by the robbers, the priest, and the Levite is countered by the actions (in reverse order) of the Samaritan: treatment, transportation, and provident care.

Both the content and the literary structure of the parable lead to the inevitable answer to the questions posed by the lawyer ("Who is my neighbor?") and by Jesus ("Which of these was the victim's neighbor?"). This humbling admission by the lawyer must have had a tremendous impact on him. And this was precisely the intention of a parable: to evoke a response from the hearer. It is not reported what effect this had upon the lawyer. However, the episode was certainly a *praeparatio evangelii*, since it attacked the deep-seated pride and arrogance which resist the gospel of redemptive love in Jesus Christ. This was the message for the lawyer: the inheritance of eternal life presupposes a humble and contrite spirit, not pride, arrogance—in fact, not even humanitarianism (as this parable is often interpreted).[22]

Conclusion

The above approach is an attempt to challenge a long-standing understanding of the parable of the Good Samaritan. It seeks to do justice to the literary structure and context of the parable. It seeks to recognize certain literary conventions, especially balance and parallelism, and by means of these to ascertain the intended message and impact. These features, as discussed above, can hardly be accidental or coincidental. They were intended for more than delightful reading or entertainment. Furthermore, by a judicious use of the "principle of identification" the original impact and purpose of the parable can often be discovered. Hopefully, these techniques can open new possibilities and dimensions in the study of a significant teaching technique found in the Gospels.

It is not without significance nor coincidence that Jesus himself later made the same journey from Jericho to Jerusalem—travelling the same road that the *dramatis personae* of the parable of the Good Samaritan travelled. Near Jericho he passed by a blind beggar (Luke 18:35-43;

identified as Bartimaeus in Mark 10:46). The crowds rebuked and tried to ignore the beggar (actions similar to the priest and Levite), but Jesus insisted on seeing him and ministering to him (actions similar to the Samaritan). The blind man responded by following Jesus and glorifying God (a demonstration of the "love-response" demanded in the parable of the Good Samaritan). This episode in Luke 18 is the message of Luke 10:25-37 acted out in a life situation.[23]

NOTES TO CHAPTER 7

1. Recent American discussions regarding the interpretation of parables have centered upon the literary structure and quality of the narratives. Some interesting insights, although influenced by certain philosophical and hermeneutical presuppositions, can be found in studies by John D. Crossan, *In Parables: The Challenge of the Historical Jesus* (New York: Harper and Row, 1973); Dan O. Via, *The Parables: Their Literary and Existential Dimension* (Philadelphia: Fortress Press, 1967); Norman Perrin, *Jesus and the Language of the Kingdom* (London: SCM Press, 1976). Some of these studies have used the parable of the Good Samaritan as a model. The Parables Seminar of the Society of Biblical Literature during the past few years has been focussed on structuralism.

2. *The Gospel According to St. Matthew* (London: Adam & Charles Black, 1960), p. 160. This purpose of parables is further elaborated in my "The Purpose of Parables According to Matthew 13:10-17," in *New Dimensions in New Testament Study*, ed. by R. Longenecker and M. Tenney (Grand Rapids: Zondervan Publishing House, 1974), pp. 180-190.

3. Some commentators have observed this striking feature in the parable, but do not work with it adequately (e.g., A. R. C. Leaney, *The Gospel According to St. Luke* [London: Adam & Charles Black, 1958], pp. 182f.; L. Morris, *The Gospel According to St. Luke* [Grand Rapids: Wm. B. Eerdmans, 1974], pp. 189f.).

4. Most recently Kenneth Bailey has urged the title "Jerusalem Document" (*Poet and Peasant* [Grand Rapids: Wm. B. Eerdmans, 1976], p. 82).

5. *Ibid.*, pp. 79-85. Bailey acknowledges his partial debt to the earlier work by M. D. Goulder. In 1974 C. H. Talbert proposed a similar structure for the Travel Narrative (*Literary Patterns, Theological Themes and the Genre of Luke-Acts* [Missoula: Scholars' Press, 1974]).

6. Talbert observes the same parallelism, but divides the material in a different manner (pp. 51-54).

7. In both accounts the nouns are modified by the indefinite *tis* (10:25; 18:18), whereas in the parallel passages of both pericopes in Matthew and Mark the numeral *heis* is used (Matt. 22:35=Mark 12:28; Matt. 19:16=Mark 10:17).

8. BAG, *s.v. nomikos.*

9. Only Mark in the parallel passage to Luke 18:18 has the same question as Luke. Matthew restructures the question in the interest of his readers. In the parallel to Luke 10:25, both Matthew and Mark introduce the dialogue with a question about the great or chief commandment.

10. A. M. Hunter observes: "Here it is necessary to remember that the pious Jews of the time regarded 'neighbour' as a term of limited liability. They could never allow that neighbour in Lev. 19:18 ('You shall love your neighbour as yourself') included Gentiles or heretical Samaritans" (*The Parables Then and Now* [Philadelphia: Westminster Press, 1971], p. 109). The Qumran sectarians were instructed in 1QS "that they may love all the sons of light" and "that they may hate all the sons of darkness" (1:9, 10).

11. Instructive here are the words in the prayer of the Pharisee in the parable of the Pharisee and Publican (Luke 18:9-14): "God, I thank thee that I am not like other men, extortioners, unjust, adulterers, or even like this tax collector. I fast twice a week, I give tithes of all that I get."

12. *Op. cit.*, pp. 73f. (n. 53). Bailey rightly observes that a "full interpretation of the parable in its Lucan setting must take into account the structure not only of the parable itself but of the dialog" (p. 74).

13. *Language, Hermeneutic, and Word of God* (New York: Harper and Row, 1966), p. 210.

14. *Ibid.*, pp. 221f.

15. *The Parables of Jesus* (New York: Scribner's, 1963), p. 205.

16. Apparently, the lawyer's extreme distaste for the Samaritans made it impossible for him to use the name employed in the parable.

17. It must be noted that Jesus used the verb *ginomai*, rather than *eimi* (as the lawyer used). This verb is used "as a substitute for the forms of *eimi*" (BAG, *s.v. ginomai*), especially for tenses where *eimi* is defective. Furthermore, the added nuance of "becoming" to indicate entering a new condition (BAG, *s.v.*) would be meaningful in Jesus' question.

18. *Rediscovering the Teaching of Jesus* (New York: Harper and Row, 1976), p. 124.

19. Perrin, however, is troubled by v. 37b ("Go and do likewise"), which he feels "transforms the parable into a general exhortation" (*ibid.*, p. 124). It is not necessary to assign this exhortation to later tradition, as he suggests; rather, it is the counterpart of the one in v. 28b, as discussed above, and specifies and reinforces the teaching of Jesus in this dialogue.

20. *Ibid.*, p. 124.

21. *Op. cit.*, pp. 72-75.

22. For helpful suggestions regarding the details of the parable proper, see Jeremias, *op. cit.*, pp. 202-205.

23. Beyond the scope of this paper is the problem of allegorization which plagued the church until Jülicher challenged this approach in 1910. Perhaps under his influence we have tended to recoil too readily from recognizing some allegorical elements in a parable. More important, and perhaps more useful, would be the fuller application of the "principle of identification," suggested above, which could avoid some of the pitfalls of allegorization and do justice to the Oriental technique of story-telling.

8: *1 Corinthians 15:20-28 as Evidence of Pauline Eschatology and Its Relation to the Preaching of Jesus*

EDUARD SCHWEIZER

Werner Georg Kümmel concludes his essay of 1964 about Jesus and Paul with the statement that Ernst Käsemann was right in saying that Jewish apocalyptic is "the mother of all Christian theology,"[1] but that one must not exempt Jesus from this view.[2]

Since 1940 Kümmel has been asserting that with regard to eschatology there is no essential difference between Jesus and Paul, even though the view of the imminence of the end-time had been "expanded" by the events of Easter and Pentecost.[3] The actual difference, however, which consists in the fact that Paul is an apostle and Jesus is Lord, now necessitates a christological explanation of the Jesus-event.[4] I therefore hope that the honored recipient of this *Festschrift* will find some pleasure in my analysis of these theses (which I consider correct), on the basis of an examination of the very apocalyptically oriented section in 1 Cor. 15:20-28.

I. The Future of the Kingdom of God

1. The God whom Jesus preaches and allows to become a reality throughout his whole life is the God who some day will set up his kingdom. Today it must again be said emphatically that Jesus distinctly spoke of that kingdom as being in the future. God is not totally encompassed in what is experienced in the present and imminent encounter with him; neither in individual discipleship which involves the "I ought" and "I can" of love for my neighbor, nor in the social action of a zealously revolutionary group or of any other modern social movement. The fact that his kingdom is one of the future shows that God cannot be confined within any human program. What Kümmel compiled in his thorough investigation[5] need not be repeated: the words about the "being-near-at-hand,"[6] about the "coming," the "day," the "judgment," and the imagery employed to describe, for example, the messianic banquet are clear enough. It might be added that Jesus proceeded

from the Baptist and his apocalyptic message and, as far as the tradition accessible to us permits a verdict, without setting himself apart from it *expressis verbis* (as, for example, in the question of fasting), and that many parables make a clear distinction between sowing and harvest, mustard seed and bush, the act of fishing and the gathering of the catch. It follows that Jesus is no ecstatic dreamer who, with a faith that scales the heavens, simply by-passes present injustice and suffering. It is of central importance to him that some day God will make good on his promises.

On this point Jesus is in agreement with the apocalypticists, but also with the pharisaic outlook: Judgment and redemption are in the future; the present is clearly distinguished from it.[7]

2. In 1 Cor. 15:23 Paul uses a technical term of apocalyptic coinage, namely, *parousia*, which first appears in 1 Thess. 2:19; 3:13; 4:15, but is rooted in the common Christian tradition. It describes the future coming of Jesus which now is clearly founded on the resurrection that has already occurred.[8] Thereby, a Hellenistic concept has evidently been introduced[9] which establishes a difference between the final coming of the apocalyptic view and that coming which was terminated with the resurrection, and which at the same time joins the latter with it. However, in contrast to the proclamation of Jesus, this far more systematic concept serves the purpose of stating plainly in the face of Corinthian enthusiasm, which thinks that the kingdom of God has already been attained,[10] that this kingdom in no way has been delivered into the hands of man. It remains at the disposition of God, who will permit it to come in his own time. Thus Paul does not submit to the force of the thought pattern, but rather changes the preceding present tense into a future tense in the subsequent phrase of v. 22: "so also in Christ shall all be made alive." There is no evidence that the Corinthian enthusiasm is in direct continuity with an even more apocalyptically oriented enthusiasm of the first congregation which saw the beginning of the phenomenon of the end-time in the resurrection of Jesus, even though this seems probable to me. Paul at any rate, in a totally new situation, reaffirmed what Jesus had stressed in the face of messianic and zealot expectations. The coming of the kingdom of God is totally God's affair and its fulfillment is not yet here.

II. The Mode and Manner of the Coming of the Kingdom of God

1. Jesus does not deliver God into the hands of men in such a way as would allow them to make apocalyptic calculations with which to pin-

point the time of his coming. Neither does he supply them with paintings of an apocalyptic landscape by which what is to come would already be at their disposal, at least for those who portray glory in the form of a fantasy. In spite of the fact that Jesus held a view that is clearly oriented toward the future, he gives no indications which could support either of the above views. Only expressions in the parables, which are clearly pictorial in character, describe what the future of the kingdom of God signifies.[11]

By way of contrast, we find in Jewish apocalyptic not only descriptions of the annihilation of the wicked, the doom of the world, and the coming glory, but also information about "weeks" which allows the approximate computation of the approaching date of the end.[12]

2. Paul seems to agree with that when he speaks in 1 Cor. 15:24 of the destruction of every rule and every authority and power, or, with the words of Ps. 110, of the enemies whom God will put under Jesus' feet.[13] Thus here Paul also operates with concepts taken over from apocalyptic writings, as has been shown in the hymn of Phil. 2:10 cited above. But precisely in doing this he renounces any kind of visual representation which might, by some mental process, give advance insight into the future actions of God. That is also shown in the fact that nothing at all is said about the fate of unbelievers. To be sure, there have been attempts to see such a statement in the mentioning of the "end" (which has been interpreted as the "remnant") in v. 24, but this is surely not its meaning.[14] When Paul portrays the condition of the redeemed as characterized by "life" which participates in the life of the risen Christ, he consciously avoids any kind of concrete description and merely states that they "shall always be with the Lord" (1 Thess. 4:17).[15] In a world which no longer takes for granted that there is an eschatological goal for the entire history of God (as was true of the world of Jesus' time), the apocalyptic terminology enables the Apostle to retain the cosmic dimension of future fulfillment which cannot be calculated in a purely individual manner, without being forced to give a more concrete description of that coming "world."

III. The Presence of the Kingdom of God

1. The new and striking element in Jesus' work, however, is that in his actions and his proclamation God becomes so imminent that it definitely can be said that the future kingdom of God has already arrived for the witnesses of those words and deeds.[16] Again it is not necessary to repeat what Kümmel himself has demonstrated.[17] It is, however, of decisive

significance that Jesus not only speaks of *events*, which in comparison to the future fulfillment are only scattered traces of a beginning development, and thus quantitatively and also qualitatively must be distinguished not only from the coming fulfillment, but also from an "eschatologically *fulfilled* presence."[18] What Jesus claims is nothing less than "that in his person, his teaching, and his deeds the salvation of the end-time, the final decision already takes place."[19] Jesus' words about the presence of the kingdom are surely not to be understood in such a way as if with him something were merely beginning, with noticeable traces here and there, which would grow beyond him toward its fulfillment. If Jesus did think of a period of time between his death and the final fulfillment, which remains a probability at least for the final stages of his ministry,[20] this intermediate period is not to be likened to the full presence of the kingdom of God as is the time of Jesus' activity. The bridegroom is no longer there and the drinking of the wine of the feast is suspended, at least for Jesus, notwithstanding the fact that he gave it to his disciples as a token of his presence.[21]

The presence of the kingdom of God which Jesus embodies and preaches is thus something different from the portrayal of Jewish apocalyptic writings. According to the latter, it is possible to point out signs of the coming victory and judgment which allow one to draw conclusions concerning the course of events which lead to the final consummation, and indeed even the terminal point of its coming.[22]

2. Again, Paul sets himself the task of stating systematically and clearly the double pronouncement of the presence of the kingdom of God, both in the period of the ministry of Jesus upon which he is now looking back and must take into account, and in the future of God which is still to be realized. In 1 Cor. 15:22f. he uses for this purpose the apocalyptic theme of an Adam-Christ correlation.[23] In this way it is indeed possible to retain the eschatological uniqueness of Jesus as the "first-fruits" of a new humanity or a new creation. But this pattern which determines the fixed course of events within the apocalyptic writings makes it possible for the Apostle to avoid portraying an automatic course of events within the last period until the time of the consummation. The bond between Christ and the new humanity inaugurated by him is indeed not one of nature but of faith. Just as Paul in v. 22, contrary to the usual employment of these concepts, changed the present tense into a future, so he now changes the "all" into "those [people] who belong to Christ." It is precisely by means of that change that the category of the new humanity is described as one of a community of faith. That, however, is a paraphrase for the fellowship with the one in whom alone the kingdom of God has already arrived and some day will come into consummation.

Thus the peculiar affinity between Jesus' statements about the kingdom which has already broken in and his person, as well as his present ministry and teaching, is appropriately sustained within a completely different theological category. This will have to be analyzed more closely in what follows.

IV. The Presence of the Kingdom of God as Suffering

1. Once again it becomes clear that for Jesus God remains God. Even where he comes with his reign over men, God, according to Jesus' words, does not deliver himself into their hands. Most emphatically he does not correspond to the standards by which people think they can comprehend him. All demands for visible signs are rejected. Indeed, the presence of the kingdom of God, according to one of the most shocking words of the New Testament, is the presence of suffering and failure (Matt. 11:12).[24] But equally shocking, and already stating the same truth, are the detailed description of the failure of the sower in the parable (Mark 4:3-7), the words about the Son of man who has no place to rest his head (Matt. 8:20) and who is rejected by all as a glutton and a drunkard (Matt. 11:19), and the portrayal of him who brings the sword (Matt. 10:34) and himself faces the fate of the prophets in Jerusalem (Luke 13:33; Matt. 23:34-39; Luke 17:25). The presence of the kingdom of God is thus of a very unusual nature. Moreover, precisely because of this, it is true that "the content of Matt. 11:12 . . . unequivocally supports the logion as authentic."[25]

This is quite different from the description of the last period of the old aeon in the apocalyptic writings. There it is normally assumed that at that time the world once more will display its worst features.[26] One can also reckon, however, with a final period of time in which the evil powers are already subjugated, although not yet fully destroyed,[27] while the just already live in heaven, so to speak.[28] These views surely supply points of departure for Jesus' teaching. In their factual contents, however, they are far removed from what Jesus expresses with them. They understand the sufferings as the last defiant convulsion of the enemy while God's victory already comes into view in the saving of the just. Jesus, however, declares that it is specifically in the suffering, the lowliness, and the rejection of the Son of man and those who belong to him that the kingdom of God breaks in.

2. Again, Paul adopts in 1 Cor. 15:24-26 a clearly apocalyptic concept of a heavenly throne of the Christ under whose feet shall be put all rule, authority, and power.[29] It is actually an image of final triumph, and

at a later time it surely has been understood as such, especially in hymnic sections.[30] Here, however, it is accompanied by the surprising statement that the rule of the risen Christ as described by these concepts of dominion indeed does not yet mean final victory and ultimate glory, but is instead a period of struggle in which death, the "last enemy," has in fact not yet been overcome.[31] Paul, in contrast to Jesus, is of course speaking here of the time after Easter. But what he says about it is rooted in his understanding of Jesus' work here on earth. V. 17 shows that. The fact that, contrary to Pauline usage, "sins" are mentioned here in the plural shows that the Apostle reverts back to the traditional *kerygma* of v. 3, according to which Christ died "for our sins."

The resurrection of Jesus is therefore the activation of the power of this death of Jesus for sins. The continuing subjugation of the powers of evil is also ultimately based on the fact that in the death of Jesus, sins have been overcome. In this sense even the risen Christ still remains the crucified Christ, and it also becomes clear that he who was exalted after Easter is not simply and only the Triumphant One. The interrelatedness of Jesus' death on the cross, his exaltation, and the subjugation of all hostile powers is far more directly expressed in mythical imagery in Col. 2:14f.[32] Although the Pauline image of the kingdom of Christ is thus closer to the Jewish apocalyptic descriptions, it nevertheless is actually rooted in the knowledge of the fact of the crucifixion of Christ for which there is no parallel in the apocalyptic writings. It therefore rejects all illusions of a life of heavenly glory already granted to the Christian community.

V. The Presence of the Kingdom of God as Overcoming the Law, Sin, and Death

1. Whether the kingdom of God is present or future is, in fact, not the decisive question; for it is both. What is decisive is the question of the manner in which it is present and the manner in which it is coming in the future. One can answer that "as a parable," i.e., "as power," it is coming over man in Jesus' ministry right now.[33] But where does it show itself as parable right now? Obviously wherever God gains power over people through Jesus' word and work. For that reason the expulsion of demons and the healing of the sick are signs of the presence of the kingdom of God. But they are this only for the person who sees God acting through them; others may see nothing but Beelzebul in them. Just as music performed is objectively present, and yet becomes music only for the person who can hear it as that rather than as an accumulation of

noises, so also the kingdom of God is objectively present in Jesus' actions and yet only for the person who recognizes it. Therefore the account of Christ's deeds is brought to a climax in Matt. 11:5f. with the words: "the poor have good news preached to them. And blessed is he who takes no offense at me."[34] This is the reason the kingdom of God also becomes present above all in those instances where it reaches its hearers in the parables of Jesus. That, however, means: (a) The kingdom becomes a reality where the law, which makes man inaccessible for God, is suspended as happens in the parable of the Pharisee and the Tax Collector, in Jesus' acts of healing on the sabbath, and finally in Jesus' trial where the innocent is condemned by a legal system that judges according to rules that have grown rigid. (b) The kingdom becomes a reality where the sin that separates man from God is overcome as happens in the parable of the Prodigal Son, in Jesus' meals with tax collectors, and as is definitively carried out in the death of Jesus. (c) The kingdom becomes a reality where death, which seems to cut man off completely from the living God, loses its power, as we see in Jesus' promise that he who loses his life will find it, and as it occurs in his healings, and then becomes forever true in his resurrection.

This marks the difference between Jesus and the apocalyptic writings which push pious adherence to the law to radical extremes,[35] expect the overcoming of sin by the destruction of the wicked,[36] and neutralize the power of death through guardian angels who protect the just against all harm.[37]

2. Here, too, Paul uses the apocalyptic category of an "order" which develops in a fixed sequence[38] in order to make clear that the redemption of the Christian community is dependent upon the Christ-event. But in so doing, he underscores once again the difference between the Exalted One who is already sitting at the right hand of God and the congregation that is still residing on earth. Actually those forces marked by such apocalyptic concepts as rule, authority, and power are the forces that still threaten to engulf man: law, sin, and death. That is made very clear in Rom. 5:12-21, and particularly so by the Adam-Christ pattern used in 1 Cor. 15:22f., which (as happens only in this context) characterizes Jesus as "man" (Rom. 5:12; 1 Cor. 15:21, 45-47). To be delivered from the power of the law is to be delivered from sin, and thereby from death, the "last enemy" (1 Cor. 15:26). As v. 56 shows, that is also precisely the background of our chapter. There, in the struggle against law, sin, and death, God's victory is attained. In this way the righteousness of God which has gained dominion in the person of Jesus establishes itself. Thus Paul once more has preserved within a quite different systematic summary what was expressed in Jesus' work and preaching.

VI. ". . . That God May Be Everything to Every One"[39]

1. The God who has become a reality in Jesus' words and deeds is the God of the First Commandment. He is the God who gives himself to man in such a way that he remains God without any limitations. The fulfillment consists in the fact that man can let him remain God without any limitations. The entire work of Jesus is the carrying out of this commandment. Every estimation of Jesus which might weaken the fact that God alone is good is rejected (Mark 10:18). Jesus teaches his disciples to ask for the glorification of the name of God and for the coming of the kingdom of God (Luke 11:2). On the sabbath he sees to it that through his action God's good will is done (Mark 3:4). The parables he tells speak wholly of God and his kingdom. As much as the latter takes shape in Jesus' very act of parabolic teaching (as well as in his entire work), so little does Jesus appear in the parables as a separate person outside of this process of the actualization of the dominion of God.[40] The theme is never the dominion of Jesus or Israel, but is always and only the dominion of God. In his dying Jesus holds fast to the First Commandment even to his final outcry, with which he nevertheless claims as his God him who has "forsaken" him (Mark 15:34). Jesus is thus not representing God in the sense that God can disappear behind him. On the contrary, in both his living and dying Jesus wants to proclaim nothing else but God as the one and only God.

This contrasts with the rare occurrence of the concept of the kingdom of God in the apocalyptic writings.[41] To be sure, the concern there is with God's intervention and his victory; but as a rule both aspects are conceived of as a dominion by Israel or by its king, which of course has been bestowed by God.[42]

2. Paul, too, has adopted in 1 Cor. 15:24-28 the apocalyptic idea of a dominion of the exalted Christ which concludes with the act of subjugation at the end of this period, not unlike that of the apocalyptic vision.[43] The real concern, however, is to reject all apocalyptic visions which could give rise to the opinion that God delegates his dominion to, or shares it with, anyone else. The dominion of Christ is already described as an act of God which subjugates all enemies to Christ. Paul also does not think that Christ ceases ruling or that he simply is absorbed into the Father.[44] The essence of the consummation is that Christ, together with all who are his (and who according to 1 Cor. 6:3 also "are to judge angels"), belongs to God so that Christ as ruler as well as the congregation sharing with him in the judgment is thus only part of the one dominion of God. This means that there can no longer be any argument about the fact that "Christ is God's," as 3:23 has already expressed it. In

what is probably an editorial addition Paul also declares at the end of the hymn in Phil. 2:6-11 that the rule of the *Kyrios* before whom every knee should bow, in heaven and on earth and under the earth in confession of his name, takes place "to the glory of God the Father." Rom. 14:11 applies the same words that are used in Phil. 2:10f. to the people who worship "God" before his judgment seat. Finally, the entire christological exposition of Rom. 1-11 comes to a climax in 11:33-36 with the praise of the God "from whom and through whom and to whom are all things."

VII. Summary

We can truly say with Kümmel that in eschatology, too, there is no essential difference between Jesus and Paul.[45] Both expect the fulfillment of all of God's promises in the future; and although both see this future as close at hand, they deny that it can be described or that its date can be fixed on the basis of apocalyptic signs. Both speak of a presence of God which, eschatologically, has already been fulfilled. According to both, however, it is manifested in suffering and persecution. For both this ultimately derives from the fact that God prevails in the overcoming of law, sin, and death; and that neither the bliss of the individual nor the triumph of God's people is the goal of all history but rather the kingdom of God in which he will be all in all.

It is difficult to decide the question of whether apocalyptic thought, in contrast to Jesus himself, came into the foreground only as a result of the Easter events. This is especially so because there is no generally accepted definition of apocalyptic thinking.[46] One can probably say with respect to clearly systematizing concepts and fixed ideas like *parousia*, or the subjugation of the powers in heaven, on earth, and under the earth, that these ideas only emerge in the post-Easter congregation, e.g., with Paul. Jesus[47] and Paul can probably be seen as sharing the same line of thought as far as a fundamental orientation toward God's future actions encompassing the entire cosmos is involved, while at the same time in the person of Jesus these actions break into the present. What then shall we say concerning Käsemann's famous assertion that apocalyptic is the "mother of all Christian theology?" Perhaps it would be better to view apocalyptic as a "midwife," bringing to light a theology that is already implied in the preaching and ministry of Christ and thus making possible its incorporation into theological language.

NOTES TO CHAPTER 8

1. *Exegetische Versuche und Besinnungen*, 3rd ed. (Göttingen: Vandenhoeck & Ruprecht, 1968), II, 100; cf. 99f., 105f., A.1, 108-112.

2. *NTS*, 10 (1963/64), 181. On pp. 173f. it is also stated that specifically in Paul's writings "apocalyptic" does not mean "anti-pharisaic." Against an all too strong distinction, viz., e.g., in D. Rössler, *Gesetz und Geschichte*, 2nd ed., in *WMANT*, 3 (Neukirchen-Vluyn: Neukirchener Verlag, 1962), 45-54, summarized, p. 110; cf. W. Harnisch, *Verhängnis und Verheissung der Geschichte*, in *FRLANT*, 97 (Göttingen: Vandenhoeck & Ruprecht, 1969), 143-221, 245f., 327 *(pharisäische Apokalyptik)*.
   Talmud and Mishna have in fact only later been expurgated anti-apocalyptically (K. W. Tröger, "Spekulativ-esoterische Ansätze," in *Literatur und Religion des Frühjudentums*, ed. by J. Maier and J. Schreiner [Würzburg: Echter Verlag/ Gütersloh: Gütersloher Verlagshaus Mohn, 1973], pp. 311f.). As little can apocalyptic thought be sharply separated from Hellenistic syncretism (H. D. Betz, "Zum religionsgeschichtlichen Verständnis der Apokalyptik," *ZThK*, 63 [1966], 394f., 408f.).

3. *ThBl*, 19 (1940), 221.

4. *Loc. cit.*, pp. 230f.

5. W. G. Kümmel, *Verheissung und Erfüllung: Untersuchungen zur eschatologischen Verkündigung Jesu*, 3rd ed., in *AThANT*, 6 (Zürich: Zwingli-Verlag, 1956), pp. 13-47.

6. Cf. also P. Gaechter, *Das Matthäusevangelium* (Innsbruck/Wien/München: Tyrolia-Verlag, 1963), p. 123, A.13; N. Perrin, *The Kingdom of God in the Teaching of Jesus* (Philadelphia: Westminster Press, 1963), pp. 64-66; R. Fuller, *The Mission and Achievement of Jesus* (London: SCM Press, 1954), pp. 20-25.
   Cf. R. F. Berkey, "*EGGIZEIN PHTHANEIN* and Realized Eschatology," *JBL*, 82 (1963), 177-187. Berkey, to be sure, is of the opinion that Mark 1:15 and Matt. 12:28, being essentially equal, see present and future as merged because eschatological fulfillment can never be confined to past, present, or future.

7. E.g., Ps. Sol. 17:11-20, 21-29; Eth. En. 90:2-16, 20-38; 1QS IV, 19-26; Test. Lev. 16f., 18; Test. Dan 5:4-8, 9-13; Mishna Soṭa 9:15 (Bill., I, 586).

8. There is much to be said for P. Hoffmann's speculation that the Easter experience did already result in Q in a strengthening of the apocalyptical expectation of the Son of man *(Studien zur Theologie der Logienquelle*, in *NTA*, 8 [Münster: Aschendorff, 1972], 139-141, 154).

9. A. Oepke, *TDNT*, V, 865.

10. 1 Cor. 4:8; about the views of the Corinthians, cf. H. Lietzmann/W. G. Kümmel, *An die Korinther I/II*, 4th ed., in *HNT*, 9 (Tübingen: J. C. B. Mohr, 1949), pp. 192f.

11. Cf. Kümmel, *op. cit.* (n. 5), pp. 45, 135, 145. Whether Jesus expressly stated that the kingdom of God would come within a generation appears questionable to me, but that does not alter the fact that he expected it soon, and that he did not think in terms of centuries.

12. E.g., Ps. Sol. 17:21-41; Eth. En. 1:3-9; 100:1-4; 1QH III, 29-36; Apoc. Bar. (syr) 51; Ass. Mos. 10:2-10; 4 Ezr. 7:26-44, 75-99; 12:10-34; 13:25-51; for the computation of time, cf. n. 22.

13. Thus, surely, v. 28b; also in the two sayings of the Psalms it is the "Lord," or rather "(the Son of) man" to whom God subjugates the enemies.

14. Cf. Kümmel, *op. cit.* (n. 10), at the place cited (p. 193); now also H.-A. Wilcke, *Das Problem eines messianischen Zwischenreiches bei Paulus*, in

AThANT, 51 (Zürich/Stuttgart: Zwingli-Verlag, 1967), esp. pp. 56-108.
Particularly in this context, it becomes clear that Paul, in spite of Rom. 2:2-11, understands the resurrection in fact only as an event of redemption that occurs to those who share in resurrection of Jesus. It is also typical that even Rev. 20:12f., in spite of v. 5, avoids the word "resurrection."

15. W. G. Kümmel, *Die Theologie des Neuen Testaments nach seinen Hauptzeugen: Jesus, Paulus, Johannes,* 2nd ed., in *NTD* Supplementary Series, 3 (Göttingen: Vandenhoeck & Ruprecht, 1972), 210f., cf. 217.

16. Kümmel, *op. cit.* (n. 2), p. 173. For Paul the expectation of the nearness of the kingdom is shown in 1 Thess. 4:17.

17. Kümmel, *op. cit.* (n. 5), pp. 98-132.

18. *Ibid.*, p. 134.

19. W. G. Kümmel, *ThBl,* 19 (1940), 219f.; cf. also R. G. Hamerton-Kelly, *Preexistence, Wisdom, and the Son of Man,* in *SNTSMS,* 21 (Cambridge: Cambridge University Press, 1973), 89.

20. Kümmel, *op. cit.* (n. 5), pp. 58-76.

21. *Ibid.*, pp. 68-70; Mark 2:18; 14:25.

22. Cf. Dan. 7:23-27; 11:2-12:4; Eth. En. 93:3-10; 91:12-17; Dam. XVI, 2-4; 4 Ezr. 4:33-5:13; also bSanh. 97a, 5 Bar. (Bill., IV, 981f.). In a certain sense Jewish apocalyptic, to be sure, also knows a merging of present and future (H. W. Kuhn, *Enderwartung und gegenwärtiges Heil,* in *StUNT,* 4 [Göttingen: Vandenhoeck & Ruprecht, 1966], 181-188); however, as a rule this is seen as restricted to the individual (G. Theissen, *Urchristliche Wundergeschichten,* in *StNT,* 8 [Gütersloh: Gütersloher Verlagshaus, 1974], 276f.).

23. Namely, L. Schottroff, *Der Glaubende und die feindliche Welt,* in *WMANT,* 37 (Neukirchen-Vluyn: Neukirchener Verlag, 1970), esp. pp. 115-118; E. Brandenburger, *Fleisch und Geist,* in *WMANT,* 29 (Neukirchen-Vluyn: Neukirchener Verlag, 1968), 50; *idem, Adam und Christus,* in *WMANT,* 7 (Neukirchen-Vluyn: Neukirchener Verlag, 1962), 68-157; E. Schweizer, *TDNT,* IX, 475f.; *idem, Neotestamentica* (Zürich: Zwingli-Verlag, 1963), pp. 274-283.
The concept of Christ as the new Adam does perhaps also linger in the background of Mark 1:12f.; cf. my commentary on the Gospel of Mark, 13th ed., in *NTD,* 1 (Göttingen: Vandenhoeck & Ruprecht, 1973), at the passage cited; Life Ad. 4; 8; Apoc. Mos. 11; bSanh. 59b (Bill., I, 138); also the parallel of Rev. 1:5 ("the faithful witness, the first-born of the dead") with 3:14 ("the faithful . . . witness, the beginning of God's creation") and of Col. 1:15a with 18b; furthermore, J. L. Sharpe, "The Second Adam in the Apocalypse of Moses," *CBQ,* 35 (1973), 35-46.

24. Concerning this interpretation cf. Kümmel, *op. cit.* (n. 5), pp. 115-117.

25. Käsemann, *Exegetische Versuche und Besinnungen,* 5th ed. (Göttingen: Vandenhoeck & Ruprecht, 1967), I, 210.

26. Cf. n. 7.

27. Eth. En. 10:11f.; 18:14-16; 88:1-3(?).

28. 1QSb III, 5; IV, 26; 11Q Melch. 14 (?); more in H. W. Kuhn, *op. cit.* (n. 22), pp. 181-188.

29. Ps. 110 apparently is not quoted in the literature on apocalyptic writings

(D. M. Hay, "The Use of Ps. 110 in the Early Church" [Diss. Typescript, Yale, 1965], p. 32).

30. It is not at all certain that this is already the case in the hymn of Phil. 2:9-11. I suspect that from the very beginning it meant the subjugation which had been started with the exaltation and terminated with the *parousia* (especially if v. 11 were to be read in the future tense). Paul at any rate did surely understand it in that sense as is evident from 1 Cor. 15:24-28 and Rom. 14:11 where the same scripture is quoted; likewise Heb. 10:12f., Col. 2:14f. (cf. n. 32), 1 Pet. 3:22, and other places speak conversely of a subjugation that has already occurred.

31. Cf. Kümmel, *op. cit.* (n. 15), pp. 209f. This is expressed with particular conciseness in 2 Cor. 5:18-6:10. The description of the apostolic sufferings is in the same context joined to the statements that God was in Christ the reconciliation of the world, and that now is the day of redemption.

32. In the same lecture hall of the University of Zürich in which I as a student in the seminar of my teacher W. G. Kümmel persistently spoke up with a *ceterum censeo*, ". . . provided The Letter to the Colossians is authentic," one of my students said last year, ". . . provided The Letter to the Colossians is unauthentic." Since then we have reaffirmed in conversations that we both still adhere to our old position without believing, however, that we have absolute assurance about it (cf. W. G. Kümmel, *Einleitung in das Neue Testament*, 17th ed. [Heidelberg: Quelle & Meyer, 1973], pp. 298-305).

33. Cf. E. Jüngel, *Paulus und Jesus*, 3rd ed. in *HUTh*, 2 (Tübingen: J. C. B. Mohr, 1967), 135, 187, who adds, to be sure, "in the parable" (of Jesus).

34. Considered an authentic saying of Jesus in Kümmel, *op. cit.* (n. 5), pp. 102-104.

35. Dan. 11:31-35; 12:1-3; Dam. VI, 2-11, etc.; also 1QS XI, 9-15 is no real exception since the righteousness of God restores new obedience to the law.

36. Ps. Sol. 17:7-10, 21-27, 36; Eth. En. 1:9; 100:4, etc.

37. Eth. En. 100:5.

38. Even if one translates with "rank" (G. Delling, *TDNT*, VIII, 32), nothing different is meant by it (Delling translates with "orders" a few lines lower). The pattern that sees Christ as the firstborn who guarantees the later resurrection of the congregation and, indeed, the joining of resurrection with *parousia*, except for the special section, Matt. 27:51-53, hardly occurs in the tradition maintained by the synoptists. Besides Paul (and Col. 1:18), it does, however, also appear in Acts 26:23; Rev. 1:5; Heb. 2:14f.; cf. G. Haufe, "Jesu persönliche Zukunftserwartung und der Ursprung der ältesten Christlichen Osterterminologie" (Diss. Typescript, Leipzig, 1959), pp. 209-230; E. Schweizer, *Jesus Christus im vielfältigen Zeugnis des Neuen Testaments*, 2nd ed., in *Siebenstern-Taschenbuch*, 126 (Hamburg: Siebenstern-Taschenbuch-Verlag, 1970), 69-71.

39. "Everything" can hardly be taken as acc. graec. (thus W. Thüsing, *Per Christum in Deum*, in *NTA*, 1 [Münster: Aschendorff, 1965], 244); cf., however, concerning the whole expression, *ibid.*, pp. 238-246 and *idem*, "Rechtfertigungsgedanke und Christologie in den Korintherbriefen," in *Neues Testament und Kirche* (für Rudolph Schnackenburg), ed. by J. Gnilka (Freiburg: Herder, 1974), p. 321.

40. Cf. A. Jülicher, *Die Gleichnisreden Jesu*, 2nd ed. (Tübingen: J. C. B. Mohr,

1910), II, 365: "In the application of our parable [Luke 15:11-32] there remains no room at all for a mediator between God and sinner."

41. Dan. 2:44; 4:22; 7:18, 27 speak only of the rule of the royal dominion that God bestows (similarly Eth. En. 92:4; 1QSb V, 21; cf. III, 5; IV, 26). Ps. Sol. 17 describes the rule of the Davidic king (vv. 21-25), whose king in turn is God (vv. 34, 46); in formulas of praise and oath, a reference to God's dominion is contained in Eth. En. 84:2 (103:1); in Ass. Mos. 10:1, however, the appearance of the dominion of God is expected (similarly Syb. 3:767). Almost throughout, the actual theme is the dominion of Israel, which ultimately is God's dominion, to be sure (W. Bousset, *Die Religion des Judentums im späthellenistischen Zeitalter*, in *HNT*, 21 [Tübingen: J. C. B. Mohr, 1926], 215-218; cf. also E. Schweizer, *TDNT*, VIII, 389f.).

42. U. Müller, *Messias und Menschensohn in jüdischen Apokalypsen und in der Offenbarung des Johannes*, in *StNT*, 6 (Gütersloh: Gütersloher Verlagshaus, 1972), 81, cf. 61-81.

43. Cf. the four hundred years of dominion of the Christ which is terminated by his death (4 Ezr. 7:28f.), after which God the Highest will appear on the throne of judgment (v. 33).

44. Correctly Thüsing, *op. cit.* (n. 39), pp. 250-252.

45. *ThBl*, 19 (1940), 221; *NTS*, 10 (1963/64), 172f., 178; *Die Theologie des Neuen Testament*, p. 221.

46. Betz, *op. cit.* (n. 2), p. 392. K. Müller, "Die Ansätze der Apokalyptik," in Maier/Schreiner, *op. cit.* (n. 2), p. 32, defines apocalyptic writings as vehement eschatologizing which under the shock of the Alexander wars of conquest erupts simultaneously and in a very similar manner in Iran, Egypt, and Palestine (pp. 33-42). With O. Plöger, *Theokratie und Eschatologie*, 3rd ed., in *WMANT*, 2 (Neukirchen-Vluyn: Neukirchener Verlag, 1968), 39f., religiously determined history, the world as a unit in opposition to God, the unilateral action of an otherworldly God, a dualism that considers the present world as evil, and the belief in the irrevocability of the day of judgment can be seen as characteristic traits, and with G. von Rad, *Theologie des Alten Testaments*, 4th ed. (München: Chr. Kaiser, 1965), II, 316f., one can add the interest in knowledge.

The expectation of an early return of the kingdom does not seem a definite criterion to me (with Harnisch, *op. cit.* [n. 2], pp. 268-321). Such things as pseudonymity, visionary reports with interpreting angels, etc., and fictitious surveys of history in futuristic form (Ph. Vielhauer, "Die Apokalyptik," in E. Hennecke, *Neutestamentliche Apokryphen in deutschen Übersetzung*, 3rd ed. [Tübingen: J. C. B. Mohr, 1964], II, 408-411), naturally do not exist in the case of Jesus and Paul. The reinterpretation of Scripture as it occasionally occurs in apocalyptic writings (W. Zimmerli, *Grundriss der alttestamentlichen Theologie*, in *ThW*, 3 [Stuttgart: W. Kohlhammer, 1972], 200), esp. of the numbers quoted in Daniel, in this form, at any rate, is not practiced by either of them; indications of it (e.g., the relating of Ps. 110 to Ps. 8 in 1 Cor. 15:25, 27), which is probably already traditional, naturally would show sooner with Paul.

47. A. Strobel, *Kerygma und Apokalyptik* (Göttingen: Vandenhoeck & Ruprecht, 1967), p. 17: not reduction but concentration of apocalyptic thinking with Jesus (cf. pp. 150-161). Käsemann, *op. cit.* (n. 1), pp. 99 and 108-110, is right on the other hand that Jesus' message proclaims "the immediacy of the God who is near" and that "apocalyptic characteristics do not strongly emerge."

9: *The Concept of Adoption in the Theology of Paul*

JAMES I. COOK

The Apostle Paul has occupied a favored place in the heart and mind of Richard Oudersluys throughout a distinguished career as a student and teacher of the theology of the New Testament. It is therefore with a study in the theology of Paul that I hope to honor him as mentor, colleague, and friend.

The challenge of understanding Paul's conception of adoption is in no small measure due to the fact that he chose to express it by the Greek word *huiothesia*. This term was coined from the classical phrase *huios tithesthai (thetos huios),*[1] and is attested from the second century B.C., with the meaning, "adoption as a child."[2] It appears frequently in pre-Christian inscriptions and is always found in the formula, *kath' huiothesian de*: A., son of B., *kath' huiothesian de*, son of C.[3] Neither this precise adoption formula nor its frequency of appearance is reflected in biblical literature. The word *huiothesia* does not appear at all in the Greek version of the Old Testament and is found only five times in the New Testament. In the latter it is confined to the Pauline corpus (including Ephesians). The passages are Rom. 8:15, 23; 9:4; Gal. 4:5; and Eph. 1:5. Only here does one encounter this word which Franz Leenhardt describes as a "juridical term which is pregnant with meaning."[4] The aim of this essay is to survey the attempts to explicate that meaning and to suggest the content that appears to be most probable both in the light of recent research and of the five passages themselves.

Commentators from Augustine to the Reformers did not find the appearance of the term *huiothesia* in any way remarkable, and were not concerned to locate its origin in one part or another of Paul's background. They were, however, very much concerned with its theological significance. Augustine, for example, perceived that by describing the sonship of the Christian with the concept of adoption, the Apostle was able to preserve the vital distinction between the Christian's sonship by grace and the sonship of Jesus by nature. In his lectures on

133

Romans, Luther confines his comments to the occurrence at 8:15, and emphasizes in particular the contrast Paul makes between the spirit of bondage and the spirit of sonship, between the fear of the servant and the love of the son.[5] His main concern is an exposition of the spirit of bondage in order to demonstrate the magnitude of the blessing that belongs to those who, as free, "have not again received the spirit of fear but, rather, the spirit of sonship which is the spirit of trusting faith." In his comments on Gal. 4:5, Luther teaches that Paul was there defining the blessing of the seed of Abraham (Gen. 22:18) as the adoption as sons and the inheritance of everlasting life. The Christian receives adoption, not by any merit of his own, but only by the redemption accomplished by Jesus Christ the Son of God.[6] Calvin also discerns significant theological content in Paul's references to adoption. He believes that the Apostle used this concept in order to make clear and certain the confidence and assurance of the Christian.[7] Such assurance is possible because the Christian's free adoption in Christ is a decisive commendation of divine grace as the ultimate cause of salvation.[8]

With the advent of modern biblical studies, more notice was taken of the word *huiothesia* itself. Opinions concerning its origin in Paul's background and the significance of that background for its interpretation began to emerge. Its treatment in the volumes of the International Critical Commentary series may be taken as representative. In their volume on Romans (1895), W. Sanday and A. C. Headlam devote a full paragraph to *huiothesia* at its initial appearance at 8:15.[9] They note its classical roots and its frequent use in Greek inscriptions of Hellenistic times, and regard the idea, like the word, as native Greek. "This," they conclude, "doubtless points to the quarter from which St. Paul derived the word, as the Jews had not the practice of adoption." T. K. Abbott's commentary on Ephesians appeared in 1897 and also offered an explanation of *huiothesia*: "The figure of adoption is borrowed from Roman law; the practice was unknown to the Jews."[10] In his commentary on Galatians (1921), E. D. Burton devotes nearly a page to *huiothesia*.[11] He notes its Greek background and its confinement to the Pauline epistles, and discusses briefly each of its five appearances. More recent commentaries tend to offer substantially the same information and opinion.

The consensus that *huiothesia* is a technical term whose form and content Paul borrowed from the legal usage of the Graeco-Roman world is also encountered in various special studies of adoption. Although an exclusively Greek background for the term has not been without its advocates, most students of the problem interpret the meaning of *huiothesia* in Paul in terms of the Roman institution of adoption. J. S. Candlish, for example, judges that "since adoption was, in Roman law, a technical term for an act that had specific legal and social effects, there is much probability that [Paul] had some reference to that in his use of the word."[12] More recently Francis Lyall, a member of the University of Aberdeen (Scotland) faculty of law, has put the case for Roman law with great force.[13] Lyall argues for a Roman content on both negative and positive grounds. Negatively, he regards Roman law as the only suitable reference for Paul because Jewish law, the obvious alternative, does not possess the concept, and because the Greek law of adoption was only a pale shadow of the Roman, existing more as a succession device than anything else. Positively, he contends that Roman law is preferable both because of Paul's undoubted knowledge of the Roman institution and because of its suitability for his purpose:

> The adoptee is taken out of his previous state and is placed in a new relationship with his new *paterfamilias*. All his old debts are canceled, and in effect he starts a new life. From that time the *paterfamilias* owns all the property and acquisitions of the adoptee, controls his personal relationships, and his rights of discipline. On the other hand he is involved in liability by the actions of the adoptee and owes reciprocal duties of support and maintenance.
>
> The Christian doctrines of election, justification, and sanctification imply that the believer is taken out of his former state, and is placed in a new relationship with God. He is made part of God's family forever, with reciprocal duties and rights. All his time, property, and energy should from that time forth be brought under God's control. The Roman law of adoption, with [the] concept of *patria potestas* inherent in it, is a peculiarly useful illustration of these doctrines in action. I conclude that Paul's use of the term "adoption" in Romans, Ephesians, and Galatians was a deliberate, considered, and appropriate reference to Roman law.[14]

In fairness to Lyall, it must be emphasized that he arrives at his conclusion in full knowledge of a considerable scholarly opinion that adoption may indeed not have been unknown to Old Testament Israel.

This opinion had its genesis in Old Testament studies that were completely unrelated to the appearance of *huiothesia* in the New Testament. Its chief catalyst was the archaeological expedition (1925-31) at Nuzi in northeast Iraq which unearthed thousands of clay tablets of the fifteenth century B.C. Among them were documents[15] which established that the institution of adoption was known and practiced at Nuzi at a time relatively close to that of the biblical patriarchs. These adoption records shed helpful light on Abram's statement that the heir of his house would be Eliezer of Damascus, a slave born in his house (Gen. 15:2ff.). The practice of adoption described in the Nuzi tablets suggests the reason for the nature of this relationship between Abram and his adopted son Eliezer. It was a custom at Nuzi for a childless couple to adopt a son to serve them as long as they lived and to bury them with proper care and mourning at their death. In exchange for these services the adopted son was designated as heir. If, however, the adopter should beget a son after the adoption, the adopted son had to yield to the real son the right of being the chief heir. This proviso appears to supply the legal background of Yahweh's reply to Abram: "This man shall not be your heir; your own son shall be your heir" (Gen. 15:4). Similar parallels between the Nuzi documents and the narrative of Jacob and Laban suggest that Jacob may have become the adopted son of Laban.[16]

This archaeological evidence prompted Old Testament scholars to reexamine other passages to discover whether or not there was evidence of the practice of adoption. Samuel Feigin[17] defended the authenticity of the Hebrew text of Judg. 11:1-3 and argued that the word *wayyōled* (v. 1) does not mean here "he begot," which is late, but "he adopted," that is, he declared Jephthah as a child. V. 1, he argues, should therefore read, "And Jephthah, the Gileadite, was a valiant warrior; but being the son of a woman, a harlot, Gilead adopted Jephthah." He proposes also that Ezra 10:44 with its difficult reading, "And they *put* children," is better rendered, "and they declared them as children," that is, they adopted them. Roland De Vaux cites and classifies a number of passages which allude to adoption.[18] The instances of Moses, who was treated as a son by Pharaoh's daughter (Exod. 2:10), of Genubath, who was reared among the sons of Pharaoh (1 Kings 11:20), and of Esther, who was brought up by Mordecai (Esth. 2:7, 15), are inconclusive for establishing the existence of adoption in Israel since they all occur on foreign soil. Clearer are the examples of Rachel regarding the two children of Bilhah as her sons (Gen. 30:3-8), Jacob considering Joseph's sons, Ephraim and Manasseh, as his own (Gen. 48:5), and putting them between his knees (Gen. 48:12), and Naomi taking Ruth's newborn child to her breast with the declaration, "A son is born to Naomi" (Ruth 4:16f.). These are examples of an adoption rite, although in somewhat less than the full sense since they all take place within the family. De Vaux regards as more significant the prophecy of Nathan about the king of David's line (2 Sam. 7:14), and as most impressive of all the one explicit text, Ps. 2:7, "You are my son, today I have begotten you." De Vaux concludes that "the notion of adoption, in the juridical sense, was known in Old Testament times, but had little influence on daily life; it was unknown in later Jewish law."[19] Arthur Weiser, also commenting on Ps. 2:7, says that the psalmist "excludes the idea of a physical begetting by adding the word 'today' and by using the ancient formula of adoption 'you are my son,' though he leaves untouched the formula 'I have begotten you' which originated in that foreign world of ideas. He transforms that alien idea into the idea of adoption, that is to say, into the declaration of the sonship of the king that took place on the day of his enthronement."[20] More recently Z. W. Falk[21] has written that references in the Bible point to the fact that adoption was known in Israel even though not treated in the law.

Among the first to suggest that these results of Old Testament research called into question the consensus that Paul's use of *huiothesia* had to be Graeco-Roman because adoption was unknown to the Old Testament was William H. Rossell.[22] The evidence from Nuzi, the Old Testament evidence referred to above, the Jewish background of Paul's readers, and the use of *huiothesia* in Rom. 9:4 combine to produce a formidable argument against this consensus. Equally problematic for the Graeco-Roman view, according to Rossell, is the appearance of the Aramaic word *Abba* in Rom. 8:15 and Gal. 4:6. How can one explain the presence of this Semitic word in adoption formulae that are supposedly Graeco-Roman? Rossell contends that a careful consideration of all these factors should lead biblical scholars to reconsider the Pauline conception of adoption as Semitic and not Graeco-Roman.

Ten years later Martin W. Schoenberg[23] reviewed the entire issue and declared himself to be in substantial agreement with Rossell. He concludes that whereas contemporary Greek literature and language supplied a convenient term, Rom. 9:4 remains the logical place to begin an exegetical inquiry into the origin and content of the Pauline notion of adoption. More recently still, C. E. B. Cranfield[24] has, in the light of the Old Testament evidence, likewise cautioned against claiming an exclusively Graeco-Roman background for this metaphor: "When Paul used the word *huiothesia* in 9:4, he must surely have had OT material very much in mind." It is, therefore, quite reasonable to suppose that the Apostle borrowed *huiothesia* from the language of the Graeco-Roman world, but poured into it a fundamentally Old Testament content. The possibility that he did precisely that is, of course, enhanced by the discovery that the notion of adoption was known in Old Testament times. That it was far less prominent in Israel than in Greece or Rome is to be expected. In a polygamous family, men were rarely childless, and leviratical marriage, which in earlier times extended to all members of the family, not merely to a brother, naturally acted as a preventative against childless families.[25] But the probability that Paul thus used *huiothesia* is established primarily by his use of the term with a clearly Old Testament content in 9:4, and secondarily by the Old Testament overtones present in its use in the remaining passages.

It would be difficult indeed to find a section of the letters of Paul more thoroughly Old Testament in nature than Romans 9-11. And there is no passage within these chapters more thoroughly Old Testament in character than 9:4-5. Here, in the process of describing his brethren, his kinsmen by race, the Apostle offers a classic inventory of their heritage: "They are Israelites, and to them belong the sonship (*hē huiothesia*), the glory, the covenants, the giving of the law, the worship, and the promises; to them belong the patriarchs, and of their race, according to the flesh, is the Christ. God who is over all be blessed forever. Amen." Of primary significance for our purpose is the fact that *huiothesia* stands at the head of this list. It is scarcely possible that in this purely Old Testament context, Paul's mind could be filled with matters Graeco-Roman. Rather, the context makes plain that *huiothesia* represents that divine act whose *locus classicus* is the scene enacted at the very beginning of Israel's national religious life: "And you shall say to Pharaoh, 'Thus says the Lord, Israel is my first-born son' " (Exod. 4:22). Israel, then, is the son of Yahweh, and there is no better way to understand or express this relationship than via the concept of adoption. To appreciate that, these words must be set against the background of the ancient Near East religions where the gods had consorts to bear their children. Living among Canaanites who worshiped a family of divinities that had at its head El and his consort Asherah and their offspring Baal and his wife Anath, Israel was brought into relationship with one God. "The first remarkable fact about the Israelite conception of God," says G. E. Wright, "is that he was believed to stand entirely alone, with no other being on his level. He is represented throughout the Old Testament as a 'jealous' God: that is, he is concerned that the people do not fall back into polytheism, that they worship and follow none but himself. He has no wife or family. In fact biblical Hebrew possessed no word for 'goddess.' "[26] Because Yahweh has no consort, he has no theogony. Instead he adopts or elects an historical people for his son. This adoptive/elective relationship between Yahweh and his people, enacted at the Exodus, is foundational for the Old Testament and, we may believe, was foundational as well for the theology of Paul. It is therefore not surprising to encounter *huiothesia* again in Eph. 1:5. Here it appears in company with the verb that is crucial to this long sentence, *exelexato*. God chose us for himself, says the Apostle. And if the phrase "in love" is taken with the words preceding it we have the theologically related participle *proorisas*, "having predestined," coming just before *huiothesian*.[27] It is followed by the purpose for which this adoption/election has been enacted, "to the praise of his glorious grace." This can hardly be understood as describing anything less than a life of obedient service, and is a significant echo of Exod. 4:23, "Let my son go, that he may serve me."

Apart from its reference to Jesus Christ, this Ephesian text is perfectly applicable to the people of God in the Old Testament. The occurrences of *huiothesia* in Gal. 4:5 and Rom. 8:15 may be taken together inasmuch as they both appear in the context of two prominent Old Testament elements that recall the history of Israel's adoption/election at the Exodus. In both contexts Paul speaks of the condition of bondage (Gal., *dedoulōmenoi, doulos*; Rom., *douleias*) which precedes adoption, and of an assured inheritance (Rom., *klēronomoi, synklēronomoi;* Gal., *klēronomos*) which follows upon it.[28]

The remaining passage, Rom. 8:23, presents a special problem to interpreters. Whereas in the other four texts adoption is regarded as an accomplished fact, as something already received, in Rom. 8:23 it is a blessing for which the Christian waits. Moreover, in this text *huiothesia* is further defined as "the redemption of our bodies." The simplest but most radical method of easing this difficulty is to accept the reading of 𝔓46, D, G, and other witnesses of the Western text, all of which omit *huiothesia*, "a word which copyists doubtless found to be both clumsy in the context and dispensable, as well as seeming to contradict ver. 15."[29] Some Roman Catholic biblical scholars have accepted this omission on the grounds that adoption is something definitive, already granted, and incapable of augmentation. For this reason the word does not appear at Rom. 8:23 in *La Bible de Jérusalem* (1956) nor in the *Jerusalem Bible* (1966). It is preferable, however, to retain the more difficult and more strongly attested reading and seek to interpret the eschatological emphasis forthrightly. The Apostle's use of *huiothesia* in Rom. 8:23 indicates that adoption is a further example of the already/not yet motif characteristic of such other New Testament concepts as kingdom, salvation, and resurrection. The Christian already possesses these blessings but not yet in their fullness. Beyond that, it is possible to understand *huiothesia* in connection with the notion of inheritance (v. 17) which for Israel at the moment of its adoption was promised concretely in the land, and for the Christian at his adoption is promised concretely in the redemption of the body.

That recent research allows Paul an Old Testament content for *huiothesia*, joined to the argument above that the texts themselves actually point to this content, means that the Apostle's concept of adoption is anchored in the supreme expression of God's love and grace, the adoption/election of a people. This in turn leads to the conclusion that the true antecedent of *huiothesia* is for Paul not a legal institution, whether Greek, Roman, or Semitic, but rather a theological confession. All too frequently overlooked is the fact that the Apostle does not use *huiothesia* for what we describe as social adoption, that is, the adoption of one human by another. He always uses it to describe what may be termed theological adoption, that is, the placing of persons into sonship to God! This theological understanding of adoption is characterized first of all by two originally Old Testament elements which are carried forward and applied to Christian adoption, and which, in the process, serve to demonstrate the inadequacy of all human legal models.

First of all, at Nuzi, Athens, and Rome, the controlling motive for adoption was the satisfaction of the needs of the adopter. In the material from Nuzi the adopter is childless. He has no one to care for him in his old age, or to bury him and mourn for him at his death. There is no indication of concern for the adoptee or his welfare. Under certain conditions the adoptee would benefit as the heir, but this seems a peripheral matter that has no role in the motivation of the adopter. The situation among the Greeks and Romans is very similar. Adoption as an institution among the Greeks was the result of a need created by their system of family organization.[30] Both Greek and Roman law stipulated that the family property could not be obtained without the obligation of cultus, nor the cultus without the property or some share of it. Equally fundamental was the principle that the family and the cultus could be continued only through male heirs. Thus, everything depended upon the presence in the family of a legitimate son. The institution of adoption was therefore a necessary outcome of the desire to perpetuate the family and the family cultus whenever the marriage produced no natural-born son. Again, the adoptee could and usually would benefit from his new status, but this was not the motive for the adoption. When these factors are compared with Yahweh's adoption/election of Israel the difference is immediately apparent. Yahweh does not adopt Israel to meet a need within himself, nor because Israel was an impressive people: "It was not because you were more in number than any other people that the Lord set his love upon you and chose you, for you were the fewest of all peoples; but it is because the Lord loves you, and is keeping the oath which he swore to your fathers, that the Lord has brought you out with a mighty hand, and redeemed you from the house of bondage, from the hand of Pharaoh king of Egypt" (Deut. 7:7f.; cf. also Hos. 11:1). Even what is required of Israel in the relationship is not for the benefit of Yahweh: "And the Lord commanded us to do all these statutes, to fear the Lord our God, for our good always, that he might preserve us alive, as at this day" (Deut. 6:24; cf. also 10:13). Israel, not Yahweh, is portrayed as the chief, if not the sole beneficiary in the relationship, and his adoption of her is an act of his love and grace. And that which was true for Israel (Rom. 9:4), Paul applied equally to his Christian readers (8:15, 23; Gal. 4:5; Eph. 1:5).[31]

Secondly, something more profound is expressed in Israel's adoption/election by Yahweh than merely being transferred from one *paterfamilias* to another. For although the adoptee was sometimes a slave, there is little evidence that his circumstances were in any way wretched or hopeless. Frequently the adoptee is briefly described as another's son. And at Rome, in cases where the natural father had died, the son enjoyed such an independent status that only a solemn act of the sovereign people could place him in the position of the son of another.[32] The Old Testament writers never tire of emphasizing that Israel's situation was very different. The adoptees at the Exodus were suffering severe affliction as helpless and hopeless slaves for whom adoption meant deliverance out of the house of bondage. At times, Israel's pre-adoption state is described as so desperate that it borders on non-existence, and what happened at the Exodus was in effect a life-giving act of divine creation: "But now thus says the Lord, he who created you, O Jacob, he who formed you, O Israel" (Isa. 43:1; cf. 44:2; Ps. 100:3). As we have seen, Paul can describe the pre-adoption state of Christians in terms of slavery and bondage;[33] he can also portray this condition as characterized by weakness or helplessness (Rom. 5:6). Moreover, in Ephesians 2 he speaks of his readers as having been dead through trespasses and sins, but having been made alive together with Christ by a new creative act of God.

The christological emphasis of these latter passages reminds us that there is something that remains to be said, for there is more to Paul's concept of adoption than a mere reiteration of Israel's experience, accompanied by a New Testament application. The four texts (and their contexts) which deal with Christian adoption manifest Paul's customary emphasis on the essential role of Christ and the Spirit. Romans 8 makes plain that adoption (v. 15) means that Christians are both children and heirs of God (v. 16); and that to be heirs of God (*klēronomoi*) is at the same time to be fellow-heirs (*synklēronomoi*) with Christ (v. 17). This christological connection is carried through to the end of the paragraph by the verbs *sympaschomen* and *syndoxasthōmen*. As was noted above, v. 23 of the same chapter links adoption with "the redemption of our bodies." Once again the christological connection is made, albeit more subtly. For apart from the resurrection of Christ there would, of course, be no Christian expectation of the redemption of the body. In Gal. 4:4f. the place of the work of Christ in the adoption of his people is made perfectly clear. The purpose for which God sent forth his Son, the goal of the incarnation itself, is "that we might receive adoption as sons." And in Eph. 1:5 it is emphasized that just as all the blessings described in that doxology are received in Christ, so also God predestined Christians for adoption "through Jesus Christ." The cumulative testimony of these passages asserts forcefully that Christians do not receive adoption apart from Jesus Christ.

Similarly, Paul emphasizes that the gift of adoption, as every other gift that flows from the work of Christ, is also mediated through the Spirit.[34] The first mention of adoption in Romans is introduced by the declaration that "all who are led by the Spirit of God are sons of God" (8:14). And in whatever way the difficult phrase "the spirit of God" (8:15) is understood (and it may well mean "the Spirit who brings about adoption"), v. 16 states plainly that "it is the Spirit himself" bearing witness with or, perhaps, to our spirit that we are children of God. In v. 23 the agonizing tension between what Christians experience *now* and the confident expectation of what they *will be* when the full blessing of their adoption is realized, is the result of the fact that they possess "the first fruits of the Spirit." And in chapter 4 of Galatians, the status of Christian sonship that stems from adoption (v. 5) is sealed (v. 6) by God when he sends "the Spirit of his Son into our hearts, crying, 'Abba! Father!' " We may say, then, that the concept of adoption in the theology of Paul belongs to the history of salvation, inaugurated at the naming of Israel as God's son, and continued and perfected in the adoption of men and women into the family of God through the work of Christ and the Spirit.

NOTES TO CHAPTER 9

1. Liddell and Scott, *A Greek-English Lexicon* (Oxford: Oxford University Press, 1940), p. 1846.

2. E. Schweizer, *TDNT*, VIII, 397.

3. G. A. Deissmann, *Bible Studies* (Edinburgh: T. & T. Clark, 1903), p. 239.

4. *The Epistle to the Romans* (London: Lutterworth Press, 1961), p. 213.

5. *Lectures on Romans* (London: SCM Press, 1961), pp. 231f.

6. *A Commentary on St. Paul's Epistle to the Galatians* (Cambridge & London: James Clarke, 1953), pp. 359f.

7. *The Epistles of Paul the Apostle to the Romans and to the Thessalonians* (Edinburgh: Saint Andrew Press, 1961), p. 168. See also the *Institutes*, where Calvin assures the Christian of the heavenly kingdom, "for the only Son of God, to whom it wholly belongs, has adopted us as his brothers" (II, xii, 2).

8. *The Epistles of Paul the Apostle to the Galatians, Ephesians, Philippians and Colossians* (Edinburgh: Saint Andrew Press, 1965), p. 126.

9. *A Critical and Exegetical Commentary on the Epistle to the Romans* (Edinburgh: T. & T. Clark), p. 203.

10. *A Critical and Exegetical Commentary on the Epistles to the Ephesians and to the Colossians* (Edinburgh: T. & T. Clark), p. 9.

11. *A Critical and Exegetical Commentary on the Epistle to the Galatians* (Edinburgh: T. & T. Clark), pp. 220f.

12. *A Dictionary of the Bible*, ed. by J. Hastings (Edinburgh: T. & T. Clark, 1898), I, 40.

13. "Roman Law in the Writings of Paul—Adoption," *JBL*, 88 (1969), 458-466. Cf. also J. D. Hester, *Paul's Concept of Inheritance*, in *SJThOP*, 14 (Edinburgh/London: Oliver and Boyd, 1968), pp. 18f., 58ff.

14. *Ibid.*, p. 466.

15. See C. H. Gordon, in *BA*, 3 (1940), no. 1. The texts are in *ANET*, ed. by J. Pritchard (Princeton: Princeton University Press, 1969), pp. 219f.

16. In his article, "Another Look at Rachel's Theft of the Teraphim," *JBL*, 81 (1962), 239-248, Moshe Greenberg disputes the usefulness of the Nuzi material for explaining Rachel's act, but does so "without prejudice to the interpretation of the Jacob-Laban relationship as a whole."

17. "Some Cases of Adoption in Israel," *JBL*, 50 (1931), 186-200.

18. *Ancient Israel* (London: Darton, Longman & Todd, 1961), pp. 51f.

19. *Ibid.*, p. 52.

20. *The Psalms* (London: SCM Press, 1962), p. 113.

21. *Hebrew Law in Biblical Times* (Jerusalem: Wahrmann Books, 1964), pp. 162f.

22. "New Testament Adoption—Graeco-Roman or Semitic?" *JBL*, 71 (1952), 233-234.

23. "*Huiothesia*: the Word and the Institution," *Scripture*, 14 (1962), 115-123.

24. *A Critical and Exegetical Commentary on the Epistle to the Romans* (Edinburgh: T. & T. Clark, 1975), I, 397.

25. Thus argue S. Feigin, *op. cit.*, pp. 193f., and Z. W. Falk, *op. cit.*, p. 162.

26. *Biblical Archaeology* (Philadelphia: Westminster Press, 1957), p. 116.

27. Markus Barth uses the phrase "election for adoption" to express Paul's thought here (*Ephesians,* in *AB* [Garden City: Doubleday, 1974], I, 105).

28. With regard to the Old Testament background for the concept of inheritance, C. K. Barrett comments on the Romans passage as follows: "Paul is still concerned to demonstrate the certainty of future salvation, and argues that if we are heirs of God our inheritance is secure. Of course the analogy is imperfect. Ordinarily an heir enters upon his inheritance only at the death of the testator; but the language of inheriting can be adopted here because in the Old Testament the word 'inheritance' is regularly used of that which God gives to his people (especially the land of Israel)" (*The Epistle to the Romans* [London: Adam & Charles Black, 1957], p. 164). Cf. also J. D. Hester, *op. cit.*, p. 29.

29. B. M. Metzger, *A Textual Commentary on the Greek New Testament* (London-New York: United Bible Societies, 1971), p. 517.

30. See W. J. Woodhouse, *Encyclopaedia of Religion and Ethics*, ed. by J. Hastings (Edinburgh: T. & T. Clark, 1908), I, 11-14.

31. Calvin uses the lovely phrase "the covenant of adoption" to describe the

circumstance of the Jews, and "the grace of adoption" to describe the circumstance of Christians (*Institutes* III, ii, 22).

32. Concerning the considerable status of the individual in adoption under Roman law see, e.g., Greer M. Taylor, "The Function of *PISTIS CHRISTOU* in Galatians," *JBL*, 85 (1966), 66f.

33. Calvin explains the adoption of Gal. 4:5 to mean "that we should not be borne down by an unending bondage, which would agonize our consciences with the fear of death" (*Institutes* II, vii, 15).

34. Markus Barth says that "Paul's utterances on adoption emphasize the causative and cognitive power of the Spirit . . ." (*op. cit.*, p. 80).

10: *The Novelty of the Gospel*

OTTO A. PIPER

The Jewish-Christian Dialogue

One of the bittersweet fruits of National Socialism is the willingness of large portions of Christians and Jews to engage in dialogue. One gets the impression, however, that with the best of will the relation of the two religions fails to bear substantial results. The reason for that stalemate still may be—it seems to me—a mistaken concept of the role that God has assigned to the Jewish people.

The emancipation of Jewry in the eighteenth century was the outcome of the Enlightenment. The leaders of that movement started from the assumption that all men are equal and that individual or racial differences do not count. Hence there was no reason for Christians to discuss the bearing that fellowship with Jews might have for their mutual relationship. As my venerable teacher Hermann Cohen of the University of Marburg, Germany, used to emphasize, all human beings are more or less on the way to ideal humanity and thus in a common situation. A similar view is adopted by the school of comparative religion, according to which all religions converge toward the ideal religion.

The Christian mission among Jews which started in the nineteenth century under the influence of the Pietistic movements implied an entirely different view of the role of Judaism. It was interpreted as a serious heretical doctrine of which Jews had to get rid in order to be saved. Either concept (Enlightenment-Pietism) has survived in modern liberal and conservative theology. Both evaluations were really interested in Judaism as theology or doctrine. Yet by seeing it in that perspective, its historical role was seriously underrated. The traditional views failed to take into consideration the way in which the two religions had dealt with each other for two millennia. Both have always considered themselves as being destined to bring about substantial changes in this world.

Irrespective of the criminal manner in which National Socialism had treated the European Jews, it had drawn attention to an element of historical truth when it defined Judaism not merely as a religion or theory, but also and above all as a movement in history. As a manifestation of divine providence, Judaism no less than Christianity has its common dynamic center, but also its common origin and common goal throughout the ages. In our days this phenomenon is blatantly obvious in modern Zionism, according to which it is the soil of Palestine (*ha-arez*) which is the common bond that unites all Jews of the earth in a common promise and a common obligation.

As recent events have shown, this interpretation of Judaism has an enormous motivating power, yet also implies a serious misunderstanding of Israel's identity. Zionism is a political dogma, a part of the Old Testament religion. This explains the ineffectiveness of Jewish-Christian dialogue in modern times. The Christian theologian cannot approach his Jewish counterpart except on the basis of holy history. According to the Jewish theologians, God's dealing with mankind has come to a standstill in his taking care of the Jewish people. Consequently, what the New Testament has to say about the ministry and the significance of Jesus for them is considered as a mere appendix to the Old Testament. According to the New Testament, however, the work of Jesus is more than the fulfillment of the promises of the Old Testament, but an absolutely new stage in the process of redemption of mankind which manifests itself primarily in the incarnation and the power of the Holy Spirit.

New Elements in the New Testament

In the Old Testament the main purpose is to record the history of God's dealings with his chosen people. So it is not primarily in the field of doctrine that we must look for new elements in the New Testament. The New Testament proclaims that new events have taken place in God's dealings with his chosen people—the incarnation and the subsequent manifestation of the power of the Holy Spirit. These two events influence and determine the whole teaching of the New Testament to such an extent that nothing in the New Testament can be understood unless it is related to these facts.

There are three aspects of the incarnation that are of equal importance for our understanding of the New Testament: first of all, that the incarnation is the personal presence of God among men; secondly, that the incarnation explains the authority of Jesus; thirdly, that the incarnation implies the work of divine reconciliation. These three aspects must be seen with equal clarity if the significance of the incarnation is to be fully appreciated.

The Old Testament in several places tells us that God appeared to men, but the later writings are anxious to show that it was not God himself but the angel of God who appeared to men; for God never was and never can be seen by anyone in this world. God is the Creator and Master of this world; this separates him from man in this fallen world. Therefore the presence of God in Jesus Christ is a unique event that has no analogy in the Old Testament.

It is true that in the pagan religions frequent mention is made of theophanies, but they are all only of a temporary character and the gods are never human beings but only appear like human beings. It is quite different in the incarnation. There we find that God identifies himself with men. In the incarnation the gulf that separates God from his creatures is bridged. This fact has no direct preparation in the Old Testament. Certainly the Old Testament speaks of the love and mercy of God, but there is no hint in the Old Testament that God the transcendent would ever identify himself with man.

It is as God present among men that Jesus is depicted in the New Testament; he is the fulfillment of Old Testament prophecy. But at the same time the New Testament writers are anxious to show that Jesus surpasses all the Old Testament prophecies. Whereas in the Old Testament we have hope, now we have experience. In the Old Testament there is anxious expectation; now there is certainty. While it is true that in this life Jesus only brings the first-fruits of the divine promise, nevertheless his presence is a guarantee of a complete fulfillment of the promise in the future. It is possible for Christians already in this life to enjoy the things to come. So Paul can say that we glory in the hope that is to be fulfilled. To him it is absolutely certain that the promise will be fulfilled.

There is a fundamental difference between the Word of God as spoken through the prophets and Jesus as the Word of God. The prophets under the old covenant could speak with supreme confidence only when they had received the Word of God for a particular occasion. It is different with Jesus. What he says is not simply a handing on of what God has told him; everything that he does and says has an authority in itself that demands absolute obedience. The ethical teaching of Jesus is thus fundamentally different from the ethical teaching of the Jewish rabbis and the Greek sages. He does not simply recommend wisdom; whatever he says in the ethical field is legislation whose authority is not to be questioned.

The eschatological view of history as held by all the writers of the

Old Testament as well as by Jesus requires ethical rules as its supplement. When God comes for judgment, man must mend his ways. But on the other hand, this close connection between ethical commands and eschatology does not mean that these ethical demands derive from eschatology. The prophets relied, in their ethical teaching, on the divine legislation of the past. The new law that is given by Jesus rests upon his nature as the Son of God.

What Jesus had to say about the nature and purpose of God was not the outcome of ecstasy, as it was in the case of the prophets, but rather rests upon introspection, for Jesus and the Father are one. God was in Jesus; therefore he could say, "He that sees me sees the Father." For this reason Jesus has a legitimate right to cleanse the temple; and above all, only he has authority to proclaim forgiveness of sins and to forgive sins himself. No human being has a right to forgive sins. I may forgive a man for harming me, but that does not remove his guilt. By forgiving sins Jesus made the sin offering of the temple worship superfluous.

Why was it that Jesus had authority to forgive sins? It is sometimes said that it was because he was the Son of God. This is not correct. It was not simply in the authority of the eternal Son of God that Jesus forgave sins. He did it as the Son of man. The forgiveness of sins that Jesus offered rested upon the anticipation of his accomplished work. He had authority to forgive sins because in his baptism he had identified himself completely with sinful mankind; therein he showed his willingness to bear all the consequences that led logically and inevitably to the cross. So in a certain regard it was indeed a presumption that during his public ministry he should forgive sins, because his work was not yet accomplished. On the other hand, when he had accomplished his task, he made himself the perfect mediator between God and man. Thus, as a result of his whole life work from the baptism to the cross, he as the mediator made superfluous the old covenant. The old covenant had lost its significance because greater benefits could now be derived from God through Jesus Christ. In him a new covenant was made between God and man.

The manifestation of the power of the Spirit in the church is a fact that has no parallel and no direct antecedents in the Old Testament. The works the Holy Spirit worked in Jesus Christ might be compared to the manifestation of the Spirit in the men of God of the Old Testament. Certainly we would say that the difference between Jesus and the Old Testament men of God was considerable, but this would be only a gradual difference. But the really new thing was that through the Spirit of Christ the church was brought into existence, and that ever since in an uninterrupted flow the Spirit is operative in believers as an edifying power (1 Cor. 14:1-19). That is to say, what had been an intermittent manifestation in the Old Testament and seemed to be an equally temporary manifestation in Jesus, now became continuous. Whereas in the old covenant the manifestation of the Spirit was limited to outstanding personalities, now it became characteristic of the average person in the church. So the New Testament describes the gifts of the Spirit by which people are able to perform the various functions for the administration and upbuilding of the church, and it speaks of the power of the Spirit to bring about a higher life. This manifestation of the Spirit is closely connected with the incarnation because through it the church is made the Body of Christ, the continuation of the earthly ministry of Jesus.

Conclusion

In the light of the above facts it should be obvious that no satisfactory result of the Jewish-Christian dialogue is to be expected as long as the discussion proceeds on a purely secular basis. Furthermore, it must be kept in mind that neither Judaism nor Christianity is a purely stationary phenomenon. Both religions are movements and live out of the conviction that their intrinsic growth, while concomitant with mental developments, is basically dependent on a succession of revelatory events.

Judaism will warn Christianity that it is often in danger of overemphasizing redemption and grace to the point where sight is lost of the fact that the God of the Bible is also the Lord of the law and of judgment. In turn Christianity is aware of a dangerous tendency in Judaism to confine election to the Jewish people. By taking the challenge of their partner seriously, both religions help each other to realize that they are mutually God's agents in history. Any agreement that is reached in their dialogue makes a contribution to the realization of God's kingdom, yet is but a provisional indication of the direction and goal God is about to accomplish. By means of these interrelations and through listening to each other, the dialogue becomes an eschatological event. Christianity seems to be superior to Judaism because it has a clearer view of man's destination through the ministry of Christ. In fact, however, the divine direction of the eschatological process precludes any kind of evaluation and mutual comparison. In both religions the devotees remain God's captives, because as the Word of God the Old Testament is paradoxically an integral and self-contained book, yet also forms the first part of the Christian Bible. The dialogue will never be finished; yet, at all times, it serves God as an instrument through which human beings have their share in realizing cosmic harmony, though in different ways.

11: *Canon and Worship*

MASAICHI TAKEMORI

I

The critical study of the New Testament has a basic problem which it cannot evade if it wants to remain a biblical study. The problem is the canonicity of the New Testament. Biblical scholars usually do not concern themselves with this problem. They believe that it does not fall within the scope of their investigation because they are convinced that what is required of them is not to testify that the New Testament is the canon of the church but rather to clarify the historical aspect of the New Testament writings. They appear to give no thought to the fact that the canonicity of the New Testament is always in danger of being threatened by their historical and critical studies. But of course these scholars can never ignore the crucial nature of this problem, although they may wish to confine it to the sphere of dogmatics. There have been frequent attempts to solve the problem of the canonicity of the New Testament on the part of New Testament scholars. The main trends of these approaches are well illustrated in the essays collected by E. Käsemann in *Das Neue Testament als Kanon.*[1] Fifteen essays (including his own) are presented together with Käsemann's comments.

The same problem is present in the younger church of Japan in a more crude but fundamental form. Dr. Zenta Watanabe[2] is the scholar who first took up this problem in Japan. Watanabe was baptized in a holiness group more than seventy years ago, and in this group he was trained to read the Bible in a fundamentalist manner. Some years later, however, he received from a Plymouth Brethren minister an English book by J. N. Darly, *On the Christian Perfection*. This book made him aware of the fact that there are radically different ways of reading the Bible. He found that what he had learned in the holiness group was not the only method of interpreting the Bible, but that there were several other methods that would produce sometimes opposing views. The holi-

150

ness group read a prescription for a holy life in Ezek. 36:25-27, for example, while the Plymouth Brethren read the same passage as a prophecy of the rebirth of Israel. Thus began Watanabe's long study of the canonicity of Holy Scripture. He went to Pasadena, California, to study the Old Testament, then to Berlin to work under Reinhold Seeberg, and then on to Freiburg where he studied philosophy under Edmund Husserl in order to find some logical means to solve his problem. Further study took him to the Sorbonne and to the Hebrew University in Jerusalem. The better his command of the disciplines of historical criticism became, the more inescapable became the problem of the canonicity of the Bible. After several years, he returned to Japan and began a long teaching career at various universities and colleges as a professor of Old Testament and/or of Systematic Theology. During the almost seventy years that Watanabe has been working as a theologian and preacher—he is said to be one of the best preachers in Japan—he has written many books. His major works are three large volumes entitled, respectively, *Teaching on the Canon* (1945), *Biblical Hermeneutics* (1954), and *The Possibility of a Biblical Theology* (1963).[3]

In the third volume Watanabe maintains that biblical theology has failed to establish the fundamental teaching which makes clear the canonicity of the Bible, and without which the whole system of biblical theology collapses: (1) While the Bible is an ancient document, it is at the same time the canon of the church. So, for example, biblical theology cannot stand when Bultmann proclaims, "The history of Israel is not a history of revelation for Christian faith,"[4] or, "The Old Testament is not a revelation any more."[5] (2) It is said that since W. Herrmann the historical-critical method is not a sufficient methodology for biblical theology. (3) Thus far a "system" has been lacking for the teaching of the Bible. The church cannot hear the unified word of the Bible by a merely historical method. (4) The only escape from this separation between the plurality of diverse witnesses based on the individual books of Scripture and the single message of the gospel is the way of *Heilsgeschichte* which has come down from J. C. K. von Hofmann. But biblical scholars have not studied it thoroughly enough. (5) Up to this time there has been no satisfying answer to the question, How can one make the Old Testament Christian?

In order to deal with these problems Watanabe, with the help of his *Basho-no-ronri* (logic of "place"), put forward the following proposals about the canonicity of the Bible. A book, he taught, is a dead thing when left alone. But once a man reads it, the book requires him to change himself in response to what he has read. This means that the book is no longer a dead thing, but something that calls out the reader as a "thou."

This is even more so in the case of a religious book. A book has a personal element in a sense, not simply because it has an author who wants to communicate something through it, but because a book is "personal" in itself. Once we understand this, we must interpret a book in the right "place" where it can call us out as a "thou." This "to-be-in-place" is the key to understanding any book, but this is especially true of the Bible. Every book of the Bible has its own "place," its *Sitz im Leben*, in the past, into which the *religionsgeschichtliche Schule* inquires; but it also has another "place" in the present as a book of the Bible, as a part of the canon. This is the "place" that is presupposed in biblical study, but never thoroughly examined. Biblical scholars often overlook or even ignore this presupposition. The fact that the canon contains sixty-six books means that the Bible limits itself to these books and thus forms itself by them. In other words, each book confines itself to the "place" which is fashioned from sixty-six constituents and from which it calls us out as a "thou." To *be* the Bible means that the book stands in that right "place," where the differentiation between the individual writings arises. To *become* the Bible, the canon of the church, means that all differences are settled in the "place" of the *Aufhebungspunkt* (point of departure). In Rom. 4:2f., for example, Abraham's faith was counted to him as righteousness, whereas in James 2:21 and 24 it is his works that are thus reckoned. And the *Aufhebungspunkt* is John 6:29: "Jesus answered them, 'This is the work of God, that you believe in him whom he has sent.' " Thus the *Aufhebungspunkt* is the right "place" of witness to Jesus Christ. Moreover, the Bible *is* the book, that is, the canon, because all the writings in the Bible bear witness to him.

Watanabe is a solitary prophet. His theology has been discussed by a limited number of theologians but he has not been very influential among specialists and lay people. Watanabe began as a fundamentalist, but he is confident that, on the one hand, he has overcome this fundamentalism through his historical-critical training as an Old Testament scholar, and that, on the other hand, he has succeeded in proving the authority of the Bible with his hermeneutic of the logic of "place."

Dr. M. Sekine,[6] however, rightly criticizes Watanabe by pointing out that he cuts off the biblical text from its historical background once he has overcome (*aufgehoben*) the *Sitz im Leben* of the individual writings and puts everything on the same level as canonical writings. Rom. 4:2f. is a clear example. The real problem behind the texts from Romans and James is hidden when they are sewn over with Johannine thread. Sekine concludes that "all this is an unavoidable outcome of the institutionalized Protestant church, which does not allow individual decision for a canon." When we are aware that Sekine is not only an outstanding Old Testament scholar but also a non-church leader in Japan, his last words are very interesting. For what he says is that if there were no (institutional) church, the problem of the canon would no longer be a serious issue. From the present writer's point of view Watanabe's failure was not determined by any unavoidable nature of the institutional church, but rather came from the fact that, perhaps because of his Pietistic background, he has not completely understood the church. It is true that his spiritual pilgrimage brought him to almost all the denominations, but unfortunately he did not see what the church really means. Canon is *par excellence* a matter of the church, not of individuals. Thus, it is ironical that neither a man of the non-church group nor a wanderer among various churches can understand the canonicity of the Bible.

II

In recent years another aspect of the problem of the canon has appeared on this side of the ocean in a quite different context. The United Church of Christ in Japan (Kyodan) has been suffering at the hands of the new-left group for several years. This group questions everything that belongs to the "establishment" but their most severe criticism is raised in connection with the confession of faith of the Kyodan. Although the Kyodan is a united church, it has a brief confession of faith that has not elicited full support from some former Congregationalist and Baptist groups. Although some ignore the written form of the confession, it remains the very basis of the life of the church.

The leftist group tries to do away with everything that binds the members to the authority of the church. One tactic they use for this purpose involves the results of recent New Testament investigation. They maintain that, according to the most up-to-date research, Christians can no longer confess that Jesus is the Christ, the Son of God, because Jesus himself had no intention of being the Messiah or of being confessed as the Messiah. Therefore, the confession of faith has no basis in history and should not exercise any authority to regulate the faith of individual members of the church. There is no single and unanimous interpretation of who Jesus was, even in the New Testament literature, so it makes no sense to pick out one of the diverse interpretations and make it the *kerygma*, or the "apostolic" faith. The issue thereby develops into the problem of the canonicity of the New Testament because it was the Old Catholic Church that produced the idea of "apostolic" authority which functioned as the criterion for the formation of the canon.

The leftist group found an able exponent in Dr. S. Arai,[7] professor of Western Classics at Tokyo University. Arai points out that the canon was formed by the church in order to defend, under the concept of "apostolic" authority, the authority of the ecclesiastical establishment (legalism) against heresies such as Marcionism and Montanism (enthusiasm). One can trace the root of this "apostolic" ideology back to the theology of Luke-Acts. For Luke-Acts harmonized the Jerusalem church (legalism) and Paul (enthusiasm) under the very idea of "apostolic" authority and *Heilsgeschichte*, and in this way provided a good example of how to save the church from confusion and disorder. That is why Arai calls the canon the product of compromise. It is true that Paul himself fought against both radical enthusiasm and legalism and that in this connection the idea of apostleship was stressed in the Pauline letters. But it was precisely the author of Luke-Acts who used this idea of "apostolic" authority to compromise the discrepancies between the Jerusalem church and Paul or, more exactly, between the many streams of first generation Christians in regard to the interpretation of the "good news" based on the words and works of Jesus of Nazareth. In doing so, however, he failed to capture what Paul really meant by "apostolic." The Paulinism of the sub-apostolic period, including Luke-Acts and the pastoral Epistles, is different from what Paul thought.

It also cannot be overlooked, Arai says, that the theology of Luke-Acts is one of many "theologies" within the New Testament. It was the social and political elements of the Old Catholic Church that used the theology of Luke-Acts as justification for regulating the interpretation of the Bible under the appealing title, "apostolic." In connection with these social and political elements Arai suggests that what the Old Catholic Church achieved was merely to compromise the existence of the church establishment within the establishment of the Roman Empire.

Accordingly, the same thing can be said of the Apostles' Creed or of the fundamental creeds produced by the councils at Nicaea and Chalcedon which overlap the formation of the canon. Each of them is the product of compromise. Thus, for Arai, to adhere to the authority of the canon means nothing more than to adhere to the *status quo*, sociologically or politically. Thus heresies in the second and third centuries are more original on the *Entwicklungslinie* (the line of development) than orthodoxy, the canonical line.[8] For this reason it is urgent that Christians relativize the absoluteness of their confession of faith or of the canon through incessant historical studies. The *kerygma* is both one and various. In other words, the interpretation of who Jesus is, is portrayed in various ways within the New Testament itself, and even more so within the non-canonical books. The individual, therefore, has always been entirely free to decide how to interpret and confess Jesus, and he should remain so. Arai himself believes that Jesus is God in the sense that he found the ground for his self-relativization in God, just as God was the ground of self-relativization for Jesus. That is, Jesus never authorized (= absolutized) his acts and words in the name of God.

The unique thing, however, is not Arai's thought but the phenomenon of how the historical approach so easily and directly influences the fundamentals of the church. Arai's academic achievements are unknown to most of the ministers and laity of Japan. Only specialists discuss his controversial thesis. But as an exponent of radical leftist groups he has had considerable impact on the problems of the canon and of the confession of faith. In this way, church life itself is moved to and fro by historical and critical studies. Arai says that as far as he is aware, no contemporary scholar maintains the absolute position of historical studies. His stand, however, exerts as strong an influence directly on many ecclesiastical problems of the church as if his position were the result of historical investigation. This proves nothing more than that the church in Japan is still young and that her tradition is not yet strong enough to enable her to stand firmly on her faith, rather than on something an historian can destroy.

For the purpose of the present paper, however, it is noteworthy that, with Arai, just as with Watanabe and Sekine, the canon seems to lose its basis when the question of how to interpret Jesus (= how to read the Bible) is made to depend on individuals. That is to say, it is again the one who does not understand the significance of the church who fails to see the canonicity of the Bible.

III

Sometimes it is more important to find out how the Bible has been received by the laity than to remain with the theological arguments of specialists concerning its canonicity, because the former reveals how the canon of Scripture is actually accepted by Japanese Christians in general. The people of Japan live in a pagan society under the influence of various religions and religious thoughts. Thus, their attitude toward the Bible is not always as it should be within the Christian church.

Shintoism, a native religion of Japan, has no canon, although there are certain books concerned with ritual. Buddhism has hundreds of sacred books, but there is no one sacred book, no canon, common to all sects and read daily by all Buddhists. There are two kinds of sacred books in Buddhism, one having to do with teaching, and the other with ritual. A limited number of these were written in Japan, mostly by great reformers from various periods, and are comparatively easy for the general public to read. Most of the remaining sacred books were written in China and use Chinese characters.[9] When imported into Japan, they are to be read in the Japanese way of reading Chinese characters (*Kanji*). Consequently only a few of them are generally used for rituals. According to Dr. Hajime Nakamura, professor emeritus of Oriental Thought at Tokyo University, Indians could read most of the original sacred books in Sanskrit or in its dialect, and Chinese could read them in Chinese translation. But when Buddhism was brought to Japan, the people read them in Chinese with the Chinese pronounciation of that time.[10] Therefore, only the educated could understand them. And by reading these books aloud with a mysterious accent, people in general expected a magical effect from them without understanding their meaning.

Hence the sacred books play a completely different role in Buddhist life. Buddhists, unlike Christians, do not gain their daily spiritual nourishment through the reading of one particular book.[11] The idea of a canon is entirely foreign to people who are reared with this background.

Confucianism, however, has contributed to the Japanese habit of reading sacred books. Visitors to Japan are often astonished at the number of book stores and the tremendous number of books published there. They see hundreds of people reading books, even on the famous rush-hour trains in Tokyo. Not only are the Japanese very fond of reading, but they do not hesitate to read important religious or philosophical works with the help of exegetical commentaries. This interest seems to be derived from their Confucian background. Confucianism as such no longer exists in Japanese society, but its influence continued until at least the turn of the century. In those days children learned to read aloud four major books and five sacred books of the Chinese classics which provided the basis for Confucianism. Sometimes they began to read at four or five years of age under the guidance of fathers and grandfathers. Usually they committed these books to memory, even though they did not understand their meaning. When they reached a certain age, they began to learn their concepts through oral exegetical comments provided by experts.[12] Today it is said that seven million copies of the Bible and Bible portions are sold annually in Japan although its Christian population numbers less than one million. Japanese people are fond of reading the Bible but most of them do not attend the worship services of the church.

One also finds among the active Christians in Japan the non-church group. It is unique, and has a certain amount of influence on educated people.[13] Its members reject all ecclesiastical institutions, sacraments, and polity. Their only concern is to read the Bible honestly. Because for them that includes reading it in its original languages, they teach individuals Hebrew and Greek. Their goal, therefore, is to read the Bible directly and personally without such human intrusions as the theology of translators or the dogma of the later church. They wish to read the original texts of the Bible with only the exegetical comments of their leaders. Should a leader force his pupils to read the Bible according to his own interpretation, however, they immediately reject it. It is entirely up to the individual to read the Bible and choose his own interpretation. Constant splits among leaders and pupils are therefore the fate of the non-church approach to Bible reading. Nevertheless, this appears to be exactly why the non-church movement is effective in Japanese society; that is, the ordinary Japanese finds the non-church attitude toward the Bible easy to accept. In fact, even those who attend church tend to exhibit the same attitude toward Scripture.

But the immediate reason why the Japanese people find it difficult to acknowledge the canon may well be the existence of idols in Buddhism and Shintoism.[14] Only those religions which have no idols—Judaism, Mohammedanism, and Christianity—can have canonical writings.

IV

There are many peculiar difficulties in Japan which hamper the reading of the Bible. The proper names in the Bible are quite foreign to the Japanese people, not to mention the absolute theism which is completely different from the pantheism familiar to them. The question of the Ethiopian eunuch to Philip is their question: "How can I [understand], unless some one guides me?" (Acts 8:31). This question becomes even more pointed when we look back on the history of the canon. Originally, the books of the canon were not written for individuals. All of Paul's letters were written to churches and were intended to be read before the congregation (Col. 4:16). Even Philemon was written not only to an individual Christian but also to "the church in your house" (v. 2). The recipient of the Gospel of Luke is Theophilus. Although he may be an historic person, yet "Luke bears in mind a mixed audience, part Jewish, part Gentile."[15]

The possiblity that writing letters may have been extremely difficult in New Testament times could explain the frequent use of the circular letter.[16] There was no attempt to make the Bible accessible to the general public individually until the Reformation period when Luther translated it for the German people and Gutenberg provided the technique to produce copies for individuals. Today it is perfectly legitimate and advisable for a sincere Christian to read the Bible for himself, but it should not be overlooked that the New Testament writings were originally written and collected for the purpose of being read in the church. This means that the writings of the New Testament were nothing but the "preaching" or "sermons" in the worship of the early church. This explains why sometimes even opposite ideas (for example, Rom. 4:2, 4 and James 2:21, 24) were expressed in different books. The variety of the literature does not destroy the significance of the canon but serves to indicate its richness. In any event, we may safely say that the New Testament books were read repeatedly at every gathering for worship. Even when they were read by individuals, this fact was always behind them. Otherwise the New Testament would not have been written, would not have been formulated, and would never have become the canon of the church. To discover the basis for the canonicity of the New Testament, then, it is necessary to clarify the relation between the New Testament and preaching, and the relation between preaching and worship.

We take up first the relation between the New Testament and preaching. By preaching we do not mean here the *kerygma* of the New Testament, but the sermon as the center of a worship service. The close relationship between the New Testament and the sermon should be demonstrated in the preaching itself. That is, texts from the New Testament should become the sermon in worship by means of preaching. The only scientific or theological means for that process is exegesis or exposition. But the problem is to understand how exegesis can make clear the meaning of the text and thus aid its transition to a sermon. Exegesis is said to be the only means of preparing a sermon. But does it really produce what is expected of it? On the contrary, recent exegesis or a rational handling of texts cannot make a sermon or provide the canonical meaning of the Bible. Therefore, the question of why a congregation can truly worship God in a church service has remained unanswered.

For the past two hundred years, exegesis has been described as the only means of discerning the gospel in a text. But many preachers have found this difficult to accomplish, for exegesis has its own limitation as an instrument for making a sermon from a text. In this connection these words of Karl Barth are often quoted: "The historical-critical method of biblical investigation has its rightful place: . . . But, were I driven to choose between it and the venerable doctrine of Inspiration, I should without hesitation adopt the latter."[17] It is said that Barth urged his students repeatedly to do exegesis. It was obvious to him that such modern commentaries as those of Lietzmann, Jülicher, Zahn, and Holtzmann are informative and useful, but that they are more concerned with the human form (*menschliche Gestalt*) of the New Testament; that is, the New Testament literature as historical documents. More important for Barth was the fact that the Word became flesh. The preacher's chief concern is to know the *Word*, and in order to do so he must also know the *flesh* by the method of exegesis. It is well known that Barth recommended that in making a sermon, preachers read the commentaries of Calvin, Luther, and Bengel.[18]

It is in a similar sense that A. Schlatter calls the historical-critical method an atheistic method.[19] A scientific method should perhaps be atheistic or neutral; that is, it should not be regulated by faith. In that case it inevitably carries the danger of producing an atheistic conclusion. There can be no surprise, therefore, if in recent years distinguished New Testament scholars[20] have "launched a broadside against historical criticism."[21] Watanabe's students study the Bible in a somewhat similar way in order to grasp its message. They first read the Scripture as it is, and then turn to the modern historical-critical method.

All this is nothing but an effort to understand the Bible as the Word of God, as the canon. The historical-critical method is fatally insufficient for reading the message of the Bible as the canon and reconstructing it into a sermon. E. Käsemann has offered this significant statement regarding the problem of the canon: "But the question 'What is the Gospel?' cannot be settled by the historian according to the results of his investigations but only by the believer who is led by the Spirit and listens obediently to the Scripture."[22] The modern method of exegesis may not be a unanimous target of critics but there seems to be a general consensus concerning the need to ask whether that method, especially with its utilization of historical criticism, is competent to bring the "good news" out of a text. In other words, modern exegetical method lacks a decisive element for handling a biblical text as canonical.

If the ultimate purpose of biblical exegesis is to interpret a text as the Word of God, the criterion of exegesis as a means of biblical interpretation must be the "sermon." Then, what makes a sermon truly "sermon" must also be the criterion of the canon. In other words, the canon of Scripture can became "canon" by way of the kind of preaching through which a sermon becomes "canon." And the only thing that makes a sermon truly "sermon" is the worship of the church. It is a sermon that makes worship truly "worship," but it is also worship that makes a sermon truly "sermon." And how the church is reading the Scripture for the congregation is demonstrated in the "sermon." In short, the best exegesis or exposition must be the sermon. Our next step, therefore, is to describe the relation between the sermon and worship in order to demonstrate that it is worship that makes clear the canonicity of the Bible.

The circumstances that surround the life of worship in Japan are different from those of the so-called Christian countries. The pagan religious temples and shrines, or the altars in private homes, are usually the places for the ordinary Japanese to encounter deities. They go to the temples or to the shrines to meet the gods and goddesses who are represented by the idols placed there. When they come into Protestant churches, however, they find no idols. If there were idols in the church, they would take it for granted that they had stepped into a place of worship! Instead, when they enter Protestant churches they get the impression that they have come into a lecture hall where people gather to listen to the stories of Christianity. The church, then, is nothing but an ordinary meeting place, and the sermon is just a speech about the Bible. They cannot find the worship they formerly experienced at the temples and shrines—idol worship—because there is no idol enshrined there. They think that they have come to study the Bible, but they do not think that they have come to worship.

Shintoism has no sermon. Buddhism has one, but not as a major part of worship. The sermon is separated from worship by usually being delivered after, or sometimes before it. Veneration and preaching are two different things. In their experience the sermon has nothing to do with worship. Naturally, then, those who come to worship in Christian churches do not regard the sermon as an integral part of the worship experience, and they listen to the sermon as a mere speech or lecture. Even Japanese Christians often do not perceive the integrity of sermon and worship. They do not mind arriving late at the Sunday morning service as long as they are in time for the sermon, for to attend church means nothing more to them than to listen to a sermon. Prayers, hymns, and offerings are simply accessories. Prayers in popular pagan religions have almost nothing to do with worship because the participants usually ask only for such personal benefits as health and wealth. Prayer belongs to individuals. There is nothing comparable to the prayers of the church.

With this background it is not difficult to understand why the non-church movements in Japan are rather influential. They have no worship. They call their Sunday gathering a meeting for Bible study. They sing hymns and offer prayer, but in a simpler way than is the church's custom. They reject formality in any sense. Instead of a sermon they have a lecture on Scripture. As was pointed out above, this lecture leads individuals to their own reading of the Bible. In these groups one glimpses how a sermon is received by Japanese Christians. Church-goers can hardly escape from the same attitudes toward both sermon and worship.

The problem for the Christians of Japan is how to believe that God is present in the worship service of the church. The only thing that makes them believe that he is present in their worship is the Word of God, that is, the scripture reading and the sermon. It was the Reformers who tried to confirm the presence of Christ in the church by their serious discussions about the Lord's Supper. By placing the sermon on the level with the sacraments as the Word of God, they put the sermon at the center of worship. Hence we assert that it is the sermon that makes worship truly "worship": "But if all prophesy, and an unbeliever or outsider enters, . . . falling on his face, he will worship God and declare that God is really among you" (1 Cor. 14:24f.). If we may be permitted to substitute "preach" in place of "prophesy" above, we may say that the sermon preached in worship makes newcomers believe that God is really in our worship. This can happen every Sunday in contemporary Christian worship, just as it has happened from generation to generation in the worship of the church.

If we believe that it is the sermon based on Scripture that makes worship truly "worship," we may also say that it is worship that makes the Bible the canon of the church. In other words, it is precisely in worship that the Bible becomes the canon of the church just as the sermon becomes truly "sermon" in worship. The sermon placed at the center of worship is what was intended by the Reformers. It was Calvin who made it clear that Scripture is the center of worship by continually preaching sermons on each book of the Bible.

There is no doubt that the New Testament consists of the books collected by the church in the first two centuries. It is also true that the New Testament *is* the canon because it was promoted by the church to be the canon after the second century. However, it *becomes* truly canon when read and preached in the worship of the church. And it is still more important to say that the New Testament writings became truly canon when written and read and preached in the worship of the first-century church. Hence we can say that it is worship that makes the canon truly "canon." We recall how the early church repeatedly read letters sent by an apostle in their worship services (Col. 4:16), and that in this way those letters became a part of the canon. The same thing should happen in the worship services of this generation. Exegesis can never be an independent task; it must always serve to make the sermon out of the Scripture and thus enable the church to worship God. If it is worship that makes the canon truly "canon," then the problem of the canon is *par excellence* a matter for the church and worship, and not merely for historical study.

Calvin is right when he says, "But those who wish to prove to unbelievers that Scripture is the Word of God are acting foolishly, for only by faith can this be known."[23] Perhaps we can cause him to say, in the language of this essay, that it is foolish to prove the canonicity of the

Bible rationally, apart from faith. It is the sermon in worship or the sermon-and-worship that proves the Bible to be the canon of the church.

NOTES TO CHAPTER 11

1. E. Käsemann, *Das Neue Testament als Kanon* (Göttingen: Vandenhoeck & Ruprecht, 1970).

2. A detailed description of Dr. Watanabe's theology is given by C. Michelson, *Japanese Contribution to Christian Theology* (Philadelphia: Westminster Press, 1960).

3. Zenta Watanabe, *Seishoron* (Tokyo: Shinkyo Shuppansha, 1946). The English translation of the title is "Teaching on the Bible."

4. *Glauben und Verstehen* (Tübingen: J. C. B. Mohr, 1954), I, 334. The English translation is mine.

5. *Ibid.*, p. 333. The English translation is mine.

6. Dr. Masao Sekine, a leading Old Testament scholar in Japan, studied in Germany for many years. He is a leader in the non-church movement.

7. Sasagu Arai is known in Japan for his study of Gnosis and the Coptic language. His view is set forth in a collected volume of essays, *Shoki Kirisutokyoshi-no Shomondai* (Tokyo: Shinkyo Shuppansha, 1973). The English translation of the title is "Problems in the History of the Early Church."

8. Arai says that this thesis was proposed by W. Bauer as early as 1930 and reasserted recently by L. Schottroff and M. Köster-J. M. Robinson.

9. Chinese characters are used as part of the Japanese language. Since 91 percent of the population of Japan enter senior high school, Buddhist books are not difficult because of a low educational level.

10. *Tôyôjin-no Shii Hôhou* (Tokyo: Shunjusha, 1961). The English translation of the title is "The Oriental Way of Thinking."

11. Instead, they have *Nenbutsu*, which they recite as often as possible. It means literally "concentrating on Buddha," a kind of Ave Maria. The whole faith of Buddhism is contained in a few Chinese characters in this particular phrase. They recite it in worship and in daily life. In some sects, believers are supposed to recite it more than one million times during their lifetime.

12. Travellers from abroad are often surprised by the fact that almost all of the world's literary, philosophical, religious, and scientific works are available in Japanese translation.

13. A spiritually-minded Christian group originating from Kanzo Uchimura which rejects the sacraments, worship, and institutional form of the church. The only thing they keep and cherish is Bible study. Emil Brunner loved this group while he was in Japan.

14. In Japan Confucianism is recognized as a type of philosophy of life instead of as a religion.

15. A. R. C. Leany, *The Gospel according to St. Luke* (London: Adam & Charles Black, 1958), p. 8.

16. Col. 4:18. Romans was probably also used in this way. Finding a proper amanuensis or even obtaining writing materials may have created additional difficulties for correspondence.

17. K. Barth, *The Epistle to the Romans*, trans. by E. C. Hoskyns (London: Oxford University Press, 1933), p. 1.

18. K. Barth, *Homiletik: Wesen und Vorbereitung der Predigt* (Zürich: EVZ-Verlag, 1966), pp. 81f.

19. "Atheistische Methoden in der Theologie," 1905, now in *Zur Theologie des Neuen Testaments und zur Dogmatik* (München: Chr. Kaiser, 1969).

20. See P. Stuhlmacher, *Schriftauslegung auf dem Wege zur biblischen Theologie* (Göttingen: Vanderhoeck & Ruprecht, 1975), and other authors. From the side of practical theology, R. Bohren, *Die Krise der Predigt als Frage an die Exegese, in dem Worts folgen* (München/Hamburg: Chr. Kaiser & Siebenstern, 1963), pp. 65-95. The English translation appears as *Preaching and Community* (Richmond: John Knox, 1965), but its place of publication is unknown.

21. This situation is briefly but clearly described by E. Krenz, *The Historical-Critical Method* (Philadelphia: Fortress Press, 1975), pp. 84ff.

22. E. Käsemann, "Begründet der neutestamentliche Kanon die Einheit der Kirche?" in *Exegetische Versuche und Bestimmungen* (Göttingen: Vandenhoeck & Ruprecht, 1960), I, 229. The English translation is from E. Käsemann, *Essays on New Testament Themes*, trans. by. W. J. Montague (London: SCM Press, 1964).

23. *Institutes* I, viii, 13.

12: *Covenant and History in the Bible**

LESTER J. KUYPER

During my many years of being associated with Richard Oudersluys in the field of biblical study at our seminary, topics of biblical interest often became subjects of conversation. A conviction shared by both of us was that the Old Testament and the New Testament together constituted the Word of God for study in the classroom and for preaching in the church. One could name many words or concepts that became God's living Word for Israel and for the church. Among these concepts covenant would be one of the foremost, if not the foremost. Consequently I am honored and delighted to offer this study on covenant and history in the Bible to honor the retirement of our esteemed colleague.

The relationship between God and Israel was often expressed in terms of covenant, a concept of relationship common in the ancient world. Studies by Mendenhall[1] show that covenants were used in the old city state of Sumer in the third millennium B.C. Their use continued in Assyrian and Hittite nations in the next millennium. The Hittite covenants, many of which still survive, were of two kinds, the suzerainty covenant and the parity covenant. The former was given by a superior, usually a ruler, to an inferior who pledged with an oath to show loyalty to his lord for benefits he had received. The parity covenant was an agreement between equals, such as the Hittite-Egyptian covenant of Rameses II drawn up at the time of the Exodus.

The suzerainty covenant began with a prologue in which the sovereign told of his benevolence toward his subjects which placed them under obligation to give unqualified allegiance to their lord. A copy of the covenant was deposited in the temple and it was to be read periodically to remind the subjects of their duty toward their king. The gods of the ruler and of the ruled people were called to witness the solemn covenant.

*This essay also appears as chapter 3 in Dr. Kuyper's recent book, *The Scripture Unbroken* (Grand Rapids: Wm. B. Eerdmans, 1978).

164

Blessings would follow obedience to the terms of the covenant and curses were pronounced over breaking the agreement.

In the Mosaic covenant (Exod. 19) we can discern interesting parallels in that the gracious favor of the LORD[2] has been demonstrated to Israel (v. 4), and that Israel is to obey the voice of the LORD (v. 5). As a reward for obedience Israel would be a special people of God to be known as "a kingdom of priests and a holy nation" (v. 6). In the Exodus account of the covenant there is no listing of blessings and curses but this does appear in Deuteronomy, and no witnesses are mentioned, for there is no witness higher than God who established the covenant. Consequently we may observe interesting similarities and differences between the covenant structures of the Old Testament and surrounding nations.

The Hebrew word *berith*, "covenant," is of uncertain derivation. It occurs most frequently with the verb *karath*, "cut," which may refer to the ceremony of cutting in two the sacrificial victim at the celebration of drawing up the covenant (Jer. 34:18, cf. also Gen. 15:7-21). Other verbs used with *berith* are *nathan*, "give, set," *qum* in the *hiphil*, "raise up, establish." Verbs that indicate that the covenant has been broken are *'abhar*, "transgress," *parar*, "break," *ma'as*, "despise," *'azabh*, "forsake," and *shakhah*, "forget." The covenant at Sinai was basically the decalogue which became known as the book of the covenant (Exod. 24:7; Deut. 4:13; 2 Kings 23:2). In a broader sense the covenant incorporated the *huqqim*, "statutes," the *mitzwoth*, "commandments," and the *mishpatim*, "ordinances" (Deut. 4:14, 40; 26:17).

The Sinaitic covenant, given at the time Israel became a nation, placed Israel under obligation to keep the covenant by obeying the law. At the solemn ratification of the covenant Moses rehearsed all the requirements of the LORD, to which Israel responded, "All that the LORD has spoken we will do, and we will be obedient" (Exod. 24:7). The covenant code (Exod. 21-23), which follows the decalogue, spelled out the requirements which Israel would keep and observe. However, early in Israel's life it became apparent that she was not able to keep the covenant, as the worship of the golden calf at Mount Sinai illustrated dramatically. Thus, at the beginning of Israel's history and throughout that history, the problem of a violated or broken covenant emerged as an important factor in the God-Israel relationship. The issue the golden calf raised can be phrased in terms of the question whether the covenant stands or falls because of Israel's obedience or disobedience. Surely we should not entertain any suggestion that God was under an illusion about Israel's ability to keep the covenant. We are closer to an understanding of this issue if we regard the keeping of the covenant as an open possibility in which God related himself to Israel. Perhaps the issue should be cast into another form by asking whether, in spite of Israel's disobedience or even her obedience, the covenantal relationship continued so that thereby God's unmerited favor for his people might repeatedly be manifested. In spite of Israel's faithlessness, God remained faithful so that the covenant instituted by God continued in effect. Thus, at the very outset, the problem of the broken covenant was solved.

Israel's loyalty to the covenant established at Mount Sinai was constantly tested as she encountered the religions of Canaan. From the time of the conquest into the early monarchy the young nation was much attracted to the religious practices of her pagan neighbors. From Joshua at Shechem to Elijah at Mount Carmel, instances where the issue of serving the LORD God of Israel was publicly raised, Israel was strangely yet understandably tempted to mix Jahwism with Baalism. This, Elijah lamented, was a forsaking of the commandments of the LORD and a forsaking of his covenant (1 Kings 18:18; 19:10, 14). In the struggle for pure Jahwism which continued up to the exile, the trend toward elaboration of worship at temples or shrines dedicated to the LORD appeared, so that the cult of the holy place with an officiating priest became the sign of covenantal loyalty.

This formalistic emphasis on ceremony and cult prevailed during the time of the eighth-century prophets, Amos, Hosea, Isaiah, and Micah. It is noteworthy that these prophets scarcely mention the covenant of Sinai in their drastic criticism of the popular religion of Israel. They did recall God's gracious choice of Israel (Amos 3:2) and God's deliverance of his son out of Egypt (Hos. 11:1), but they did not recall the covenant established with Israel at Mount Sinai. To understand this curious omission we have but to see these prophets in their violent opposition to the routine performance of external acts of worship which supposedly took the form of keeping the covenant. Amos therefore inveighed against the pilgrimages to popular shrines; Hosea denounced the priests for getting rich off worshippers' sense of guilt; Isaiah scorned the frequenting of temples and the offering of prayers; and Micah poured contempt on offering thousands of rams and ten thousand rivers of oil. What these prophets wanted instead of the much displayed rites of worship was a living relationship to God and a personal concern for the oppressed and needy. The covenant, as these prophets observed, had degenerated into a bargain counter religion in which Israel, through sacrifices and ritual, purchased from God her license to live in disregard of human need. Hence it is not difficult to see that these prophets made little use of the covenant.

In the century following that of the above-mentioned prophets another attitude which placed the covenant in high esteem appeared. It was then that the law book, commonly regarded as Deuteronomy, which was found in the temple, became the basis for the great reformation under the direction of King Josiah. The law book was called the book of the covenant and was read in the hearing of the people (2 Kings 23:2). The generation preceding the reign of Josiah was stigmatized by the historian as more iniquitous than the Amorites who formerly inhabited the land (2 Kings 21:11). The law and the covenant which had been Israel's heritage and tradition had been thoroughly disregarded, so that Judah and Jerusalem had become entirely filled with sin. Thus the demands for a reformation made a return to the law and covenant most necessary. Consequently Josiah made the discovered book of the law the basis for the reformation.

Some features of the Sinaitic covenant also appear in Deuteronomy. In both the covenant was identified with the law, and the covenant described the relationship of God to Israel in terms of the redemption from Egypt. However, a significant addition which we do not have in the Exodus account appears in Deuteronomy. This addition is the acknowledgment of the covenant made with Abraham, Isaac, and Jacob. The LORD's choice of Israel to become his people was founded both on his sovereign love for Israel and on his oath sworn to the patriarchs (Deut. 7:8). The possession of the land with its cities and fields was evidence that the LORD remembered the oath to the fathers (6:10f.; 9:5). The covenant with the patriarchs and the covenant at Sinai appeared as interrelated acts of God that set the course of Israel's history within the faithfulness and reliability of God.

At this point in our discussion we ought to review the patriarchal narrative concerning the establishment of the covenant with Abraham. The account (Genesis 17) declares that God, whose name is *El Shaddai,* translated God Almighty, made a covenant with Abram. The covenant's prominent feature involved a promise of a multitude of descendants who would come from Abram and his wife Sarah. Since they were childless and well-advanced in years, the promise of a large posterity was either a mockery or pointed to a miraculous intervention of God in their lives. This intervention did indeed take place and further underscored God's approach to man in establishing the covenant. To confirm the promise of many descendants the name of Abram was changed to Abraham, which is made to mean a father of a multitude of nations (17:5). The descendants would comprise kings and nations that would continue into endless generations. The descriptive quality, "everlasting," was attached to the covenant and to the possession of the land in which Abraham moved about as a sojourner. And finally the relationship established between God and Abraham would be continued between God and Abraham's children. In summary, the covenant promised a multitude of descendants, the possession of Canaan, and the continuing bond between God and Abraham's posterity.

The covenant was to be kept, not by obeying the law as in the case of the Sinai covenant, but by the sign of circumcision. This sign, made on all male children at their eighth day and on all foreigners brought within the tribe of Abraham, indicated in their flesh that God's everlasting covenant was upon them.[3]

Deuteronomy associated the oath of God with the covenant he established with Abraham. The oath, as narrated in the Genesis account, involved the repetition of the promise of descendants and the possession of the land (22:16-18; 24:7; 26:3). Although the oath was not given in the setting of the covenant, yet it intended to underscore God's reliability in the keeping of his covenant. Consequently, as we read of the oath in Deuteronomy (4:31; 7:8, 12; 8:1, 18) we are in effect reminded of the patriarchal covenant.

Although the Sinaitic covenant is clearly recognized in Deuteronomy (4:13f.), it appears that another covenant with Israel was established in the land of Moab (29:1, 9, 12, 14), forming what would amount to the third in a series of covenants. If this is a correct surmise, then the relationship of God with Israel appears to rest on three pillars which presented Israel's history as having begun with the gracious acts of God to the patriarchs, as having continued with the establishing of Israel as a people, and as stressing the necessity of each new generation's response in faithful and loving obedience to God who keeps covenant and faithfulness toward his people (7:9-11).

The recognition that the prophets Jeremiah and Ezekiel gave to the covenant undoubtedly reflected the influence of Deuteronomy that had inspired the Josiah reformation, although we have no clear indication that either of them took an active part in it. Since the historical narratives do not mention them but only note that Jeremiah composed a lament for the death of Josiah (2 Chron. 35:25), we may conclude that they had no active part in the great movement. Jeremiah nevertheless accorded the covenant some significance in his preaching, contrasting the condescending grace of God toward Israel at the time of the Exodus with the base ingratitude revealed in Israel's covenant-breaking. He did not speak of the covenant as the everlasting and continuing relationship between God and Israel. Rather he employed other figures such as the marriage bond, the relationship of father and son, and the shepherd and flock to describe the covenant (Jer. 31:3-4, 9, 20, 32; 23:1-4). Viewed in historical perspective, especially in the post-Josiah period when the gains of the reformation were already lost, the covenant could not be regarded as the enduring bond uniting people with God.

SALES SLIP

Customer's Order No. _____ Phone No. _____ Date _____ 19 ___

Sold To _Nolan Palsmey_

Address _____

SOLD BY	CASH	C. O. D.	CHARGE	ON ACCT.	MDSE. RETD.	PAID OUT	

QUAN.	DESCRIPTION		PRICE	AMOUNT	
			TAX		
			TOTAL	7	50

ALL claims and returned goods MUST be accompanied by this bill.

07623   Rec'd by

GrayLine PRODUCT OF WILSON JONES, U.S.A.   CARBONLESS PAPER   FORM 50-461

In view of Jeremiah's less than enthusiastic view of the covenantal relationship, we may be somewhat surprised that he nonetheless used the covenant concept to describe the future age of Israel's redemption in the prophecy of the new covenant (31:31-34). The covenant would be established as an act of God's redemptive concern for his people Israel, even as the first covenant expressed God's redemptive love. The law would again be given by God, not written on tables of stone but on the inner self, on the heart. No response needed to be made to the giving of the law as had been the case in the first covenant, for that response would flow spontaneously from the inner self. The knowledge of God, which was indicated in deeds of mercy and justice (cf. 22:15f.), would not be taught because God himself would implant that knowledge in all the people within the covenant. Since sins and iniquities would be fully forgiven, the people would be fully aware of the forgiving grace of God. The emphasis of "I will forgive their iniquities and I will remember their sin no more" would not describe the constant waywardness of the people but rather their constant awareness of God's forgiveness. As a forgiven people living in appreciation of pardon, all would manifest a forgiving compassion for others. In summary, the new covenant presents God in redemptive action patterned on the redemptive act of the Exodus, yet wondrously changed. Here the God-people relationship grows out of God's gracious forgiveness and produces the people's response in demonstrations of forgiveness based on mercy and righteousness, which are the knowledge of God.

The new covenant prophecy of Jeremiah has clear similarities with the Sinai covenant, especially in that both describe the action of God to establish Israel as his people. The terminology of covenant, law, and the God-people bond is common to both. The unique element in the new covenant was not the gracious act of God to redeem his people, but rather the taking into account of Israel's inability to obey the law and to keep the covenant. As Jeremiah pondered the history of Israel's faithlessness to the LORD who had redeemed her, as he saw that covenantal renewal or reformation was like the morning dew which quickly vanishes away, he declared that mankind as seen in Israel was so corrupt and perverse that it would be impossible for Israel to be obedient and faithful to any covenant which God might make with her. The prophet as appointed tester of the ways of Israel (6:27) declared that "the heart is deceitful above all things, and desperately corrupt; who can understand it?" (17:9). So it becomes impossible for Israel to change her ways and to return into fellowship with God, even as it would be impossible for an Ethiopian to change his skin and a leopard his spots (13:23). Any covenant requiring the obedience of the people has no chance for survival; it carries its own seeds of failure. Jeremiah, more than any prophet before him, had clearly discerned the problem of man's inability to remain within the covenantal fellowship of God.[4]

Ezekiel shared Jeremiah's "low" view of the sinfulness of Israel and her consequent inability to keep the law as seen in a review of Israel's history (chap. 20). Israel was called a "house of rebellion" (2:7). Because of Israel's sinful disposition this prophet projected the future restoration of Israel in terms of inner cleansing and change. "A new heart I will give you, and a new spirit I will put within you; and I will take out of your flesh the heart of stone and give you a heart of flesh" (36:26). The inner disposition would be changed radically by the implanting of a new spirit. The new spirit would create the ability to walk according to the ordinances of God. Ezekiel, like Jeremiah, saw no restoration of covenantal fellowship based on the requirements of Deuteronomy or of the Sinaitic covenant. The new fellowship would have its base in the creation of a new heart and in the giving of a new spirit.[5]

In the reference quoted above, Ezekiel did not use the term covenant for the new relationship between God and Israel. It was for the vindication of his holy name rather than out of regard for his covenant that the LORD would bring back all the dispersed out of the lands in which the name of God had been profaned. The honor of the LORD had been reviled by nations who declared, "These are the people of the LORD, and yet they had to go out of his land" (36:20), and the restoration would be a response to this.

However, in other instances (34:25; 37:26), Ezekiel prophesied the establishing of "the covenant of peace," which implied the perfect welfare of Israel in a future time characterized by abundant fertility of fields, freedom from slavery, and blessed welfare in all relationships. Ezekiel thus filled out the new covenant utterance of Jeremiah with some practical details concerning common life. We may here underscore a previous observation that the forgiveness of God would be constantly kept in mind in the people's response to God and in their behavior to others. The prophet did not envision a "sinless" people who would enjoy the covenant of peace, but rather a people whose sin would always be forgiven. This people would be filled with the spirit of forgiveness and would demonstrate forgiveness and compassion to others in that new covenant community.

In our survey of the place of the covenant in the future hopes of Israel we need to discuss the covenant made with David. The occasion that led to the establishing of this covenant was David's desire to build a house for the ark of God, which was then kept in a tent. The narration of the event (2 Sam. 7) states that David had overcome his enemies and was living in his house of cedar. The king's desire to build a house for the ark of the LORD was communicated to Nathan the prophet, who at first encouraged him to do as he desired. During that night the word of the LORD instructed Nathan to tell David that he should not build the house he had planned but that his son would do that. The main point of Nathan's message was that the LORD and not David would build a house which would be the house or lineage of David to be established on the throne of Israel. In this interesting play on the word "house" we discern that the LORD was establishing a special relationship with David, a relationship that had all the basic elements of a covenant: God's choice of David, his favor which prospered David, his promise of faithfulness to David's descendants, and the establishing of his throne forever. Even though all these covenantal features are present in the narrative, the word "covenant" does not appear. Why the historian should refrain from using it here is not easy to determine. Apparently the Deuteronomist narrator intended to restrict the use of the word to the relationship of God either to the patriarchs (2 Kings 13:23), or to Israel at the time of the Exodus (1 Kings 8:21; 2 Kings 17:15; 23:2f.). It was for later writers such as the Chronicler and the psalmists to declare that God had indeed established an eternal covenant with David (2 Chron. 7:18; 13:5; 21:7; Ps. 89:28, 34, 39 [29, 35, 40, Heb.]; 132:11f.). In the psalm (2 Sam. 23:1-7) known as the last words of David, the words "For he has made with me an everlasting covenant" reflect the time of the Chronicler when the relationship God established with David was readily described as a covenant.

The above psalm, with its reference to the everlasting covenant, may have been the inspiration for Psalm 89, which enthusiastically celebrates the covenant with David. Covenantal vocabulary, which is so strangely absent and restricted in 2 Samuel 7, now comes to full expression in such words as *ḥesed,* "steadfast love," *'emunah,* "faithfulness," *'olam,* "everlasting," and *shaba',* "swear." A significant and unique feature in this covenant description is that its endurability is compared with the sun, moon, and skies (89:36f.), a comparison that also appears in Jeremiah under the terms of a covenant with the day and the night (33:19-21).

Extolling the covenant is not the primary purpose in this psalm, for the praise of the covenant becomes the background upon which the psalmist projects his moving lament. He greatly deplores that God has renounced his covenant, for God has manifested his wrath to bring dishonor upon the king, the descendant of David. King and city have been despoiled by the enemy, and the glory of David's throne has been cast to the ground. All this appears to reflect the time of Judah's exile when Jerusalem was destroyed and the king was taken captive. However, out of the lament the psalmist calls on God to remember his steadfast love, his faithfulness, and his oath which are the tokens of the covenant made with David. Hope arises out of the lament, for God will surely not forget the covenant once established with David. Israel's future hope lies in the restoration of that covenant (cf. also Ps. 132).

Deutero-Isaiah, the prophet of the exile, appeared on the stage of Israel's history when her glory and fame had vanished. The nation languished overcome with despair in the Babylonian captivity. Some of her godly-minded people were deeply conscious of her sin and guilt and accepted the disgrace of the exile as God's just visitation upon them. The more secular among them followed the instructions of Jeremiah (29:1-7) and established themselves in the life and commerce of Babylon so that they had little concern for the restoration of the chosen people. In the mighty grip of Babylon Israel's national hopes had reached their nadir; in that dark night she saw no dawn of hope. Yet in that darkness the great prophet of the exile arose to proclaim that God's dawn would break in upon the night and herald the beginning of a new day.

This prophet had pondered with careful discernment the records of God's redemptive acts in Israel's history. The traditions, both written and oral, declared that God had entered history to act on behalf of Israel to establish her as a people and a kingdom so that she might mediate the blessings of God to the nations of the world. It is both remarkable and significant that the prophet alludes to three special occasions when God established relationships in which the covenant played a prominent part. These are the covenants with Abraham, with Israel through Moses, and with David.

The prophet refers to Abraham twice. The first reference, "But you, Israel, my servant, Jacob, whom I have chosen, the offspring of Abraham, my friend" (41:8), intends to parallel God's call of Israel to be his servant with the call of her forebear Abraham. The second, "Look to the rock from which you were hewn, and to the quarry from which you were digged. Look to Abraham your father and to Sarah who bore you; for when he was but one I called him, and I blessed him and made him many" (51:1b-2), stresses the calling of Abraham from an unpromising origin. Yet in spite of this God blessed him to make him many. Although the prophet does not mention the covenant made with Abraham, yet he and his hearers, then living at the place of Abraham's origin, would be reminded of the oath and promise God made to Abraham when he established the covenant.

Although neither Moses nor the Exodus is named, the prophet makes clear allusions to the Exodus history. The highway prepared through the desert (40:3) recalls the way Israel took when she left Egypt;

the thirsty drinking water from the rock (48:21) alludes to the people quenching their thirst during their wilderness journey; and the destroying of Rahab at the sea and the drying up of the great deep (51:9f.) pictures the great deliverance of Israel's crossing the Red Sea. Further, in the descriptions of the Servant of the Lord the prophet alludes to Moses as a teacher (50:4; 53:11), as a man of the spirit (42:1), and as an intercessor (53:12).

The prophet of the exile makes but one reference to David and the covenant. "Incline your ear, and come to me; hear, that your soul may live; and I will make with you an everlasting covenant, my steadfast, sure love for David" (55:3). Here we find the full covenant vocabulary used: *'olam,* "eternal," *hesed,* "steadfast love," and *'emunah,* "faithful," here given in the *niphal* participial form. David's covenant as described in Psalm 89 is here compressed into one line. The prophet thus points out that even though David's line was not on the throne yet God had not forgotten the covenant. The covenant shall again be restored, not with a representative of David's house, but with David's people then in exile, for they are being addressed in this context. The LORD shall bring the trustworthy benefits of the Davidic covenant upon the weary exiles who shall become a witness and an attraction to the nations (55:4f.). The covenantal blessings are here interpreted messianically and are to be realized in the future ministry of the redeemed people.

The exiles, who are referred to as a widow forsaken by her husband, are comforted to know that although the LORD in overflowing wrath had for a brief moment forsaken them, he will now gather them with great compassion to restore them to their land. Much like the restoration of the earth after the flood in the days of Noah, so shall Israel experience the faithfulness of the LORD, for his "covenant of peace" shall not be removed from her (54:10). The association of peace, *shalom,* with the covenant points out the welfare and good the covenant relationship is designed to promote.

This covenant carries with it the bestowal of the LORD's spirit, which was placed upon the Servant (42:1), and which now through the mediation or mission of the Servant is also upon the redeemed community (59:21). Moreover, the words of the LORD, formerly placed in the mouth of the prophets (Jer. 1:9) and in the mouth of the Servant (Isa. 49:2; 50:4), are now put in the mouth of the restored people. Furthermore, the covenant people are assured that the spirit and the word of God, formerly the tokens of prophetic revelation, would continue to be present in their descendants. Besides, the eunuch who is faithful within the community shall enjoy a recognition beyond that of one with many sons and daughters; and the foreigner shall likewise participate in the covenantal blessings (56:4-7). The covenant shall extend to many generations and those formerly excluded shall fully share in all the covenantal benefits of the redeemed community.

In two other instances Deutero-Isaiah makes use of the covenant to be realized in a similar futuristic manner. "I have given you as a covenant to the people, a light to the nations, to open the eyes that are blind, to bring out the prisoners from the dungeon, from the prison those who sit in darkness" (42:6b-7). From the context we learn that the Servant of the LORD is here addressed. The Servant's identity, which in the history of interpretation of Deutero-Isaiah has received much discussion, may be both Israel the people of God and an individual of messianic import. The Servant has been made a covenant which is in effect a God-ordained mission to bring light to the nations, sight to the blind, and freedom to prisoners. The other reference declares that, "I have kept you and given you as a covenant to the people, to establish the land, to apportion the desolate heritages; saying to the prisoners, 'Come forth,' to those who are in darkness, 'Appear' " (49:8f.). This last passage rather clearly describes the return of the captives to their homeland. However, the full context looks for people coming from many distant places to enjoy the favor and blessings of the LORD. In both instances the covenant carries within itself a task more than a relationship. This task placed upon the Servant includes on the one hand the return of Israel from her exile and on the other hand the bringing of God's light and revelation to nations beyond the community of Israel.

In the above survey of the use the prophet made or did not make of the covenants established in Israel's history we ought to determine from the little data what significance the covenant had in his preaching. In his references to Abraham he made no mention of the covenant or promise as a possible God-given assurance for Israel's return to her homeland as did the psalmist (Pss. 105:8-10, 42; 106:45-47). Likewise, in his more frequent allusions to the history of the Exodus, the covenant established at Mount Sinai was not mentioned. Although mentioned but once, the Davidic covenant with its everlasting faithfulness of God shall again come into being. In this covenant the Servant people shall become a witness and shall attract many nations because of the LORD their God. This covenant, formerly established with David and his house, is now to be established with David's people, here called Servant. In this covenant we can clearly detect that a double purpose was to be realized: The first was that the special favor of God, once promised to David and his house, shall now come upon the Servant people; and the second was that the Servant people were to be appointed for mission to the nations. The second purpose was plainly stated in 42:6 and 49:8 where the Servant has become the covenant, that is, the ministry of God to the peoples. This double usage of covenant may be stated as follows: *God makes his covenant with the Servant, and God makes the Servant himself his covenant.*

Deutero-Isaiah therefore made a significant transition in the understanding of covenant, which has become identified with the mission of the Servant. We can best understand covenant as we come to know the ministry of the Servant.

As described by the prophet this ministry reached universal proportions that surpassed the concepts of former prophets. Previously, Isaiah (2:2-4) and Micah (4:1f.) had envisaged the nations going to Mount Zion to hear the word of the LORD and to be taught his ways. The Servant, however, has been appointed to bring justice, *mishpat,* which may mean practical religion, to the nations (42:1). These nations are waiting to receive his law, *torah,* possibly meaning instruction (42:4). The Servant's ministry is not to be restricted to Israel for her restoration and salvation, for that would be too small a task; his ministry shall bring light and salvation to the ends of the earth (49:6). Also in the Davidic covenant passage it is stated that this Servant shall become a witness that shall attract many nations (55:4f.). Further, many nations and kings, as they gaze upon the spectacle of the Suffering Servant in dumb amazement (52:15), shall be told that the suffering of the Righteous One shall be for the forgiveness and healing of sinful people, and that by his knowledge the many shall be declared righteous (53:11). The Servant's ministry will bring the revelation of God to the nations, and through his vicarious suffering the nations will experience the forgiving and healing grace of God.

This vicarious suffering will be the apex of the Servant's covenantal ministry. Here we observe that the covenant becomes more than God's gracious favor established with Israel in the giving of the law at Mount Sinai, for the covenant expresses itself in terms of an individual who identifies himself with Israel and the nations in terms of suffering and affliction. The covenant thus becomes a bond in life which takes hold of mankind in the depth of human need. That need, as seen in the breaking and forsaking of covenants in Israel's past, was the restoration and healing of a rebellious people. To be sure, God in his faithfulness and his steadfast love did remember his covenant and did restore his people. But now this restoration will mean more than a return to the beloved Jerusalem; it will mean that Israel shall be restored into a covenantal fellowship that rests upon forgiveness mediated through the vicarious atonement of the Servant. Covenant therefore has become more than a formal contract or ratified agreement between God and Israel; it has become a person whose life of teaching and vicarious suffering brings God's peace and healing upon a sinful and broken people.

A brief resumé of our study may help summarize the significance of the covenant and its development in the Old Testament.

1. The covenant was instituted by God in history. The relationship between the LORD and Israel was never regarded as a natural bond that united a nation with her god. Ancient religions frequently speak of tribes which had been united to their gods by a natural bond arising from a myth in which the tribe or clan was considered to be offspring from its god. Although in a few instances the LORD is called the father of Israel and Israel is called son, in no instance could Israel claim to be related to her God by ties of birth. In every case of the covenant, such as with Abraham, or with Israel, or with David, God established a bond with people who were in no way "naturally" related to him. God chose people who had no more claim to this privilege than any other and brought them into the covenant.

The covenant took place in Israel's history and at significant points in that history. The covenant with Abraham was instituted after the breakdown of human history at Babel, and this marked the beginning of redemptive history. The covenant with Israel took place at the deliverance from Egypt, at the beginning of Israel's history as a people. The covenant with David happened when Israel was established as a kingdom and when the center of worship and of the state was placed in Jerusalem. The new covenant, or the covenant for the end time with its roots in covenantal history, anticipates the consummation of history when a renewed and Spirit-filled people shall fully realize the benefits of the covenant. Thus it is that the covenant in the Old Testament underscores the redemption and revelation of God in the events of Israel's history.

2. The covenant demonstrates the LORD's election of Israel for mission. This may be seen in the covenant established with Abraham which embodied God's promise that all the families of the earth should be blessed. This promise implied that the covenanted seed of Abraham would be the channel of blessing and would become God's mission for redemptive history in the world (Gen. 12:2f.; 17:4-6; 18:18; 22:18). At Mount Sinai Israel was designated to be a "kingdom of priests" (Exod. 19:6), which in effect placed Israel in the world to represent the God of the covenant to the nations. Israel's law, known as the book of the covenant, was to be her wisdom among the nations (Deut. 4:6), who would flow to Jerusalem in the final days to be instructed in the law (Isa. 2:2-4). Covenant was equated with mission in the descriptions of the Servant of the LORD who would bring restoration to Israel and the

light of salvation to the ends of the earth (Isa. 49:6).

3. In its legal obligations the covenant could be distorted into formalism. When Israel was enjoined to keep the covenant by obeying the law formalism became a tempting possibility. Preoccupation with the requirements of the law did indeed lead to cultic formalism that reduced the covenant to a "bargain-counter" religion in which God's favor was thought to be regulated according to the magnificence of ceremonial observances. During the time of the eighth-century prophets the covenant had been degraded to a *"Do ut des"* (I give that you may give) performance which produced an irreverent calculation of winning God's favor rather than a trustful surrender to his covenantal faithfulness.

4. Israel's breaking of the covenant did not destroy the relationship God had established. The keeping or the breaking of the covenant posed a serious problem in the relationship between God and Israel. The keeping of the covenant could, and in some instances did, produce a legalism that destroyed the inner graces of compassion and righteousness, as we have noted in the preceding paragraph. However, the wanton breaking of the covenant in worshipping other gods raised the problem of the covenant's durability. And this problem arose shortly after the Sinai covenant had been consummated when Israel worshipped the golden calf. God's wrath was aroused and he threatened to destroy Israel. However, the destruction was changed to a plague that was sent upon the people (Exod. 32:35). This Sinai incident became a pattern, a cycle of wrath, punishment, and restoration, which historians used as they narrated Israel's covenant-breaking, as in the case of the Achan incident (Josh. 7:11, 15), in the defeat during the time of the Judges (Josh. 23:16; Judg. 2:20), in the case of Solomon's apostasy (1 Kings 11:11), and in the going into exile (2 Kings 17:15-18).

Israel's breaking of the covenant brought on punishment, but in no instance was the covenant abrogated by the LORD. "Man cannot annul the covenant; if he breaks it, this only means that he is violating its conditions. The majesty of divine love shows itself in this, that God alone has the power to dissolve the relationship, yet never makes use of it."[6]

Israel's conduct, whether it be covenant-breaking or covenant-forsaking, would not cause the LORD to abandon his people (Deut. 4:31). As transgressor Israel came under the chastisement of God, as was the case with the exile. Yet chastisement was not the end of the covenantal relationship, for Israel's restoration came about through the LORD's remembering the covenant. Covenant-breaking, therefore, was never ignored, since to do so would call the LORD's ethical integrity into question. Moreover, covenant-keeping, to which Israel was constantly enjoined, could not become the base on which the covenant relationship rested, for this would promote self-righteousness, an attitude of heart not acceptable in the God-Israel relationship (cf. Deut. 8:17f.; 9:4-6). We may consequently observe that, on the one hand, the giving of the covenant gave proper recognition to both God's moral integrity and to his bestowal of grace upon a sinful people, and that, on the other hand, Israel in her relationship with God was always commanded both to keep the covenant through moral living, and to receive the covenant and all its benefits as bestowals of God's favor, thereby keeping herself free from self-righteousness.

5. The new covenant for the end time would bring about inner renewal. The descriptions given by Jeremiah emphasized the writing of the law on the heart, the inner self, which is to say that God would implant his ideals and ways for life within man. Ezekiel spoke of a new spirit, and a heart of flesh instead of a heart of stone; by this he meant a ready receptivity for the revelation and instruction of God. God would freely grant forgiveness, which implies that perfection of life would not be achieved. Yet forgiveness would qualify all "to know" God. This knowledge, which could not be imparted by the formal teaching of priests, would be expressed in deeds of compassion and justice. The community envisaged by these prophets would apparently not be free from human frailty and error, yet the appreciation of forgiveness and the inner direction of the will would bring about the conditions of peace.

6. The Servant of the Lord in Deutero-Isaiah would be God's covenant for Israel and the nations. It is significant to note that here the covenant is not an agreement, but a person, the Servant. We are told that this Servant receives the covenantal benefits once promised to David, and that the Servant himself becomes the covenant in his ministry to Israel and the nations. This mission includes the giving of the Torah, as was also true in Jeremiah's new covenant; but his mission goes further in that he shall bring salvation and deliverance to those in prisons of darkness. His ministry shall astonish kings and nations, who shall gaze in dumb amazement at the despised and afflicted Servant. They shall learn that the Servant thus despised and afflicted suffers for those who despise him. It is through his chastisement that peace and healing shall come upon Israel and the many. In the hymn of joy that follows chapter 53, the prophet declares that "the LORD's covenant of peace" (54:10) shall not be removed from the people. Peace, which connoted the fullness of God's favor in all areas of life, shall be the eternal possession of the redeemed people. Truly the Servant as covenant shall accomplish fully

what other covenants realized only in part. This is God's covenant at its highest fruition.

The Covenant at Qumran

The concept of covenant played an important role in the monastic community at Qumran established in the Judean wilderness west of the Dead Sea at the close of the second century B.C. This community was founded by priests banished from Jerusalem by the Hasmonean priesthood, descendants of the Maccabean priest-kings, who were in political power. The exiled priests set up a monastic order under rigorous regulations derived from the law of Moses. As interpreted by the Qumran priests the law became the framework of the covenant which everyone entering the community placed himself under oath to obey.

The references to the covenant in the writings of Qumran regard the covenant either as the continuation of the Old Testament covenant or as the new covenant. The covenant made with the patriarchs is thought to be indissoluble; however, it is to be remembered that Israel constantly forsook the covenant so that only the remnant, the elect of God, remained within it. The restoration of some Jews to Jerusalem after the Babylonian exile becomes the basis of the Qumran teaching concerning covenant and remnant. As God saw the penitence and purity of heart of the remnant, and remembered his covenant to bring back his people, so he remembers the penitent and faithful remnant of his people to establish them in his covenant. The counterpart to this understanding of the covenant is that the rest of the Jews have no part in the fellowship of the sons of light, but are the sons of darkness who are destined to come under the judgment of God. The monastics at Qumran thus regarded themselves as the preserved remnant with whom God was continuing his covenant.

Poverty was a sign of faithfulness to the covenant. According to the teachings of the sect unchastity and desire for material riches were the sins that brought on the downfall of the apostates who were once within the covenant. The newly admitted members were obliged to surrender their personal property into the control of the community. The readiness with which the new member would surrender his goods was an indication of being in a state of grace and he could therefore be identified with the group. Thus it appears that the poor in worldly goods were very similar to the "poor in spirit," which is to say that poverty brought on humility and that riches encouraged pride. The future glory of the community would be brought on through the poor, for God would demonstrate his power through their weakness as they waged the war of vengeance against the enemies of God. In the not-too-distant future God would use these members of his covenant to exterminate all the heathen nations and to bring punishment upon the apostates who no longer lived within the covenant.

The title "new covenant" appears at least twice in their literature, which would indicate that the prophetic ideal of Jeremiah (31:31f.) was in their thinking. Further, they speak of "the covenant of steadfast love" (*ḥesed*) and "the covenant of repentance," which seem to refer to the prophecies of Jeremiah and Ezekiel. If they indeed considered this to be the new covenant, it was not instituted at the organization of their community, for they refer to the followers of the man of the lie who had previously rejected the covenant of God in the land of Damascus. It seems clear, therefore, that the new covenant had already come into existence before they withdrew to the wilderness, and that they were the faithful remnant of that new covenant.[7]

The use of covenant at Qumran to describe the God-people relationship has a remarkable affinity to the concept of covenant in the New Testament. As we shall see in the next part of this study, the relationship of God with the church came through Jesus Christ, who was the mediator of the new covenant. As at Qumran, the people of God in the New Testament were the members of the new covenant. However, the difference between Qumran and the New Testament on the point of covenant is extremely interesting and important. For the monastics in the Judean wilderness, the new covenant was in existence before they were driven from Jerusalem and were established in communal life. They carried on the true line of the new covenant; the rest of the Jews were apostates. In contrast, the New Testament declares that the new covenant came into being through Jesus Christ. Further, Qumran as the community of the new covenant was awaiting the coming of the messiah, or more accurately the messiahs; the New Testament confessed that Jesus of Nazareth was the Messiah who had come to institute the new covenant. Perhaps the most noteworthy difference appears in the particularism of the Qumran covenant which restricted membership in the covenant to the ascetics at the monastery, as compared to the universalism of the New Testament covenant which embraced all Jews and Gentiles who, through faith in Jesus Christ, became heirs of the covenant and promise made to Abraham (Gal. 3:16-29). Thus, at Qumran the members of the sect entered the covenant of God and awaited the coming of the promised messiah; in the New Testament all believers as members of the church were in the new covenant because the Messiah had come and had established it.

It becomes clear, therefore, that the New Testament emphasis on the covenant not merely highlights the expected realization of a new God-people relationship, but also contradicts the claims of Qumran to be the people of the covenant. The authentic continuation of the Old Testament covenant is not to be found in the monastic community but in the church established by Jesus Christ through the apostles.

The Covenant in the New Testament

The New Testament, which may more accurately be called New Covenant (cf. the title page of English versions of the New Testament), makes use of the word "covenant" only thirty-three times, of which seventeen appear in the Epistle to the Hebrews. Apart from Hebrews the covenant is given incidental attention, which is especially to be noticed in contrast to words like "law," "righteousness," and "holiness." However, the idea of covenant as descriptive of a God-people relationship was not ignored, for this relationship appears frequently and under different names and descriptions.

In the Epistle to the Hebrews the author's thesis is that the new covenant of which Christ is the Mediator is better than the old covenant mediated through Moses. The new covenant passage of Jeremiah is quoted in full and in the author's line of argument yields the conclusion that the old covenant is obsolete and ready to vanish away (8:8-13). The new covenant is superior to the old since it is enacted on better promises (8:6), and since the blood of the sacrifice of Christ secures eternal redemption which is also effective for those under the first covenant (9:12, 15). The sacrifice of Christ is made but once under the new covenant, for the words of the Old Testament prophecy state that God will no longer remember the sins and misdeeds of his people (10:11-18). In these covenant passages we learn that the author intends to contrast the new covenant established in Christ with the old covenant given through Moses, according to the interpretation derived from the new covenant prophecy of Jeremiah.

In the writings of the apostle Paul the covenant does not receive such formal treatment as he gives to themes such as righteousness. In his references to the covenant Paul relates it to the promises made in the Old Testament which have come to fruition in the gospel. This means that Jew and Gentile alike have the eschatological hope for both the future and the present in this world. Since Paul does not delineate the covenant, we may assume that he has all the covenants in mind (Eph. 2:12). These covenants and promises are a much-to-be-appreciated heritage (Rom. 9:4). Similarly, in Galatians Paul relates promise to covenant, in this case to the covenant with Abraham. The point to be made is that, in giving the law 430 years later, God did not annul the promise made to Abraham (3:16-18). Paul does not mention the covenant with its attendant promise at the giving of the law since he is establishing the theme of Abraham's righteousness by faith. The other use of covenant in Galatians has a figurative sense by which Paul differentiates between the freedom of those in the church and the servitude of those in Judaism (4:24-26). In his discussion about a letter of recommendation, a letter that he declares to be written for him on the hearts of the members of the church at Corinth, Paul is quite naturally led to think about being ministers of the new covenant since the new covenant speaks of the law being written on the heart. This new covenant with its special kind of writing induces Paul to contrast the life-giving writing of the Spirit on the heart with the external writing of the law on tablets of stone, which writing brings death (2 Cor. 3:1-7). The ministers of the new covenant, therefore, possess the Spirit whose writing on the heart results in life. In the Apostle's extended consideration of Israel's place in the purpose of God (Romans 9-11), he combines a covenant-deliverance passage (Isa. 59:20f.) with the passage from Jeremiah concerning the forgiveness of sins found in the new covenant, in order to establish the point that all Israel shall be saved (Rom. 11:26f.).

Finally we need to examine the use made of covenant in Jesus' institution of the Last Supper. In Mark Jesus declares, "This is my blood of the covenant poured out for many" (14:24). To this Matthew adds, "for the forgiveness of sins" (26:28). In both Gospels the adjective "new" which appears in late manuscripts is not found in the early manuscripts. The intrusion of this "new" covenant in the later manuscripts may be due to Paul's version of the institution: "This cup is the new covenant in my blood" (1 Cor. 11:25), a text that has no variant reading. If we may regard the Mark-Matthew text with its omission of the adjective "new" as the earliest tradition, then we may not have an allusion to the new covenant prophecy of Jeremiah. And it may well be that in the use of the word "covenant" Jesus did not intend to allude to Jeremiah, for other prominent features of Jeremiah's oracle such as the writing of the law on the heart, the knowledge of God, and the God-people relationship are conspicuously absent in the institution of the Last Supper. Moreover, the breaking of the bread and the pouring of the cup with their symbolic interpretations as the broken body and the poured out blood are not found in Jeremiah. To be sure, the "for the forgiveness of sins" found in the Matthean version may reflect Jeremiah's "I will forgive their iniquity, and I will remember their sin no more" (31:34). However, the theme of forgiveness of sins can equally well be related to other Old Testament references as will be done below. Our preliminary observation about the covenant in the Last Supper is that it may not refer to the new covenant oracle of Jeremiah. The covenant that comes into clear focus is that prophesied by Deutero-Isaiah about the Servant whom God had set as a covenant for Israel and the nations. Jesus had previously identified himself with the servant of the LORD in that he had forewarned his disciples of his rejection, death, and resurrection (Mark 8:31). The anointing of Jesus at Bethany for burial, as he interpreted it, and the plotting for the betrayal continued the theme of the Servant rejected and put to death. At the supper itself Jesus employs the bread and the cup as symbols for his suffering and death which reflect the suffering and death of the Servant. The body broken like bread and the blood poured out like the cup depict one much like the great Sufferer in Isaiah 53. Since the Servant motif dominates the setting and the institution of the Last Supper, the covenant mentioned in it would be that spoken of by Deutero-Isaiah. As we noted above, the prophet of the exile had declared that the LORD had set the Servant as a covenant, which was to say that the covenant was the mission of the Servant. If we understand covenant as mission, then Jesus is here stating, through the symbolism of the cup, the pouring out of his blood, that he is accomplishing the mission of the Suffering Servant. Matthew's addition, "for the forgiveness of sins," emphasizes the portrait of the Servant who makes himself an offering for sin and bears the sins of many.

As given by Jesus in the institution of the Holy Supper the covenant reflects and fulfills the covenantal mission of the Servant. The Sinaitic covenant on which the Jewish passover was established has here given way to a covenant concept which is more than the bond between God and people, for, as the prophet of the exile has made clear, this covenant is the mission in which the Servant offers himself as the ransom for many. This mission has universal dimensions which the covenant in the Last Supper brings to consummation through the pouring out of the Servant's blood.

In summary, the Old Testament covenants come into fulfillment and fruition as they are incorporated in particular themes of New Testament writers. Since promise and covenant are parts of the same fabric in the Old Testament, the blessings of Abraham's covenant are promises of God realized through faith in Christ. Believers are children of Abraham who inherit the promises made to the patriarch. The Sinaitic covenant represents a Judaism that must give way to the new covenant as foretold by Jeremiah. This fits in with the thesis of Hebrews which shows that the dispensation of Jesus Christ far exceeds the servants and service of the dispensation of the old covenant. Although the Davidic covenant is not mentioned in the New Testament, it may well be included in the Servant covenant of Deutero-Isaiah (Isa. 55:3). The high point of covenant consummation involves the Servant whose covenantal ministry Jesus took upon himself and meaningfully symbolized in the institution of the Last Supper.

NOTES TO CHAPTER 12

1. G. E. Mendenhall, *Law and Covenant in Israel and the Ancient Near East* (Pittsburgh: The Biblical Colloquium, 1955); "Covenant," in *IDB*, 1 (New York: Abingdon), 714f.

2. The LORD is a translation of *the* Name of God associated with the giving of the covenant at Mount Sinai. The Hebrew consonants without vowels are YHWH. With vowels the spelling becomes Yahweh or Jahweh. Translators have generally preferred the translation, the LORD, to the transliteration of the Hebrew, Yahweh. The LXX has *KURIOS* and the Vulgate *DOMINUS*, both meaning the LORD. The English versions have the same translation—except the American Revised Version (1901), which has Jehovah.

   Yahweh is built on the verbal root *HYH*, the verb "to be," which suggests the background meaning of the Existing One, or the One Causing to Be, derived from the causative stem of the verb. The extensive literature about the Name and its meaning produces no consensus, although most scholars accept one of the above derivations. The interpretation taken from the causative stem, the One Causing to Be, or the One Bringing into Existence, has much to commend it since at Mount Sinai the LORD brings into existence the nation of Israel and establishes his covenant with her.

3. The Sinaitic covenant also had a sign which was the sabbath (Exod. 31:13-17).

4. Cf. G. von Rad, *Old Testament Theology* (London: Oliver and Boyd, 1965), II, 216f.

5. *Ibid.*, pp. 270f.

6. W. Eichrodt, *Theology of the Old Testament* (Philadelphia: The Westminster Press, 1961), I, 54.

7. The teachings on the covenant and the remnant are prominent in the following writings of the sect: The Damascus Document and The Manual of Discipline. Translations are given by M. Burrows, *The Dead Sea Scrolls* (New York: The Viking Press, 1955). For a discussion on the covenant theology at Qumran read K. Schubert, *The Dead Sea Community* (New York: Harper & Brothers, 1959), pp. 80-88; also A. R. C. Leaney, *The Rule of Qumran and Its Meaning* (Philadelphia: The Westminster Press, 1966), pp. 119ff.

A Bibliography of the Writings of Richard C. Oudersluys

Articles published in the *Western Seminary Bulletin:*

"The Unity of the Church," I, no. 4 (March, 1948), 3-7.

"Fundamentalism and the Evangelical Faith," II, no. 3 (December, 1948), 4-7.

"The Resurrection and the Christian Life," II, no. 4 (March, 1949), 3-5.

"The Polity of the Church," III, no. 2 (September, 1949), 5-7.

"Preaching the Parables and Miracles of Jesus," V, no. 2 (September, 1951), 5-8.

"Biblical History and Faith," VII, no. 2 (September, 1953), 1-4.

"The Revision of Our Liturgy," VIII, no. 4 (March, 1955), 1-4.

Articles published in the *Reformed Review:*

"Liturgy in the New Testament," IX, no. 4 (June, 1956), 45-55.

"Celebrating the Genevan Bible," X, no. 4 (June, 1957), 23-31.

"Paul's Use of the Adam Typology," XIII, no. 4 (May, 1960), 1-10.

"Old Testament Quotations in the New Testament," XIV, no. 3 (March, 1961), 1-12.

"Eschatology and the Church," XVI, no. 4 (May, 1963), 8-18.

"Eschatology and the Holy Spirit," XIX, no. 2 (December, 1965), 3-12.

"The New Testament in Greek," XX, no. 1 (September, 1966), 41-44.

"Some Reflections on the New Hermeneutic," XXI, no. 3 (March, 1968), 26-28, 45-53.

"The Renewal of Worship," XXII, no. 4 (May, 1969), 44-48.

"The Parable of the Sheep and Goats (Matthew 25:31-46): Eschatology and Mission, Then and Now," XXVI, no. 3 (Spring, 1973), 151-161.

"Charismatic Theology and the New Testament," XXVII, no. 1 (Autumn, 1974), 48-59.

"The Future Present: Worship is Always Eschatological Worship," XXVII, no. 2 (Winter, 1974), 70-73.

"The Purpose of Spiritual Gifts," XXVIII, no. 3 (Spring, 1975), 212-222.

Articles published in the *Leader:*

"Christian Endeavor," August 2, 1933, pp. 2-3.

"God, the Holy Spirit and Purity in Life," October 24, 1934, pp. 4-5.

Articles published in the *Intelligencer-Leader:*

"Facing the New Year with God," December 30, 1936, p. 2.
"The Christian and His Conscience," December 17, 1937, pp. 7-8.
"Missions in the World Today," January 17, 1941, pp. 18-19, 23.
"Read it Again!" (A series of short expositions on familiar texts frequently misunderstood): April 30, 1943, p. 8; May 21, 1943, p. 13; May 28, 1943, p. 5; July 16, 1943, p. 5; July 23-30, 1943, p. 7; August 20, 1943, p. 5.

Articles published in the *Church Herald:*

"The New Translation of the New Testament," April 19, 1946, p. 7.
"The Place and Need of a Formulated Liturgy in the Reformed Church," May 18, 1951, p. 24.
"The Suffering of Our Lord Jesus Christ," April 3, 1953, pp. 12-13.
"The Ordination of Women and the Teaching of the New Testament," Part 1, March 15, 1957, pp. 8-9; Conclusion, March 22, 1957, pp. 10-11, 22.
"Back to Bethlehem," December 19, 1958, pp. 5, 20.
"Reformed Theology and Church Architecture," May 22, 1964, pp. 10-12, 29-30.
"The New Liturgy: The People's Book," June 14, 1968, p. 14.
"Which Bible Shall We Read?" April 7, 1972, p. 16.

Articles published in various periodicals:

"The Gospel of Offense" (A Sermon), *Religious Digest,* December, 1936, pp. 67-70.
"Jesus, the Man," *Forward,* February 18, 1940.
"Jesus, the Teacher," *Forward,* February 25, 1940.
"Jesus, Revealer of God," *Forward,* March 3, 1940.
"Jesus, the Saviour," *Forward,* March 10, 1940.
"Jesus, Lord of My Life," *Forward,* March 17, 1940.
"The Basis of Immortality," *Forward,* March 24, 1940.
"What is Protestant Christianity?" *The United Presbyterian,* March 18, 1946, pp. 11ff.
"The Doctrinal Significance of the New Revision," *Calvin Forum,* August-September, 1946, pp. 18-20.
"Increasing Use of the RSV Indicates Its Integrity," *Earnest Worker,* November, 1957, pp. 12-13, 23.
"The C. E. Topic," *The Sunday School Guide,* 1935-1961 (A series appearing weekly).
"The International Sunday School Lesson," *The Boys' and Girls' Guides,* 1935-1961 (A weekly lesson exposition).
"Insight into Difficult Passages," *Adult Uniform Lessons,* A Quarterly

published by the Presbyterian Church U.S., the United Presbyterian Church, and the Reformed Church in America, 1948-1962 (A series appearing weekly).

Book Reviews published in the *Western Seminary Bulletin:*

The Pastoral Epistles: Introduction, Translation, Commentary and Word Studies, by Burton Scott Easton. II, no. 2 (October, 1948), 14-15.

The Biblical Doctrine of Infant Baptism: Sacrament of the Covenant of Grace, by Pierre Ch. Marcel. VIII, no. 4 (March, 1955), 13-15.

Book Reviews published in the *Reformed Review:*

Principles and Problems of Biblical Translation: Some Reformation Controversies and their Background, by W. Schwarz. IX, no. 1 (October, 1955), 47-50.

Jesus Christ the Risen Lord, by Floyd V. Filson. X, no. 2 (January, 1957), 44-47.

The Letter to the Hebrews, by Johannes Schneider. XI, no. 1 (October, 1957), 49-51.

The Epistle to the Hebrews, by Gleason L. Archer. XI, no. 1 (October, 1957), 49-51.

Theological Dictionary of the New Testament, I, by Gerhard Kittel and Gerhard Friedrich. XVIII, no. 3 (March, 1965), 45-47.

The Form of a Servant: A Historical Analysis of the Kenotic Motif, by Donald G. Dawe. XVIII, no. 4 (May, 1965), 53-56.

The Liturgy of the Reformed Church in America Together with the Psalter Selected and Arranged for Responsive Reading, ed. by Gerrit T. Vander Lugt. XXII, no. 1 (September, 1968), 22-24.

Corporate Worship in the Reformed Tradition, by James Hastings Nichols. XXII, no. 1 (September, 1968), 28-30.

The Pre-existence of Christ in the New Testament, by Fred B. Craddock. XXII, no. 1 (September, 1968), 30-32.

Interpreting God's Word Today, ed. by Simon Kistemaker. XXV, no. 2 (Winter, 1973), 101-103.

Book Reviews published in various periodicals:

Jesus, by Charles Guignebert, trans. by S. H. Hooke, in the *Westminster Theological Journal,* XIX, no. 2 (1957), 238-242.

The Coming of the Kingdom, by Herman N. Ridderbos, in *Christianity Today,* VII, no. 13 (March 29, 1963), 655-656.

Other publications:

Our Father in Heaven: A Catechetical Book for Beginners, Ages 5 and 6 (Grand Rapids: Zondervan, 1935).

Stories of Beginnings: A Catechetical Book for Primary Children, Ages 6 and 7 (Grand Rapids: Zondervan, 1935).

Stories of a People: A Catechetical Book for Primary Children, Ages 7 and 8 (Grand Rapids: Zondervan, 1935).

Hero Stories of the Old Testament: A Catechetical Book for Junior Children (Grand Rapids: Zondervan, 1937).

The Church of God: A Brief Study of the Meaning of Ekklesia in the New Testament (Holland, Michigan: 1945). Inaugural Address.

"The Rediscovery of Forgiveness" (Matt. 6:12); in *Sermons on the Lord's Prayer by Ministers of the Reformed and Christian Reformed Churches,* ed. by Henry J. Kuiper (Grand Rapids: Zondervan, 1956), pp. 106-120.

"Exodus in the Letter to the Hebrews," in *Grace Upon Grace: Essays in Honor of Lester J. Kuyper,* ed. by James I. Cook (Grand Rapids: William B. Eerdmans, 1975), pp. 143-152.

"The Theology of the New Testament: A Syllabus" (mimeographed, Holland, Michigan, 1962).

"Essential Books for New Testament Study: A Bibliographical Guide for the Seminarian and Preacher" (mimeographed, Holland, Michigan, 1962).